THE TRUTH IS

1. Leveling up your craft to write a story that lives long after you've left the planet is what some might call a ridiculous goal.

2. You know that you will not tell that story after reading just one how-to-write book.

3. You know that you will not tell that story as the result of taking one seminar.

4. You know that creating a timeless work of art will require the dedication of a world-class athlete. You will be training your mind with as much ferocity and single-minded purpose as an Olympic gold medal hopeful. That kind of cognitive regimen excites you, but you just haven't found a convincing storytelling dojo to do that work.

5. The path to leveling up your creative craft is a dark and treacherous course. You've been at it a long time, and it often feels like you're wearing three-dimensional horse blinders. More times than you'd wish to admit, you're not sure if you are moving north or south or east or west. And the worst part? You can't see anyone else, anywhere going through what you're going through. You're all alone.

WELCOME TO THE STORY GRID UNIVERSE. HERE'S HOW WE CONTEND WITH THOSE TRUTHS:

1. We believe we find meaning in the pursuit of creations that last longer than we do. It is *not* ridiculous. Dedicating our work to seizing opportunities and overcoming obstacles as we stretch ourselves to reach for seemingly unreachable creations is transformational. We believe this pursuit is the most valuable and honorable way to spend our time here. Even if ... especially if ... we never reach our lofty creative goals.

2. Writing just one story isn't going to take us to the top. We're moving from point A to Point A^{5000}. We've got lots of mountains to climb, lots of rivers and oceans to cross, and many deep dark forests to traverse in our way. We need topographic guides on demand, and if they're not available now, we'll have to figure it out and write them ourselves.

3. While we're drawn to seminars to consume the imparted wisdom from an icon in the arena, we leave with something far more valuable than the curriculum. We get to meet the universe's other pilgrims and compare notes on the terrain.

4. The Story Grid Universe has a virtual dojo, a university to work out and get stronger—the place to stumble, correct the mistakes, and stumble again until the moves become automatic, lethal, and mesmerizing to outside observers.

5. The Story Grid Universe has a performance space, a publishing house dedicated to leveling up the craft with clear boundaries of progress, and the ancillary reference resources to pack for each project mission. There is an infinite number of paths to where you want to be with a story that works.

Seeing how others made it down their own private yellow brick roads to release their creations into the timeless creative cosmos will help keep you on the straight and narrow path.

All are welcome—the more, the merrier. But please abide by the golden rule:

Put the work above all else, and trust the process.

TREASURE ISLAND BY ROBERT LOUIS STEVENSON

A STORY GRID MASTERWORK ANALYSIS GUIDE

LESLIE WATTS

Edited by
ALLISON FAIRHURST

STORY GRID

STORY GRID

Story Grid Publishing LLC
223 Egremont Plain Road
PMB 191
Egremont, MA 01230

First Story Grid Publishing Paperback Edition April 2021

For Information About Special Discounts for Bulk Purchases,

Please visit www.storygridpublishing.com

ISBN: 978-1-64501-067-8
Ebook: 978-1-64501-068-5

For

All Past, Present, and Future Story Nerds

HOW TO READ TREASURE ISLAND BY ROBERT LOUIS STEVENSON: A STORY GRID MASTERWORK ANALYSIS GUIDE

There are two ways to read this book.

1. Enjoy the novel without worrying about any of the Story Grid stuff.
2. Read each chapter thinking about the Story Grid principles.

   a) The bolded words in each scene correspond to a particular element that Story Gridders would include on their Story Grid Spreadsheet. To see the entire Story Grid Spreadsheet for *Treasure Island* (it's far too long and detailed to include in this book), visit https://www.storygrid.com/masterwork/Treasure-Island/.

   Please note some bolded sections within the text are not part of the Story Grid Spreadsheet. I've highlighted them to point out a particularly telling passage from the book.

   b) Occasionally, you'll see an italicized notation within the text. They indicate particular creative choices the writer made or pinpoint storytelling techniques, like point of view or the controlling idea.

c) At the conclusion of each scene, I've included an additional section entitled "Analyzing the Scene." By answering four Socratic questions, I'll walk you through how to determine the critical information for the Story Grid Spreadsheet—*Story Event* and *Value Shift*.

d) Another section I've included at the end of each scene is "How the Scene Abides by the Five Commandments of Storytelling."
For each and every scene in *Treasure Island* I indicate the Inciting Incident, Turning Point Progressive Complication, Crisis, Climax, and Resolution.

For those unfamiliar with Story Grid's Five Commandments of Storytelling, you can read about them in the book *Story Grid 101* (free download on the Story Grid site), in *The Story Grid: What Good Editors Know*, or in articles about them on the site. Just access the "start here" or "resources" section of https://www.storygrid.com/ to read at your leisure.

e) In addition to the Story Grid Spreadsheet for *Treasure Island*, you can view the Story Grid Foolscap and the actual Story Grid Infographic at https://www.storygrid.com/masterwork/Treasure-Island/.

INTRODUCTION

When we think of pirates, we tend to imagine they are resourceful rogues or "gentlemen of fortune" as Long John Silver would say. They live exciting lives unconstrained by polite society with their own social structure, culture, and code. It's safe to say these spirited characters have captured our imaginations. The Pirates of the Caribbean ride at Disneyland opened more than fifty years ago and still promises to transport riders to "a swashbuckling cruise through seas plagued by scoundrels."[1] The film series spins the ride into a narrative promising nautical adventure with a dose of slapstick humor. Kids dress up as pirates for Halloween, and we're encouraged to talk like a pirate on September 19, each year.[2]

The typical pirate bears signs of hard living: weathered skin, scars, and sometimes missing fingers or limbs. They drink rum, sing songs, tell stories of close scrapes with death, and fight. A parrot may perch on a pirate's shoulder, and the Jolly Roger, a black flag with skull and crossbones, flies from the masts of their ships.

Why are we so interested in them?

Piracy has a long history, with activity recorded as long ago as 1400 BCE. People like Edward Teach (Blackbeard), John Rackham (Calico Jack), and the brothers Oruç and Hizir Reis (also known by the name Barbarossa) appear in historic records as violent pirates who steal and kill without remorse. But the fictional accounts of piracy are probably what keep pirates alive in our imaginations.

Although it was not the first novel to feature pirates (stories like *Robinson Crusoe* by Daniel Defoe and *The Pirate* by Sir Walter Scott were published decades earlier), much of what we think of when we think of pirates is the result of the details Robert Louis Stevenson included in his 1883 novel, *Treasure Island*. From a map drawn with stepson Samuel Lloyd Osbourne for inspiration, Stevenson wrote a story we're still reading more than 140 years after it was published. *Treasure Island* was Stevenson's first commercial success. It supported his family and made him and his characters legendary.

The life of the story's protagonist, Jim Hawkins, has little in common with our lives today, but it still resonates with us because *Treasure Island* is a what we in the Story Grid Universe call a Masterwork. This story has been around for a long time—a perennial seller. Something about stories like this speaks to us in a way that transcends the time and culture of their authors.

Readers still buy and read copies of this nautical adventure tale, and *Treasure Island* has given rise to dozens of adaptations including sequels and a compelling "prequel" in the television series *Black Sails*. We are captivated by a romantic idea of pirates, but there must be more to it because the story is still in print.

There are plenty of reasons why this story endures. One important one is that it meets reader expectations of the Action content genre. We can use our Story Grid toolbox to find out how and apply those lessons in our own stories. This Masterwork Guide focuses on the Action genre, but *Treasure Island* is a valuable resource, a solid map for storytellers, even if we're not writing an Action story or if our primary readers are adults. I'll show you how.

WHAT'S THE STORY?

Treasure Island is an excellent model of an exciting Action story.

These stories are all about survival, and unsurprisingly, that never gets old. Life and death stakes are compelling to us because we're mortal. No matter how safe and secure we feel, we're drawn to "Action scenes" in life and in the stories we consume. It's hard to turn away from a car collision on the highway because our mind says, "Pay attention to this." We have a vested interest in living and our minds and bodies are wired to look for threats, even if we're not consciously aware of it and don't prefer Action stories.

Treasure Island opens when a seafaring man, Billy Bones or "the captain," comes to stay at the Admiral Benbow inn where Jim lives with his parents. We soon learn that Bones is pursued by a group of men who are willing to use violence to get what's in the sea chest Bones brought with him. We later learn what they want is a map and instructions that lead to a treasure hoard on a Caribbean island. When Jim takes possession of the chest, these violent men pursue him.

But *Treasure Island* isn't only about how Jim manages to survive when confronted with life-threatening pirates while on a quest for treasure. It's also about what happens when we're so focused on a goal that we overlook a huge problem right in front of us. We've all been there even if we haven't stood between pirates and what they want.

Jim keeps the map even though giving it up could probably eliminate the threat and save the inn from ruin. Then he pursues the treasure with the help of some adults, despite the repeated warning that a vicious pirate with one leg wants it. Jim doesn't speak up when he learns his friends have hired someone fitting that terrifying man's description to be their cook on the voyage. Jim also ignores or explains away information that could help him make better decisions. But by the end of the story, Jim takes responsibility for his actions and is willing to sacrifice his life to help his friends survive.

Treasure Island is also a coming-of-age story. Jim must look beyond a person's appearance and manners to tell friend from foe and must learn to think for himself. In the beginning, Jim follows the lead of Livesey and Squire Trelawney even when he possesses more information than they do. He's a close observer of people's appearance and behavior, and his input and actions are required for the party to survive.

Finally, this story is about how we persevere when it looks as if we have no way out of our troubles. When they realize they are stuck on the island and won't have enough provisions to sustain them until help arrives, Jim and his friends don't give up. Instead they take stock of their circumstances, weigh their options, and take the actions they can again and again. Captain Smollett maintains order and morale, Livesey offers friendship to the abandoned sailor Ben Gunn, Trelawney is a crack shot, and Jim uncovers the plot and secures the ship. Each person must use their skills and abilities to contribute to the survival of the group.

Treasure Island was inspired by a map, and that's fitting for our purposes because our Story Grid analysis is a kind of map of the terrain of the story. What is the nature of what we're mapping? It's all about change.

MAPPING SPECIFIC CHANGE

Stories are about change. Small changes within scenes add up over the course of the story to cause big changes in the lives of the characters and in their world. If nothing changes, it's less like watching a film and more like viewing a photograph.

Changes in scenes are important to us as readers because the ups and downs of the characters' circumstances keep us interested in the story. Jim's situation from scene to scene in the story follows a pattern we feel as readers, deep inside us, and usually on a subconscious level.

As writers we can use this because we know *Treasure Island* is a story that works (it's been selling for over a century), and readers are drawn to experiences that are familiar but different. Once we see the pattern of change in a well-loved story, we can use that pattern as a skeleton in our own stories with our own settings, characters, and events.

Paying attention to these changes is critical. If a scene doesn't affect Jim's survival in some way—be it through action or revelation—the reader would probably wonder why the scene is being included, and it would probably make the reader lose interest in the story, at least temporarily. Though some people are patient and will read through to the end, your goal as a writer should be to keep your readers engaged in the story so they don't for a second consider putting the book down.

As Story Grid writers, we describe the change in a scene so it's meaningful to us. For example, life to death, confident to doubting, or on land to at sea. You'll see a description with a brief explanation in the Story Event analysis for each scene in this Masterwork Guide to *Treasure Island,* and the same description is entered in the *value shift* column of the Story Grid Spreadsheet.

If you find you would describe the change in a scene differently than I have, don't worry. This is a subjective process, and no two Story Grid Spreadsheets of the same story will look exactly the same. Just do the best you can to identify the most important change in the scene. How do you know what that is? Because *Treasure Island* is a global Action story, look for the shift that has the biggest impact on the survival of Jim and his friends.

We make our subjective descriptions objective by converting them to the *polarity shift*, which we also add in its own column in the Story Grid Spreadsheet. You'll see this as movement from positive to negative (+/-) or negative to positive (-/+). Less often, we identify movement from positive to even more positive (+/++) or negative to even more negative (-/--). This notation shows how Jim is doing from scene to scene.

If you want to see what how the micro changes add up across the entire story, check out the *life/death* value line on the Story Grid Infographic. You'll notice we end in positive territory, that is *life*, but it's lower than when the story began. This reflects the cost in human life of the journey.

Stories are about change, and we use the Story Event analysis, Spreadsheet, and Infographic to map this quality. But what's our destination? Action stories are about changes in our need and ability to survive.

MAPPING THE ACTION TERRAIN

In *Treasure Island*, we can say, when attacked by pirates who want the treasure map he holds, Jim needs to *survive* (core need), which creates change on the *death-life* spectrum (core value), generating *excitement* (core emotion) when he outwits the pirates in the *Luminary Agent at the Mercy of the Shadow Agent Scene* (core event).[1] These core elements make up Story Grid's content genre Four Core Framework.[2] Much of this statement probably makes intuitive sense, but we need to break it down to really understand it.

Action stories are concerned with human survival, our most basic need.[3] Across the entire story, Jim confronts threats to his life (and his friends' lives) from dangerous pirates who come to the inn and follow him on his voyage. An ocean voyage raises the risk of falling overboard, being shipwrecked or stranded on an island, or dying of starvation or thirst. The tropical island destination in this story adds the danger of malaria and yellow fever. In every scene, Jim and his friends must act in response to unexpected events, and their choices make survival more or less likely.

For a clear example, consider when Jim informs Livesey, Trelawney, and Smollett about what he overheard in the apple barrel. Once they know of the threat of mutiny and murder, they move from unaware to aware, and it becomes a lot more likely they will survive because they can do something about it.

Survival is the core need that is threatened in an Action story. We can translate that need to a gradient of value that includes death and life, the core value, to see how Jim and his friends are doing within each scene. A gradient of value is like a spectrum with clear negative and positive outcomes. In an Action story, it's fairly easy to identify and apply these values to what's happening.

The extreme negative value is a fate worse than death. We call this the negation of the negation because it's a positive value, life, that feels negative because of the circumstances. After Jim falls into the hands of the pirates in the stockade, Jim fears they will torture him into revealing the location of the ship. A fate worse than death for him is knowing he's caused the death of his friends by his own mistakes.

The extreme positive value is a meaningful life, which Jim approaches once he returns home. He survives the ordeal and helps his friends survive, though he deeply regrets the lives the treasure has cost.

In between the extremes are death (e.g., those of Redruth, O'Brien, and Hands), the threat of death, which happens in several scenes (e.g., during Jim's trip from land to the ship), unconsciousness (e.g., when Jim goes unconscious while lying in the coracle after cutting the *Hispaniola* free), and injury (Smollett is shot, and Jim is cut with a knife).

Your story may include events across the entire range of value. For example, the protagonist—or *luminary agent*, like Jim—may never experience a fate worse than death. We know what that condition is for him, but he's not physically tortured in the story. That's appropriate for a younger audience and the questions explored in this story. In *The Road* by Cormac McCarthy, a disturbing dystopian Action story crafted for an adult audience, we spend a lot time walking the line between death and a fate worse than death in part because that's the question we're exploring when we read that story. How do we keep going when we risk a fate worse than death in a horrific landscape?

Do you see how the Four Core Framework can help you focus your ideas and provide a kind of rudimentary map of your story's territory and the character's destination, which in this case is attaining their core need? Maps show us how to reach our destination, and the story's *controlling idea* is a brief statement of Jim's journey and how he manages to survive. We'll look at that next.

CONTROLLING IDEA

Knowing how the protagonist survives (or not if the story ends in negative territory) is important in an Action Story. As readers we want to know this because we're humans who want to survive. But the point of telling a story is to dramatize or show through action the truth of the story's lesson. That lesson is what we call the *controlling idea*.

We sometimes use the terms controlling idea and theme interchangeably, but *theme* outside of Story Grid is not always well-defined. Writers or critics might talk about themes of *family* or *redemption* or *courage* in a story. That's useful to know, but the controlling idea serves a different purpose. This brief statement reveals the change in universal human value related to the core need in the story and its cause. It's what happens and why.

As writers we deliver the story's message through actions and their results on the page, stage, or screen. We don't usually state the controlling idea openly, but it helps to know the primary cause and effect operating in the story before we try to show them.

Here are the typical positive and negative versions of the controlling idea for Action stories.

Meaningful life prevails when the luminary agent overpowers or outwits the shadow agent.

Death prevails when the luminary agent fails to overpower or outwit the shadow agent.

Let's take a minute to define a few of these terms.

Meaningful life is the positive result because a character can be alive but experience a fate worse than death. If *Treasure Island* had ended with Jim alive after being tortured to reveal the whereabouts of the ship, that would not be a meaningful life to him. He would have to live with the fact that he doomed his friends to death by starvation.

Luminary agent is what we call the protagonist in the Story Grid Methodology. This term helps us better understand the role the protagonist plays in most stories, but for now, realize this is the protagonist. Jim is the protagonist and luminary agent of the story. Although others contribute to the group's survival, Jim is the only character whose change makes it possible for them to survive.

Shadow agent is what we call the primary force of antagonism in the story. Violent pirates are the primary threat to Jim's survival here. We'll come back to these agents again soon.

The two sentences above sum up the change in a positive (prescriptive) or negative (cautionary) Action story, but it's possible and useful to be more specific. The specifics of the controlling idea's "how" are often provided through the internal genre, which here is Worldview Maturation.

In the beginning, Jim justifies anything that takes him closer to what he wants. (We've all been there, right?) Jim had the knowledge he needed to make a good decision—alerting the authorities and turning the captain's papers over to them—but he pursued adventure without considering the consequences. Focusing on what we want at the expense of our survival needs is an immature approach to life, and in certain settings, we can risk death or a fate worse than death.

This is how I've combined the external and internal genres to describe *Treasure Island*.

Meaningful life prevails when a young person outwits the shadow agents by giving up what he wants and seizing and applying his agency.

Jim's life is threatened when Bones moves into the inn, but Jim secures a meaningful life after he returns. He survives and helps some of his friends survive too.

A cautionary tale where the luminary agent or protagonist doesn't learn the lesson might go like this. A fate worse than death results when we relentlessly pursue what we want at the expense of what we need.

But Jim has an additional challenge. In the beginning he relies on the adults, even when he possesses important information they don't have. Jim's failure to act early on gives rise to problems that put him and his friends on a ship with a group of violent pirates.

Jim is able to outwit the pirates because he quickly stops focusing on the treasure *and* begins to think and act for himself. Defeating the pirates requires the actions of several people, but Jim uncovers the pirates' plot, finds Ben Gunn, and secures the ship. If Jim doesn't begin to rely on himself, he and his friends can't survive.

The controlling idea can be difficult for us to see in our own work and distill into a brief statement. But the typical positive or negative version is a good place to start and will help you make decisions and stay within the boundaries of the Action genre. You can refine the statement as you gain insights about your story.

Let's do a recap before we move on. When we choose a global content genre, Story Grid's Four Core Framework tells us *what the story is about*. That helps us determine the type of problem the protagonist or luminary agent will face in the story. *Treasure Island* is a global Action story about survival (core need) and the change that happens is on a gradient of value that includes death and life.

With the global genre in mind, we begin to know how the story should start (a force of antagonism is a threat to life) and even how it ends because the core event is the luminary agent at the mercy of the shadow agent. Life is threatened in the first scene when Bones arrives, and Jim must deal with dangerous characters until the end of the story when he returns home. The controlling idea expresses that change and its cause. *Meaningful life prevails when a young person outwits the shadow agency by giving up what he wants and seizing and applying his agency.*

The external and internal changes Jim experiences don't happen for no reason or without some preexisting conditions that we call *conventions*. These help us see the lay of the land of our genre and more specifically what kinds of people and features we'll find. Let's look at them next.

CONVENTIONS

Genre conventions[1] create the potential for a specific change in the story that will turn the abstract concept of the controlling idea into a concrete experience your reader can feel. That might sound complicated, but once you know what to look for, you'll start seeing conventions in every story you read and watch. Genre conventions hide in plain sight.

For an Action story, the setting should be a place where survival is threatened, we must populate that world with multidimensional characters whose desires are in conflict, and we need circumstances that force that conflict to the surface. Genre conventions help you as a writer set up the story you want to write (and help you course correct during revision). For readers, they serve as unconscious signals that set up their expectations for the story.

How do conventions establish the possibility for change in a way that readers easily recognize? They narrow a general problem related to human needs. You already know this is survival in an Action story, but other content genres are about changes that threaten or provide opportunities to meet other needs. In a crime story (like *Murder on the Orient Express* by Agatha Christie), an inciting crime threatens *justice*. In a Performance story (like the 2000 film *Billy Elliot*) the luminary agent is offered an inciting performance opportunity that allows him to meet his need for *respect*.

The first step to generate the genre-specific problem is to constrain the environment, for example a deserted tropical island in the eighteenth century, a train caught in a blizzard, or a working-class neighborhood.

Conventions also give rise to possible solutions within the environment, like a crafty threshold guardian who knows the lay of the land, clues a criminal has left behind, or a supportive mentor who guides the luminary agent through unfamiliar circumstances.

We can separate genre conventions into two big buckets of constraints.

Selective constraints are elements of the setting, or *arena*, that help define the problem in a story and put the core need at stake. We call them selective because they narrow the field of potential big-picture problems.

Enabling constraints are the characters and circumstances that allow the protagonist or luminary agent to solve the problem. The setting or arena exists from the start, and enabling constraints, or *characters* and *catalysts*, arise from within the arena. These characters and catalysts enable solutions by increasing external conflict. That doesn't sound very helpful, but it is because the struggle forces characters to see what they've been missing and change for the better.

The external conflict reveals that the luminary agent's typical way of dealing with problems won't work in their current situation. They must do some housecleaning when it comes to the way they approach unexpected events. Sometimes this means acquiring a new skill or adapting an existing one, but more often this means the luminary agent must change the way they think about and see the problem. They have some propositions that may have worked in another setting but that don't work in their current circumstances.

For example, Jim believes if a person has a neat appearance and is polite, they must be worthy of trust. That makes sense when it comes to most customers who visit the inn. Silver's appearance and manner trick Jim, even though he was specifically warned on many occasions about the seafaring man with one leg. We could say Jim went from believing he could see to believing what he could perceive and as a result learned to trust himself.

Let's get more specific about the selective and enabling constraints in *Treasure Island* to see how Stevenson sets up the change in the story and shows us the lay of the land, its features, and people.

SELECTIVE CONSTRAINTS

The Action genre narrows the universe of possible problems the luminary agent could face to one focused on survival. It makes sense that the setting must include the potential for life-or-death problems, but they must arise from the environment organically.

The selective constraints set up an environment with *disturbed unbalanced physical and social environment* and *beneath the surface asymmetry*. Note that these characteristics are tangible and intangible, each giving rise to multiple levels of conflict.

The Admiral Benbow inn is located on the coast near a cove where pirates who have a ship can temporarily threaten the safety of others easily (personal conflict) as they pursue the map. But the hamlet is located within England where authorities like revenue agents can be of help to citizens even if they aren't immediately on the scene.

The primary conflict between the pirates and Jim and his friends is personal. A small group of individuals attack other individuals to get something they want. So this lands us in the *Duel* subgenre of the Action genre that deals with conflict between individuals or small groups. The plot is Hunted, where the shadow agent(s) chases the luminary agent(s).[1]

Jim and his friends quickly move out of reach of official channels of assistance. Once at sea and then on the island, they are in grave danger, and not only from the pirates. Ships are sometimes lost in storms, they can run aground, seafarers can become stranded, and the island is a place where death by disease, starvation, or thirst are all possibilities (extra personal conflict).

That's the physical environment, but the social and cultural context creates conflict too. When in England, people like Livesey and Trelawney have an advantage. Livesey is a doctor who represents the middle class and a magistrate who represents the government and law. Trelawney is the local squire, a landowner and powerful man in the area. They both have skills they don't use every day that they can apply in the broader world. Trelawney is a crack shot, and Livesey is a former soldier with tactical skills. But despite certain hypocritical positions, they each possess a cultural and moral code that limit the actions they're willing to take. For example, Livesey and Trelawney choose to use deadly force only when their lives are directly threatened.

Pirates are people who by necessity or preference work outside sanctioned channels to meet their basic needs and desires. They are much more powerful away from England but can still operate on the mainland in secret. Pirates don't hesitate to take a life if it helps them get what they want.

Another challenge within the setting is the difficulty for young people to learn to trust themselves to think and act for themselves. This is a big social problem present in the story that sets up the problem of the Worldview secondary genre. Jim relies on the adults for most decisions, even when he has more information. It's hard for adolescents to meet their need for actualization and fulfill their potential as individuals when they look to adults for the answers.

This interpersonal conflict gives rise to inner conflict for Jim. He has information and ideas that could help him and his friends survive. But his default mode is to rely on the adults as authority figures to decide what's important and what to do. The need to survive while alone forces Jim to begin to trust his intuition and to act for the good of himself and his friends.

The selective constraints of *Treasure Island* provide a setting ripe for responsive conflict and life-and-death problems for Jim. Now let's see how the enabling constraints force more conflict that leads to a solution.

ENABLING CONSTRAINTS

Once the world is established, we can look at enabling constraints—the characters and catalysts that make it possible for the luminary agent to solve the problem. Enabling constraints ultimately help, but they can make the luminary agent miserable in the process. Remember the goal is to impose conflict from the outside to turn up the heat on Jim's inner conflict.

CHARACTERS

What characters force Jim to confront his inner conflict about trusting himself? The luminary agent(s) is required, as is the shadow agent(s), and the agency deprived. An Action story without these three roles tends to be unsatisfying.

The protagonist or luminary agent fulfills a role that's been called the hero in the past. A hero is someone who sacrifices their wants and/or needs for the benefit of someone else. That's been a useful term, but it leaves a little too much room for moral ambiguity. One person's hero is another person's shadow agent or villain.

At Story Grid, instead of calling the main character the hero or protagonist, we like the term *luminary agent*. This is someone who shines a light by helping as many people as possible exercise their agency. Agency is simply the ability to solve the problems we encounter. When we aren't able to apply our agency, we can identify and solve the problems that get in the way of survival, thriving (that is, pursuing goals beyond survival), and deriving meaning in our lives.[1]

Jim is a luminary agent who responds to the threat of death by growing. Because he wants to save the innocent members of the party, he is willing to expand his cognition. That means Jim considers the way he's approaching the problem (second order thinking), which allows him to better understand what's happening and learn to apply his skills more effectively. He realizes he must risk death to regain possession of the ship and increase the chances his friends will get home safely. They survive because he applies his powers of observation and acts decisively at the right time.

Jim's willingness to begin trusting himself makes possible the insights that save as many people as possible. For example, when Jim goes ashore with the pirates, he finds Gunn, whose help is critical to survival. Livesey can enlist Gunn's help because Jim made the connection (and this also saves Gunn from being stranded on the island). When Jim finds Gunn's coracle, he has a tool to regain possession of the ship. Then by agreeing to work with the pirates after he stumbles into their camp, Jim ensures he'll be able to deliver knowledge of the ship's location to Livesey.

The *shadow agent* is the role we used to call the villain. Shadow agents are external forces of antagonism that limit other characters' agency. That is, they prevent others from doing the things that will help them survive, thrive, and/or derive meaning. It can be an indifferent force like a cyclone or shark, or an individual or group whose goal is to increase their power by constraining other individuals or groups. Shadow agents accomplish this in a wide variety of ways—by force, coercion, or persuasion—but their nature or goal is designed to take agency from others.

The pirates who served under Captain Flint are a group of shadow agents willing to kill to obtain the treasure. Silver is also a *shapeshifter* who leads the pirates. Silver's ability to disarm people with his friendly manner makes him especially dangerous. He pursues the physical security that wealth will bring him at the expense of others' lives.

The *agency-deprived* is the role we used to identify as the victim. Their ability to solve problems, meet their needs, and adapt to a changing environment has been constrained by the shadow agent. The luminary agent works to save the agency deprived. In *Treasure Island*, Jim saves Livesey, Trelawney, Smollett, Gray, Gunn, and even Silver. Before the journey, Jim attempts to protect his ill father from the stressful activity that Bones engages in. Jim stays with his mother when Pew and other pirates arrive at the inn even though she told him to take the money from the sea chest and leave. Jim even attempts to save Bones from his own excessive drinking and from Black Dog and Pew when they come to the inn.

These three roles—luminary agent, shadow agent, and agency-deprived—do not exist in a vacuum. Their relationships are the key to understanding Action stories. The luminary agent has no reason to improve their cognitive capacity or skills without the shadow agent's threat to the agency deprived. The shadow agent is much more powerful than the luminary agent at the beginning, is not susceptible to the luminary agent's usual tools and skills and is not shackled by moral considerations. The luminary agent cares about the greatest common good. Otherwise they have no reason to engage in what appears to be a losing battle.

Can you see how Jim's attempts to achieve his goal are made harder because his own agency is restricted? If Jim hadn't relied on Livesey in the opening scene, Jim might have sounded the alarm before Black Dog arrived at the inn. Of course, it wouldn't be much of a story if he had!

We refer to these enabling constraints as characters, but it's more precise to consider them as roles that can shift from character to character. For an Action story, you must have a global luminary agent, shadow agent, and agency-deprived, but within individual scenes, different characters might try these roles on for size, which adds dimension to the story and the characters.

Even Jim plays the role of shadow agent when he lashes out at the boy who will work at the inn while Jim is on his adventure. He's is awful to the boy, delivering harsh criticism that isn't designed to help. People with more power agency in a particular setting or moment can play the role of luminary agent or shadow agent.

Now let's examine the catalysts that make things even harder for the luminary agent.

CATALYSTS

Catalysts are circumstances that arise from the environment and ensure responsive conflict in the story.

In an Action story, the **speech in praise of the shadow agent** establishes the large power divide between the shadow and luminary agents. We also learn the shadow agent's point, or what they want and why. The shadow agent wants to gain power by seizing agency.

The luminary agent's *object of desire* is to save the agency-deprived and defeat the shadow agent. That goal drives the protagonist forward despite the *power divide* between the two agents, which is also a catalyst. These conflicting goals mean both will fight to the very end.

In *Treasure Island*, Stevenson sets up the power divide between the luminary agent and shadow agent in the first scene when Bones warns Jim about a seafaring man with one leg. The description terrifies Jim at first. But the more critical speech is delivered by Silver himself while recruiting Dick, a young member of the crew. Jim learns that Silver wants the treasure for financial security and that he risks being hanged if caught by the British authorities. As a result, Silver plans to kill the innocent members of the crew. Even among the fiercest pirates, Silver is feared because he is ruthless and cunning, and he faces death if he doesn't prevail.

The **Deadline** or *ticking clock* is a catalyst that adds tension by giving the luminary agent very little time to solve their primary or secondary problems. Time pressure forces the luminary agent to consider options they wouldn't consider otherwise and to act without overthinking. The deadline (a specific time) or ticking clock (time pressure without a certain time) are useful devices to add excitement in any story as long as they emerge organically from the setting and circumstances.

Jim and his mother face a deadline when the pirates tell Bones they will return in six hours (of course, they don't wait that long). Jim and the others face a ticking clock because they must outwit the pirates before they find the treasure. If the pirates secure what they want, they will leave Jim and his friends stranded on the island, and there is not enough food for all of them to survive until help can arrive. Jim leaves the stockade to find Gunn's coracle partly because he's uncomfortable and feeling ignored but also because he believes time is running out. If they don't secure a way to access the ship, they will be stuck on the island. The deadline and ticking clock make the story more exciting. Jim can't just wait out Silver and the other pirates. He must act.

Set-Piece Action Sequences are mini-stories of two or more scenes in which the luminary agent demonstrates changes in their skills and worldview. They tackle a small task to make progress on their global goal.

In one sequence in the middle build, Jim and his friends are stuck on the island in the stockade, and the pirates have control of the ship. Jim slips out and finds the *Hispaniola* attended by two drunk pirates. He rows a small boat to the ship, cuts it adrift, and later boards the ship and deals with the pirate who remains alive.

In an earlier sequence, when Jim goes ashore with the pirates, he is scared and runs away when he observes Silver kill a member of the crew. By the time Jim encounters Hands and O'Brien alone on the *Hispaniola*, he risks engaging in a fight and survives.

Now that we've established the territory and features of our map, let's explore the landmarks of change.

OBLIGATORY MOMENTS

Once you've established setting, characters, and catalysts, you've created the conditions for change. The potential for change you set up with conventions are realized through the obligatory moments. We've sometimes called them obligatory scenes or events, but they can often be reduced to a single moment in time.

We can identify the change in the core value from the beginning of the story to the end. In *Treasure Island*, Jim's life is threatened in the beginning, and he's safe at home in the end. That global change happens incrementally within each scene. But during key moments the value shifts more dramatically. They are obligatory moments because they are required if the luminary agent is going to have the insight needed to outwit or overpower the shadow agent and save the agency deprived.

What kinds of moments are we talking about? They are *unexpected events, revelations, decisions, and actions*. These moments align with the Five Commandments of Storytelling, which create patterns of change within each unit of story. They include the following:

- The Inciting Incident, an unexpected event that kicks off the action;

- The Turning Point Complication, an unexpected event or revelation that changes the global value in a significant way;
- The Crisis, which is a big question or dilemma for one of the characters;
- The Climax, which is the decision and action a character takes in response to the Crisis; and
- The Resolution, which is the outcome of the action that happens in the Climax.

To see these in action globally within the story, we would say:

Inciting Incident: Bones, a dangerous pirate, moves into the Admiral Benbow inn with his giant sea chest and a map that attracts other pirates. He causes chaos until Livesey stands up to him. Jim keeps quiet about the dangerous seafaring man with one leg.

Turning Point Progressive Complication: Once Jim and his friends make it to Treasure Island, he goes ashore with the pirates. He spies on Silver, who kills one of the faithful members of the crew. Jim runs because he realizes Silver is willing to kill him too.

Crisis: After a battle in which they lose two men and Smollett is injured, Jim leaves the safety of the cabin to confirm the existence of Gunn's boat. When he reaches it and learns the *Hispaniola* is held by two drunk pirates, he must decide whether to risk his life to try and secure the ship.

Climax: Jim agrees to join Silver against the other pirates to survive. When Livesey arrives to treat the mutineers, Jim won't break his word by escaping, but he reveals the location of the ship. He cedes agency to adults only when necessary.

Resolution: Jim and his companions secure the treasure and leave for England. Silver escapes on the way, and Jim is done with adventures.

The obligatory moments taken together align with the structure of the Five Commandments of Storytelling within each of the four main quadrants of the story (beginning hook, middle build one, middle build two, and ending payoff). This is true of any story. But the nature of these events is influenced by the genre's core need (survival) and core value (death-life).

The quadrant titles inform us about the purpose of each part in our relationship with the reader. In the first quadrant, we hook the reader, and then we build conflict through both halves of the middle. Ultimately, we pay off the reader's expectations.

But each quadrant exemplifies a theme and serves a purpose to create story form. The conventions that set up the changes and the obligatory moments that pay them off are the elements that communicate to a reader that what they have is a story not just a series of interesting events.

- *Beginning Hook:* The status quo of the luminary agent's life is upset by an unexpected event that threatens a need or provides an opportunity to meet one. The luminary agent reluctantly chooses to engage with the problem, but they don't understand it's nature.
- *Middle Build One:* The luminary agent attempts to solve the problem using their best skills and propositions, but they still don't understand it. The arena and forces of antagonism break the luminary agent down until they reach a point of no return when they make sense of the unexpected event.
- *Middle Build Two:* The luminary agent is dropped into chaos. The problem is finally understood, but they have no idea how they will solve it. In the all is lost moment, the luminary agent realizes there are no guarantees they will be successful and, in a positive story, chooses to go on anyway.
- *Ending Payoff:* Fully committed, the luminary agent joins with others to face the force of antagonism willing to sacrifice to increase the agency of others.

The quadrant themes influence the obligatory moments, which give us the bones of the story. It may seem that several important events have been left out, but we're looking at the moments in Action stories that meet reader expectations for the genre. Of course, there is more to the story, but focusing on these significant moments of change allows us to think about the story as a whole and begin to consider what we need for the maps of our own stories.

Beginning Hook

- **Attack (inciting incident):** Bones arrives at the Admiral Benbow inn, warns Jim about a seafaring man with one leg, and pulls a knife on Livesey.
- **Sensing disorder (turning point progressive complication):** Bones dies, leaving Jim with his sea chest. Pirates descend on the inn searching for the contents of the chest.
- **Running away to reluctant engagement (crisis):** Should Jim take the captain's packet of papers or leave it? Jim suspects the papers are of great value, but if he takes them, the pirates could come after him.
- **Agreeing to fight (climax):** Jim takes the papers, and he and his mother hide near the inn until revenue officers arrive and kill one of the pirates and the other pirates escape.
- **Fix-it-and-forget-it mission (resolution):** Jim brings the papers to Livesey and Trelawney. They learn the papers include a map and instructions to a great treasure. They decide to embark on a voyage to obtain it.

Middle Build One

- **A whole new world (inciting incident):** Jim travels to Bristol and meets Long John Silver, a seafaring man with one leg, who will be the cook on their crew aboard the *Hispaniola*.
- **Luminary agent becomes target (turning point progressive complication):** Jim learns that Silver is the leader of a group of pirates masquerading as crew members on the ship. They plan to kill Jim and the innocent crew members after obtaining the treasure.
- **Comply or defy? (crisis):** When they reach the island and Smollett allows crew members to go ashore, should Jim stay on the ship with Livesey or go ashore to keep an eye on the

pirates? Jim might be safer with his friends, but then they won't know what the pirates are doing on shore.

- **Luminary agent responds in an unexpected way, and shadow agent attacks again (climax):** Jim jumps into one of the boats going ashore. Silver tries to catch him on the island, but Jim runs.
- **Point of no return (resolution):** Jim escapes from the pirates by running into the center of the island. Honest members of the crew are killed, and soon the faithful party loses control of the ship.

Middle Build Two

- **Encounter with the unexplained (inciting incident):** Jim meets Ben Gunn, a pirate abandoned on the island years before who gives Jim information.
- **All is lost (turning point progressive complication):** Jim and the other innocent members of the crew shelter within the stockade on the island when the pirates attack, killing a member of the crew and wounding others.
- **How can my death be meaningful? (crisis):** When Jim finds Gunn's boat and the *Hispaniola* almost unguarded, should he row out and cut the ship loose or not? If Jim takes the boat, he may be lost at sea or captured or killed by the pirates. If he doesn't, they may never have another chance to take back control of the ship and avoid being abandoned on the island.
- **Absolute commitment (climax):** Jim sets the ship adrift but then boards and dispatches the last pirate left guarding it.
- **Preparations to enter the ultimate arena (resolution):** Jim secures the ship in a safe place and returns to the stockade where he's captured by the pirates.

Ending Payoff

- **No holds barred (inciting incident):** Silver convinces the pirates not to kill Jim. He holds the map, and Jim may be an asset later. Jim promises to speak up for Silver if he's ever caught by the British authorities.

- **Death is imminent (turning point progressive complication):** When the pirates follow the map, they find the treasure has already been taken. They turn on Silver and Jim.
- **Do the ends justify the means? (crisis):** Does Jim work with Silver to outwit the other pirates or not? If Jim trusts Silver, he could be betrayed, but if Jim doesn't work with Silver, he's alone and even more outnumbered.
- **Luminary agent at the mercy of the shadow agent (climax and core event):** Jim joins Silver, and the two fight the other pirates. Livesey, Gray, and Gunn arrive, and soon they kill or chase away the pirates.
- **The reward (resolution):** Jim and the faithful party leave the island with much of the treasure, and Silver escapes when they stop for supplies. Jim continues to have nightmares about Silver after he returns to England.

Can you see how the conventions and obligatory moments come together to set up and pay off the reader's expectations of the core need of survival, the core value of life-death, and the core emotion of excitement? The obligatory moments provide you with a skeleton of the story. And you might be able to see how to apply this to other Action stories. But what if you're writing a different kind of story?

YOUR OWN STORY MAP

Treasure Island is not just one story.

It is the story of how an adolescent outwits pirates to survive. This story is incredibly relevant today. Pirates live among us—people who are willing to take the agency of others to increase their own power. Like Silver, they don't look or act like pirates at first glance, but that doesn't make them less dangerous. Silver is a great model for a shadow agent in any story because metaphoric (if not actual) pirates can inhabit any setting and threaten any of the basic human needs threatened in the Story Grid content genres. The way Jim outwits Silver and the other pirates is a useful lesson for life *and* writing.

Treasure Island is also a story about how to expand our cognitive abilities to enable us to focus on what's important in our current circumstances. When it comes to identifying friend and foe, we should sometimes default to friend, but not always, and that is particularly true when we enter new territory. All luminary agents in stories that work enter an actual or metaphoric extraordinary world where they must adapt to situations they've never encountered before. This is not unique to Action stories.

Treasure Island is also about what to do when you figure out the people or guidance systems you've relied on to navigate the world are imperfect and you need to think and act for yourself. This is incredibly hard whether we're fifteen or forty-five. All characters (and people) must decide what to do when they hit bottom and all is lost. Do they embrace uncertainty and do the best they can, or do they give up?

When you can see *Treasure Island* from these different perspectives, you can use the story as scaffolding for an Action Story or Crime Story or Worldview Story. As writers we need to be able to see masterworks and our own stories through multiple lenses. We look at each story unit at its most concrete, with all the details—another writer's or our own—and at its most abstract, as the Five Commandments of Storytelling. And like Jim, we need to consider *how we're thinking* about the way we navigate.

We can dismiss *Treasure Island* because it's an Action Story with pirates or because it was written for boys or because it's old, but then we miss out on learning how Stevenson crafted an entertaining and multilayered story that has endured far beyond his own lifespan. No matter what we read, writers can choose to remain curious to see what lessons a book has to offer and apply those lessons to our own work.

The masterwork is a map, but the journey is up to us.

TREASURE ISLAND BY ROBERT LOUIS STEVENSON

DEDICATION

To
S.L.O.,

an American gentleman in accordance with whose classic taste the
following narrative has been designed, it is now, in return for numerous
delightful hours, and with the kindest wishes, dedicated by his
affectionate friend, the author.

TO THE HESITATING PURCHASER

If sailor tales to sailor tunes,
    Storm and adventure, heat and cold,
    If schooners, islands, and maroons,
    And buccaneers, and buried gold,
    And all the old romance, retold
    Exactly in the ancient way,
    Can please, as me they pleased of old,
    The wiser youngsters of today:
    —So be it, and fall on! If not,
    If studious youth no longer crave,
    His ancient appetites forgot,
    Kingston, or Ballantyne the brave,
    Or Cooper of the wood and wave:
    So be it, also! And may I
    And all my pirates share the grave
    Where these and their creations lie!

PART ONE: THE OLD BUCCANEER

1

THE OLD SEA-DOG AT THE ADMIRAL BENBOW

Squire Trelawney, Dr. Livesey, and **the rest of these gentlemen** having asked me to write down the whole particulars about **Treasure Island**, from the beginning to the end, keeping nothing back but the bearings of the island, and that only because there is still treasure not yet lifted, I take up my pen in **the year of grace 17_** and go back to the time when my father kept **the Admiral Benbow inn** and **the brown old seaman with the sabre cut** first took up his lodging under our roof.

I remember him as if it were yesterday, as he came plodding to the inn door, his sea-chest following behind him in a hand-barrow—a tall, strong, heavy, nut-brown man, his tarry pigtail falling over the shoulder of his soiled blue coat, his hands ragged and scarred, with black, broken nails, and the sabre cut across one cheek, a dirty, livid white. I remember him looking round the cove and whistling to himself as he did so, and then breaking out in that old sea-song that he sang so often afterwards:

"Fifteen men on the dead man's chest—
Yo-ho-ho, and a bottle of rum!"

in the high, old tottering voice that seemed to have been tuned and broken at the capstan bars. Then he rapped on the door with a bit of stick like a handspike that he carried, and when **my father** appeared, called roughly for a glass of rum. This, when it was brought to him, he drank slowly, like a connoisseur, lingering on the taste and still looking about him **at the cliffs** and up at our signboard.

"This is **a handy cove**," says he at length; "and a pleasant sittyated grog-shop. Much **company**, mate?"

My father told him no, very little company, the more was the pity.

"Well, then," said he, "this is the berth for me. Here you, matey," he cried to **the man who trundled the barrow**; "bring up alongside and help up my chest. I'll stay here a bit," he continued. "I'm a plain man; rum and bacon and eggs is what I want, and that head up there for to watch ships off. What you mought call me? You mought call me **captain.** Oh, I see what you're at—there"; and he threw down three or four gold pieces on the threshold. "You can tell me when I've worked through that," says he, looking as fierce as a commander. [*Jim is so focused on the captain he doesn't record what must have been his father's attempt to find out how the newcomer planned to pay for room and board.*]

And indeed bad as his clothes were and coarsely as he spoke, he had none of the appearance of **a man who sailed before the mast**, [*This phrase refers to living quarters aboard ship. Ordinary crew members would bunk in the forecastle.*] but seemed like **a mate or skipper** accustomed to be obeyed or to strike. The man who came with the barrow told us the mail had set him down the morning before at **the Royal George**, that he had inquired what inns there were along the coast, and hearing ours well spoken of, I suppose, and described as lonely, had chosen it from the others for his place of residence. And that was all we could learn of our guest.

He was a very silent man by custom. All day he hung round the cove or upon the cliffs with a brass telescope; all evening he sat in a corner of the parlour next the fire and drank rum and water very strong. Mostly he would not speak when spoken to, only look up sudden and fierce and blow through his nose like a fog-horn; and we and **the people who came about our house** soon learned to let him be. Every day when he came back from his stroll he would ask if any **seafaring men** had gone by along the road. At first we thought it was the want of **company of his own kind** that made him ask this question, but at last we began to see he was desirous to avoid them. When **a seaman** did put up at the Admiral Benbow (as now and then some did, making by the coast road for Bristol), he would look in at him through the curtained door before he entered the parlour; and he was always sure to be as silent as a mouse when any such was present. For me, at least, there was no secret about the matter, for I was, in a way, a sharer in his alarms. He had taken me aside one day and promised me a silver fourpenny on the first of every month if I would only keep my "weather-eye open for **a seafaring man with one leg**" and let him know the moment he appeared. Often enough when the first of the month came round and I applied to him for my wage, he would only blow through his nose at me and stare me down, but before the week was out he was sure to think better of it, bring me my four-penny piece, and repeat his orders to look out for "the seafaring man with one leg."

How that personage haunted my dreams, I need scarcely tell you. On stormy nights, when the wind shook the four corners of the house and the surf roared along the cove and up the cliffs, I would see him in a thousand forms, and with a thousand diabolical expressions. Now the leg would be cut off at the knee, now at the hip; now he was a monstrous kind of a creature who had never had but the one leg, and that in the middle of his body. To see him leap and run and pursue me over hedge and ditch was the worst of nightmares. And altogether I paid pretty dear for my monthly fourpenny piece, in the shape of these abominable fancies.

But though I was so terrified by the idea of the seafaring man with one leg, I was far less afraid of the captain himself than anybody else who knew him. There were nights when he took a deal more rum and water than his head would carry; and then he would sometimes sit and sing his wicked, old, wild sea-songs, minding nobody; but sometimes he would call for glasses round and force all the trembling company to listen to his stories or bear a chorus to his singing. Often I have heard the house shaking with "Yo-ho-ho, and a bottle of rum," **all the neighbours** joining in for dear life, with the fear of death upon them, and each singing louder than the other to avoid remark. For in these fits he was the most overriding companion ever known; he would slap his hand on the table for silence all round; he would fly up in a passion of anger at a question, or sometimes because none was put, and so he judged **the company** was not following his story. Nor would he allow anyone to leave the inn till he had drunk himself sleepy and reeled off to bed.

His stories were what frightened **people** worst of all. Dreadful stories they were—about hanging, and walking the plank, and storms at sea, and the **Dry Tortugas**, and wild deeds and places on **the Spanish Main**. By his own account he must have lived his life among **some of the wickedest men** that God ever allowed upon the sea, and the language in which he told these stories shocked **our plain country people** almost as much as the crimes that he described. My father was always saying the inn would be ruined, for people would soon cease coming there to be tyrannized over and put down, and sent shivering to their beds; but I really believe his presence did us good. People were frightened at the time, but on looking back they rather liked it; it was a fine excitement in a quiet country life, and there was even **a party of the younger men** who pretended to admire him, calling him a "**true sea-dog**" and a "**real old salt**" and such like names, and saying there was **the sort of man that made England terrible at sea.**

In one way, indeed, he bade fair to ruin us, for he kept on staying week after week, and at last month after month, so that all the money had been long exhausted, and still my father never plucked up the heart to insist on having more. If ever he mentioned it, the captain blew through his nose so loudly that you might say he roared, and stared my poor father out of the room. I have seen him wringing his hands after such a rebuff, and I am sure the annoyance and the terror he lived in must have greatly hastened his early and unhappy death.

All the time he lived with us the captain made no change whatever in his dress but to buy some stockings from **a hawker**. One of the cocks of his hat having fallen down, he let it hang from that day forth, though it was a great annoyance when it blew. I remember the appearance of his coat, which he patched himself upstairs in his room, and which, before the end, was nothing but patches. He never wrote or received a letter, and he never spoke with any but the neighbours, and with these, for the most part, only when drunk on rum. The great sea-chest none of us had ever seen open.

He was only once crossed, and that was towards the end, when my poor father was far gone in a decline that took him off. **Dr. Livesey** came late one afternoon to see the patient, took a bit of dinner from **my mother**, and went into the parlour to smoke a pipe until his horse should come down from **the hamlet**, for we had no stabling at the old Benbow. I followed him in, and I remember observing [*This is a reference to Jim's vantage point when he's recording the story.*] the contrast the neat, bright doctor, with his powder as white as snow and his bright, black eyes and pleasant manners, made with **the coltish country folk**, and above all, with that filthy, heavy, bleared scarecrow of a **pirate** of ours, sitting, far gone in rum, with his arms on the table. Suddenly he—the captain, that is—began to pipe up his eternal song:

"Fifteen men on the dead man's chest—
Yo-ho-ho, and a bottle of rum!
Drink and the devil had done for the rest—
Yo-ho-ho, and a bottle of rum!"

At first I had supposed "the dead man's chest" to be that identical big box of his upstairs in the front room, and the thought had been mingled in my nightmares with that of the one-legged seafaring man. But by this time we had all long ceased to pay any particular notice to the song; it was new, that night, to nobody but Dr. Livesey, and on him I observed it did not produce an agreeable effect, for he looked up for a moment quite angrily before he went on with his talk to **old Taylor, the gardener**, on a new cure for the rheumatics. In the meantime, the captain gradually brightened up at his own music, and at last flapped his hand upon the table before him in a way we all knew to mean silence. The voices stopped at once, all but Dr. Livesey's; he went on as before speaking clear and kind and drawing briskly at his pipe between every word or two. The captain glared at him for a while, flapped his hand again, glared still harder, and at last broke out with a villainous, low oath, "Silence, there, between decks!"

"Were you addressing me, sir?" says the doctor; and when the ruffian had told him, with another oath, that this was so, "I have only one thing to say to you, sir," replies the doctor, "that if you keep on drinking rum, the world will soon be quit of **a very dirty scoundrel!**"

The old fellow's fury was awful. He sprang to his feet, drew and opened a sailor's clasp-knife, and balancing it open on the palm of his hand, threatened to pin the doctor to the wall.

The doctor never so much as moved. He spoke to him as before, over his shoulder and in the same tone of voice, rather high, so that all the room might hear, but perfectly calm and steady: "If you do not put that knife this instant in your pocket, I promise, upon my honour, you shall hang at the next assizes."

Then followed a battle of looks between them, but the captain soon knuckled under, put up his weapon, and resumed his seat, grumbling like a beaten dog.

"And now, sir," continued the doctor, "since I now know there's such a fellow in **my district**, you may count I'll have an eye upon you day and night. I'm not a doctor only; I'm **a magistrate**; and if I catch a breath of complaint against you, if it's only for a piece of incivility like tonight's, I'll take effectual means to have you hunted down and routed out of this. Let that suffice."

Soon after, Dr. Livesey's horse came to the door and he rode away, but the captain held his peace that evening, and for many evenings to come.

• ANALYZING THE SCENE •

STORY EVENT

A Story Event is an active change of a universal human value for one or more characters as a result of conflict (one character's desires clash with another's, or an environmental shift changes the value positively or negatively).

A Working Scene contains at least one Story Event. To determine a scene's Story Event, answer these four Socratic questions:

1. **What are the characters literally doing—that is, what are their micro on-the-surface actions?**

The captain (Bones) comes to the Admiral Benbow inn looking for lodging. Jim observes the newcomer as he strolls around the cove during the day and drinks rum, sings songs, and tells tales at night. Bones frightens (but also intrigues) the regular patrons with his stories and pays Jim to look out for a seafaring man with one leg.

2. **What is the essential tactic of the characters—that is, what above-the-surface macro behaviors are they employing that are linked to a universal human value?**

Bones wants to hide from other pirates, but he is a lonely man who craves the attention he receives for telling his stories. Jim's father is sick and worried about the bottom line but avoids confronting the old pirate. Some of the regular patrons of the inn wish the pirate would leave, but most appreciate his exciting stories. Livesey wants to lay down the law and maintain order in his district. Jim is curious about Bones and observes him closely. When Bones warns him of the seafaring man with one leg, Jim is terrified but not enough to mention it to the adults. He's living vicariously through the captain's stories.

3. **What beyond-the-surface universal human values have changed for one or more characters in the scene? Which one of those value changes is most important and should be included in the Story Grid Spreadsheet?**

Overall the atmosphere at the inn changes from a state of order to chaos, but you could also describe the change as boredom to excitement. We want to focus on how the universal human value for the global story, in this case *life*, is enhanced or threatened.

Though he's afraid of being discovered, Bones enjoys giving the locals a fright until Livesey shuts him down. Jim is intrigued by Bones and terrified of the seafaring man with one leg, but he doesn't tell his parents or Livesey about the potential danger.

Afraid to False Sense of Safety

4. The Scene Event Synthesis: What Story Event sums up the scene's on-the-surface, above-the-surface, and beyond-the-surface change? We will enter that event in the Story Grid Spreadsheet.

The captain comes to stay at the inn with his giant sea chest and causes chaos, but Livesey stands up to him, and Jim keeps quiet about the danger.

HOW THE SCENE ABIDES BY THE FIVE COMMANDMENTS OF STORYTELLING

Inciting Incident: Causal. The captain arrives at the Admiral Benbow inn.

Turning Point Progressive Complication: Active. After the captain pulls a knife on Livesey, the doctor tells the captain he'll have him hung if he doesn't put the knife away.

Crisis: Best bad choice. If the captain attacks Livesey, he risks bringing unwanted attention to himself from both the law and other pirates, but if he gives in, he'll lose face.

Climax: The captain puts his knife away and sits down.

Resolution: Livesey informs the captain he'll be keeping an eye on him. He's the magistrate as well as the local doctor. Peace is restored for a while.

NOTES

- Jim is mostly a passive observer in this scene, and he focuses on what's new to him. He reveals what life was like before the captain arrived by showing us what's changed. This is efficient storytelling. We can show the ordinary world by contrast.

- The first lines of this scene set up the story's narrative device. Jim is recording the events from memory for an official record. This allows Jim to see these events in hindsight. In a way, it's as if he's trying to understand his own actions and his process of maturation and individuation.
- Can you see how Jim's life is similar to Dorothy's in *The Wonderful Wizard of Oz* before she is transported by the cyclone? The captain transports Jim through stories, and Jim shows us how others are transported. In Jim's opinion, Bones is good for the locals and is shaking them out of their mundane reality. But some are frightened, and Jim's father is worried the captain will ruin their business.
- When the unexpected event of the Turning Point Progressive Complication happens here, the character sees it a certain way because of the frame through which they view the world. Jim is a keen observer of appearance and manner throughout, but his lack of sophistication means he doesn't see the knife and the captain's anger as a danger to himself.
- Livesey restores order here, but it appears he doesn't have the full picture of what's happening. Jim has a better idea of the danger, but it doesn't occur to him to speak up. He is so taken in by the romance of adventure and thinks he can judge friend and foe accurately.
- Notice that the inn's regular customers are afraid of the captain and a bit shocked by his behavior, but they keep showing up because they can't get enough of his stories. Jim recognizes this in hindsight because he is as drawn in by the adventure as the others. Jim thinks he's a good judge of character.
- One mystery is what's in that great chest Bones brought with him. The suggestion is that he doesn't have clothes in there because the captain is always wearing the same outfit. If he possesses great wealth, why doesn't he pay his bills? What have his years of adventure done for him? He seems to have no friends or loved ones. He's alone with only his stories and

a sea chest. What Jim can't see is that adventure won't give you what's important, and it's easy to romanticize the danger involved.

2

BLACK DOG APPEARS AND DISAPPEARS

It was not very long after this that there occurred the first of the mysterious events that rid us at last of **the captain**, though not, as you will see, of his affairs. It was a bitter cold winter, with long, hard frosts and heavy gales; and it was plain from the first that **my poor father** was little likely to see the spring. He sank daily, and **my mother and I** had all **the inn** upon our hands, and were kept busy enough without paying much regard to our unpleasant guest.

It was one January morning, very early—a pinching, frosty morning—**the cove** all grey with hoar-frost, the ripple lapping softly on the stones, the sun still low and only touching the hilltops and shining far to seaward. The captain had risen earlier than usual and set out down the beach, his cutlass swinging under the broad skirts of the old blue coat, his brass telescope under his arm, his hat tilted back upon his head. I remember his breath hanging like smoke in his wake as he strode off, and the last sound I heard of him as he turned the big rock was a loud snort of indignation, as though his mind was still running upon **Dr. Livesey**.

Well, mother was upstairs with father and I was laying the breakfast-table against the captain's return when the parlour door opened and **a man** stepped in on whom I had never set my eyes before. He was a pale, tallowy creature, wanting two fingers of the left hand,

and though he wore a cutlass, he did not look much like a fighter. I had always my eye open for **seafaring men**, with one leg or two, and I remember this one puzzled me. He was not sailorly, and yet he had a smack of the sea about him too.

I asked him what was for his service, and he said he would take rum; but as I was going out of the room to fetch it, he sat down upon a table and motioned me to draw near. I paused where I was, with my napkin in my hand.

"Come here, sonny," says he. "Come nearer here."

I took a step nearer.

"Is this here table for **my mate Bill**?" he asked with a kind of leer.

I told him I did not know his mate Bill, and this was for a person who stayed in our house whom we called the captain.

"Well," said he, "my mate Bill would be called the captain, as like as not. He has a cut on one cheek and a mighty pleasant way with him, particularly in drink, has my mate Bill. We'll put it, for argument like, that your captain has a cut on one cheek—and we'll put it, if you like, that that cheek's the right one. Ah, well! I told you. Now, is my mate Bill in this here house?"

I told him he was out walking.

"Which way, sonny? Which way is he gone?"

And when I had pointed out the rock and told him how the captain was likely to return, and how soon, and answered a few other questions, "Ah," said he, "this'll be as good as drink to my mate Bill."

The expression of his face as he said these words was not at all pleasant, and I had my own reasons for thinking that the stranger was mistaken, even supposing he meant what he said. *But it was no affair of mine, I thought; and besides, it was difficult to know what to do.* The stranger kept hanging about just inside the inn door, peering round the corner like a cat waiting for a mouse. Once I stepped out myself into the road, but he immediately called me back, and as I did not obey quick enough for his fancy, a most horrible change came over his tallowy face, and he ordered me in with an oath that made me jump. As soon as I was back again he returned to his former manner, half fawning, half sneering, patted me on the shoulder, told me I was a good boy and he had taken quite a fancy to me. "I have **a son** of my own," said he, "as like you as two blocks, and he's all the pride of my 'art. But the great thing for **boys** is discipline, sonny—discipline. Now, if you had sailed along of Bill, you wouldn't have stood there to be spoke to twice—not you. That was never Bill's way, nor the way of sich as sailed with him. And here, sure enough, is my mate Bill, with a spy-glass under his arm, bless his old 'art, to be sure. You and me'll just go back into the parlour, sonny, and get behind the door, and we'll give Bill a little surprise— bless his 'art, I say again."

So saying, the stranger backed along with me into the parlour and put me behind him in the corner so that we were both hidden by the open door. I was very uneasy and alarmed, as you may fancy, and it rather added to my fears to observe that the stranger was certainly frightened himself. He cleared the hilt of his cutlass and loosened the blade in the sheath; and all the time we were waiting there he kept swallowing as if he felt what we used to call a lump in the throat.

At last in strode the captain, slammed the door behind him, without looking to the right or left, and marched straight across the room to where his breakfast awaited him.

"Bill," said the stranger in a voice that I thought he had tried to make bold and big.

The captain spun round on his heel and fronted us; all the brown had gone out of his face, and even his nose was blue; he had the look of a man who sees a ghost, or the evil one, or something worse, if anything can be; and upon my word, I felt sorry to see him all in a moment turn so old and sick.

"Come, Bill, you know me; you know an old shipmate, Bill, surely," said the stranger.

The captain made a sort of gasp.

"**Black Dog!**" said he.

"And who else?" returned the other, getting more at his ease. "Black Dog as ever was, come for to see his old shipmate Billy, at the Admiral Benbow inn. Ah, Bill, Bill, we have seen a sight of times, us two, since I lost them two talons," holding up his mutilated hand.

"Now, look here," said the captain; "you've run me down; here I am; well, then, speak up; what is it?"

"That's you, Bill," returned Black Dog, "you're in the right of it, Billy.

I'll have a glass of rum from this dear child here, as I've took such a liking to; and we'll sit down, if you please, and talk square, like **old shipmates.**"

When I returned with the rum, they were already seated on either side of the captain's breakfast-table—Black Dog next to the door and sitting sideways so as to have one eye on his old shipmate and one, as I thought, on his retreat.

He bade me go and leave the door wide open. "None of your keyholes for me, sonny," he said; and I left them together and retired into the bar.

For a long time, though I certainly did my best to listen, I could hear nothing but a low gattling; but at last the voices began to grow higher, and I could pick up a word or two, mostly oaths, from the captain.

"No, no, no, no; and an end of it!" he cried once. And again, "If it comes to swinging, swing all, say I."

Then all of a sudden there was a tremendous explosion of oaths and other noises—the chair and table went over in a lump, a clash of steel followed, and then a cry of pain, and the next instant I saw Black Dog in full flight, and the captain hotly pursuing, both with drawn cutlasses, and the former streaming blood from the left shoulder. Just at the door the captain aimed at the fugitive one last tremendous cut, which would certainly have split him to the chine had it not been intercepted by our big signboard of Admiral Benbow. You may see the notch on the lower side of the frame to this day. [*Addressing Jim's audience here lends authenticity to Stevenson's narrative device.*]

That blow was the last of the battle. Once out upon the road, Black Dog, in spite of his wound, showed a wonderful clean pair of heels and disappeared over the edge of the hill in half a minute. The captain, for his part, stood staring at the signboard like a bewildered man. Then he passed his hand over his eyes several times and at last turned back into the house.

"**Jim,**" says he, "rum"; and as he spoke, he reeled a little, and caught himself with one hand against the wall.

"Are you hurt?" cried I.

"Rum," he repeated. "I must get away from here. Rum! Rum!"

I ran to fetch it, but I was quite unsteadied by all that had fallen out, and I broke one glass and fouled the tap, and while I was still getting in my own way, I heard a loud fall in the parlour, and running in, beheld the captain lying full length upon the floor. At the same instant **my mother**, alarmed by the cries and fighting, came running downstairs to help me. Between us we raised his head. He was breathing very loud and hard, but his eyes were closed and his face a horrible colour.

"Dear, deary me," cried my mother, "what a disgrace upon the house! And your poor father sick!"

In the meantime, we had no idea what to do to help the captain, nor any other thought but that he had got his death-hurt in the scuffle with the stranger. I got the rum, to be sure, and tried to put it down his throat, but his teeth were tightly shut and his jaws as strong as iron. It was a happy relief for us when the door opened and **Doctor Livesey** came in, on his visit to my father.

"Oh, doctor," we cried, "what shall we do? Where is he wounded?"

"Wounded? A fiddle-stick's end!" said the doctor. "No more wounded than you or I. The man has had a stroke, as I warned him. Now, Mrs. Hawkins, just you run upstairs to your husband and tell him, if possible, nothing about it. For my part, I must do my best to save this fellow's trebly worthless life; Jim, you get me a basin."

When I got back with the basin, the doctor had already ripped up the captain's sleeve and exposed his great sinewy arm. It was tattooed in several places. "Here's luck," "A fair wind," and "Billy Bones his fancy," were very neatly and clearly executed on the forearm; and up near the shoulder there was a sketch of a gallows and a man hanging from it—done, as I thought, with great spirit.

"Prophetic," said the doctor, touching this picture with his finger. "And now, **Master Billy Bones**, if that be your name, we'll have a look at the colour of your blood. Jim," he said, "are you afraid of blood?"

"No, sir," said I.

"Well, then," said he, "you hold the basin"; and with that he took his lancet and opened a vein.

A great deal of blood was taken before the captain opened his eyes and looked mistily about him. First he recognized the doctor with an unmistakable frown; then his glance fell upon me, and he looked relieved. But suddenly his colour changed, and he tried to raise himself, crying, "Where's Black Dog?"

"There is no Black Dog here," said the doctor, "except what you have on your own back. You have been drinking rum; you have had a stroke, precisely as I told you; and I have just, very much against my own will, dragged you headforemost out of the grave. Now, Mr. Bones—"

"That's not my name," he interrupted.

"Much I care," returned the doctor. "It's the name of **a buccaneer of my acquaintance**; and I call you by it for the sake of shortness, and what I have to say to you is this; one glass of rum won't kill you, but if you take one you'll take another and another, and I stake my wig if you don't break off short, you'll die—do you understand that?—die, and go to your own place, like **the man in the Bible**. Come, now, make an effort. I'll help you to your bed for once."

Between us, with much trouble, we managed to hoist him upstairs, and laid him on his bed, where his head fell back on the pillow as if he were almost fainting.

"Now, mind you," said the doctor, "I clear my conscience—the name of rum for you is death."

And with that he went off to see my father, taking me with him by the arm.

"This is nothing," he said as soon as he had closed the door. "I have drawn blood enough to keep him quiet awhile; he should lie for a week where he is—that is the best thing for him and you; but another stroke would settle him."

• ANALYZING THE SCENE •

STORY EVENT

A Story Event is an active change of a universal human value for one or more characters as a result of conflict (one character's desires clash with another's, or an environmental shift changes the value positively or negatively).

A Working Scene contains at least one Story Event. To determine a scene's Story Event, answer these four Socratic questions:

1. What are the characters literally doing—that is, what are their micro on-the-surface actions?

Black Dog comes looking for Bones, who is out for a walk. When the captain returns, Black Dog confronts him, and the men argue. The captain chases him from the inn but suffers a stroke. Livesey shows up in time to bleed him and save his life.

2. What is the essential tactic of the characters—that is, what above-the-surface macro behaviors are they employing that are linked to a universal human value?

Black Dog confronts the captain though Jim doesn't know what it's about. Livesey issues a stern warning because he wants to preserve life. Jim is afraid of injury or death but is also curious about what the men are discussing.

3. What beyond-the-surface universal human values have changed for one or more characters in the scene? Which one of those value changes is most important and should be included in the Story Grid Spreadsheet?

The captain moves from hidden to found and from life to unconsciousness and illness. Although the captain is very ill, the shift that has the greatest impact on survival for the most people is Black Dog's escape. With confirmation that the captain is staying at the inn, he will bring the other pirates.

Hidden to Found

4. The Scene Event Synthesis: What Story Event sums up the scene's on-the-surface, above-the-surface, and beyond-the-surface change? We will enter that event in the Story Grid Spreadsheet.

Black Dog seeks the captain and gets away with his life. The captain has a fit.

HOW THE SCENE ABIDES BY THE FIVE COMMANDMENTS OF STORYTELLING

Inciting Incident: Causal. Black Dog shows up looking for the captain.

Turning Point Progressive Complication: Active. Black Dog confronts the captain.

Crisis: Best bad choice. From the captain's perspective, if he gives Black Dog what he seeks, he might be safe, but the treasure map is all he has left in the world. The reader and Jim don't know what Black Dog wants, but they know it's in that mysterious chest.

Climax: The captain runs after Black Dog but has a stroke and falls unconscious.

Resolution: Livesey shows up and bleeds the captain, ostensibly saving his life. The captain regains consciousness, Livesey gives him advice, and he's is put to bed.

NOTES

- Jim opens the scene with some foreshadowing, that they would be rid of Bones soon. This raises the question, how will they be rid of him? Although the global value for the story is life-death, as well as unconsciousness, and the captain is unconscious during this scene, the value that is relevant to the global story seems to be the fact that the captain had been hidden and is now exposed because he can't run. The scary men who are after him have confirmed his location and will surely come knocking again.
- This chapter and the last establish Livesey's character. He won't withhold medical care just because he doesn't like the captain. This sets up his later care of the wounded and ill pirates on the island, which allows an important exchange of information.

- These scenes also set up a pattern of Livesey's presence being a support to Jim. If he's present, everything works out alright, at least temporarily. But Jim doesn't question Livesey or inform him about Black Dog, which is also a pattern in the story.
- Bones wants to hide, but rum is a weakness that causes him to lose his inhibitions.
- Jim's position when faced with Black Dog is so relatable. We've all been in a situation when we don't know what to do so we do nothing. It's easy to dismiss something as not our concern when we're afraid we may do the wrong thing. Part of maturation and individuation is acting even when we can't know if we're doing what's right.
- Jim accurately identifies Black Dog as a foe, but he doesn't think about the consequences of what's taken place beyond the inn. He hasn't yet realized that he and his family are in danger. He's concerned about the captain but blind to his own peril.

3

THE BLACK SPOT

About noon I stopped at **the captain**'s door with some cooling drinks and medicines. He was lying very much as we had left him, only a little higher, and he seemed both weak and excited.

"Jim," he said, "you're the only one here that's worth anything, and you know I've been always good to you. Never a month but I've given you a silver fourpenny for yourself. And now you see, mate, I'm pretty low, and deserted by all; and Jim, you'll bring me one noggin of rum, now, won't you, matey?"

"**The doctor**—" I began.

But he broke in cursing the doctor, in a feeble voice but heartily. "Doctors is all **swabs**," he said; "and that doctor there, why, what do he know about **seafaring men**? I been in places hot as pitch, and mates dropping round with Yellow Jack, [*yellow fever*] and the blessed land a-heaving like the sea with earthquakes—what do the doctor know of lands like that?—and I lived on rum, I tell you. It's been meat and drink, and man and wife, to me; and if I'm not to have my rum now I'm a poor old hulk on a lee shore, my blood'll be on you, **Jim**, and that doctor swab"; and he ran on again for a while with curses. "Look, Jim, how my fingers fidges," he continued in the pleading tone. "I can't keep 'em still, not I. I haven't had a drop this blessed day. That doctor's a fool, I tell you. If I don't have a drain o' rum, Jim, I'll have the horrors; I seen some on 'em already. I seen **old Flint** in the corner there, behind you; as plain as print, I seen him; and if I get the horrors, I'm a man that has lived rough, and I'll raise **Cain**. Your doctor hisself said one glass wouldn't hurt me. I'll give you a golden guinea for a noggin, Jim."

He was growing more and more excited, and this alarmed me for **my father**, who was very low that day and needed quiet; besides, I was reassured by the doctor's words, now quoted to me, and rather offended by the offer of a bribe.

"I want none of your money," said I, "but what you owe my father. I'll get you one glass, and no more."

When I brought it to him, he seized it greedily and drank it out.

"Aye, aye," said he, "that's some better, sure enough. And now, matey, did that doctor say how long I was to lie here in this old berth?"

"A week at least," said I.

"Thunder!" he cried. "A week! I can't do that; they'd have the black spot on me by then. **The lubbers** is going about to get the wind of me this blessed moment; lubbers as couldn't keep what they got, and want to nail what is another's. Is that seamanly behaviour, now, I want to know? But I'm a saving soul. I never wasted good money of mine, nor lost it neither; and I'll trick 'em again. I'm not afraid on 'em. I'll shake out another reef, matey, and daddle 'em again."

As he was thus speaking, he had risen from bed with great difficulty, holding to my shoulder with a grip that almost made me cry out, and moving his legs like so much dead weight. His words, spirited as they were in meaning, contrasted sadly with the weakness of the voice in which they were uttered. He paused when he had got into a sitting position on the edge.

"That doctor's done me," he murmured. "My ears is singing. Lay me back."

Before I could do much to help him he had fallen back again to his former place, where he lay for a while silent.

"Jim," he said at length, "you saw **that seafaring man** today?"

"**Black Dog**?" I asked.

"Ah! Black Dog," says he. "*He's* a bad un; but there's worse that put him on. Now, if I can't get away nohow, and they tip me the black spot, mind you, it's my old sea-chest they're after; you get on a horse—you can, can't you? Well, then, you get on a horse, and go to—well, yes, I will!—to that eternal doctor swab, and tell him to pipe all hands—**magistrates** and sich—and he'll lay 'em aboard at the Admiral Benbow —all **old Flint's crew**, man and boy, all on 'em that's left. I was first mate, I was, old Flint's first mate, and I'm the on'y one as knows the place. He gave it me at Savannah, when he lay a-dying, like as if I was to now, you see. But you won't peach unless they get the black spot on me, or unless you see that Black Dog again or **a seafaring man with one leg**, Jim—him above all."

"But what is the black spot, captain?" I asked.

"That's a summons, mate. I'll tell you if they get that. But you keep your weather-eye open, Jim, and I'll share with you equals, upon my honour." *[Note that Bones doesn't say what he's sharing, and it's unlikely that Jim knows it's a treasure map unless he mentioned it some other time.]*

He wandered a little longer, his voice growing weaker; but soon after I had given him his medicine, which he took like a child, with the remark, "If ever **a seaman** wanted drugs, it's me," he fell at last into a heavy, swoon-like sleep, in which I left him. What I should have done had all gone well I do not know. Probably I should have told the whole story to the doctor, for I was in mortal fear lest the captain should repent of his confessions and make an end of me. But as things fell out, my poor father died quite suddenly that evening, which put all other matters on one side. Our natural distress, the visits of **the neighbours**, the arranging of the funeral, and all the work of the inn to be carried on in the meanwhile kept me so busy that I had scarcely time to think of the captain, far less to be afraid of him.

He got downstairs next morning, to be sure, and had his meals as usual, though he ate little and had more, I am afraid, than his usual supply of rum, for he helped himself out of the bar, scowling and blowing through his nose, and no one dared to cross him. On the night before the funeral he was as drunk as ever; and it was shocking, in that house of mourning, to hear him singing away at his ugly old sea-song; but weak as he was, we were all in the fear of death for him, and the doctor was suddenly taken up with a case many miles away and was never near the house after my father's death. I have said the captain was weak, and indeed he seemed rather to grow weaker than regain his strength. He clambered up and down stairs, and went from the parlour to the bar and back again, and sometimes put his nose out of doors to smell the sea, holding on to the walls as he went for support and breathing hard and fast like a man on a steep mountain. He never particularly addressed me, and it is my belief he had as good as forgotten his confidences; but his temper was more flighty, and allowing for his bodily weakness, more violent than ever. He had an alarming way now when he was drunk of drawing his cutlass and laying it bare before him on the table. But with all that, he minded people less and seemed shut up in his own thoughts and rather wandering. Once, for instance, to our extreme wonder, he piped up to a different air, a kind of country love-song that he must have learned in his youth before he had begun to follow the sea.

So things passed until, the day after the funeral, and **about three o'clock of a bitter, foggy, frosty afternoon**, I was standing at the door for a moment, full of sad thoughts about my father, when I saw someone drawing slowly near along the road. He was plainly blind, for he tapped before him with a stick and wore a great green shade over his eyes and nose; and he was hunched, as if with age or weakness, and wore a huge old tattered sea-cloak with a hood that made him appear positively deformed. I never saw in my life a more dreadful-looking figure. He stopped a little from the inn, and raising his voice in an odd sing-song, addressed the air in front of him, "Will any kind friend inform **a poor blind man**, who has lost the precious sight of his eyes in the gracious defence of his native country, England—and God bless **King George!**—where or in what part of this country he may now be?"

"You are at the Admiral Benbow, **Black Hill Cove**, my good man," said I.

"I hear a voice," said he, "a young voice. Will you give me your hand, my kind young friend, and lead me in?"

I held out my hand, and the horrible, soft-spoken, eyeless creature gripped it in a moment like a vise. I was so much startled that I struggled to withdraw, but the blind man pulled me close up to him with a single action of his arm.

"Now, boy," he said, "take me in to the captain."

"Sir," said I, "upon my word I dare not."

"Oh," he sneered, "that's it! Take me in straight or I'll break your arm."

And he gave it, as he spoke, a wrench that made me cry out.

"Sir," said I, "it is for yourself I mean. The captain is not what he used to be. He sits with a drawn cutlass. Another gentleman—"

"Come, now, march," interrupted he; and I never heard a voice so cruel, and cold, and ugly as that blind man's. It cowed me more than the pain, and I began to obey him at once, walking straight in at the door and towards the parlour, where our sick old buccaneer was sitting, dazed with rum. The blind man clung close to me, holding me in one iron fist and leaning almost more of his weight on me than I could carry. "Lead me straight up to him, and when I'm in view, cry out, 'Here's a friend for you, Bill.' If you don't, I'll do this," and with that he gave me a twitch that I thought would have made me faint. Between this and that, I was so utterly terrified of the blind beggar that I forgot my terror of the captain, and as I opened the parlour door, cried out the words he had ordered in a trembling voice.

The poor captain raised his eyes, and at one look the rum went out of him and left him staring sober. The expression of his face was not so much of terror as of mortal sickness. He made a movement to rise, but I do not believe he had enough force left in his body.

"Now, Bill, sit where you are," said the beggar. "If I can't see, I can hear a finger stirring. Business is business. Hold out your left hand. Boy, take his left hand by the wrist and bring it near to my right."

We both obeyed him to the letter, and I saw him pass something from the hollow of the hand that held his stick into the palm of the captain's, which closed upon it instantly.

"And now that's done," said the blind man; and at the words he suddenly left hold of me, and with incredible accuracy and nimbleness, skipped out of the parlour and into the road, where, as I still stood motionless, I could hear his stick go tap-tap-tapping into the distance.

It was some time before either I or the captain seemed to gather our senses, but at length, and about at the same moment, I released his wrist, which I was still holding, and he drew in his hand and looked sharply into the palm.

31

"Ten o'clock!" he cried. "Six hours. [*A deadline.*] We'll do them yet," and he sprang to his feet.

Even as he did so, he reeled, put his hand to his throat, stood swaying for a moment, and then, with a peculiar sound, fell from his whole height face foremost to the floor.

I ran to him at once, calling to **my mother**. But haste was all in vain. The captain had been struck dead by thundering apoplexy. It is a curious thing to understand, for I had certainly never liked the man, though of late I had begun to pity him, but as soon as I saw that he was dead, I burst into a flood of tears. It was the second death I had known, and the sorrow of the first was still fresh in my heart.

STORY EVENT

A Story Event is an active change of a universal human value for one or more characters as a result of conflict (one character's desires clash with another's, or an environmental shift changes the value positively or negatively).

A Working Scene contains at least one Story Event. To determine a scene's Story Event, answer these four Socratic questions:

1. **What are the characters literally doing—that is, what are their micro on-the-surface actions?**

Jim is running the inn and caring for Bones. The captain begs for rum and warns Jim about the seafaring man with one leg again. He tells Jim to go for help if a black spot (a summons) is delivered. A blind man arrives with the black spot and a deadline, and the captain dies.

2. **What is the essential tactic of the characters—that is, what above-the-surface macro behaviors are they employing that are linked to a universal human value?**

Bones wants Jim to give him rum (because he's suffering from withdrawal symptoms) but also to send for help if a black spot is delivered. When Jim's father dies, Jim becomes distracted with his duties. The blind man gets Jim to do his bidding by physically harming him. The blind man lays down the law with the captain.

3. **What beyond-the-surface universal human values have changed for one or more characters in the scene? Which one of those value changes is most important and should be included in the Story Grid Spreadsheet?**

Jim's father and the captain move from grave illness to death in this scene, and even though this change is on the global value spectrum for Action Story, we want to look at Jim's position. The danger to him at this point is that Pew has promised to return in fewer than six hours, and Jim is alone except for his mother.

Potential Danger to Imminent Danger

4. **The Scene Event Synthesis: What Story Event sums up the**

scene's on-the-surface, above-the-surface, and beyond-the-surface change? We will enter that event in the Story Grid Spreadsheet.

Jim's father dies, and then a blind pirate delivers the black spot and a deadline before the captain dies.

HOW THE SCENE ABIDES BY THE FIVE COMMANDMENTS OF STORYTELLING

Inciting Incident: Coincidental. The captain is recovering from his stroke.

Turning Point Progressive Complication: Active. The captain tells Jim to sound the alarm if someone delivers the black spot but to keep the sea chest secret unless that happens.

Crisis: Best bad choice. If Jim tells Livesey about the danger, the captain will be angry with him, but if he doesn't, no other adult will know of the danger to him and his mother.

Climax: Jim's father dies and he is distracted by grief and work and doesn't mention anything to the doctor.

Resolution: The blind man delivers a black spot summons giving them six hours until the pirates return. The captain has a stroke and dies.

NOTES

- Jim is on the lookout for dangerous sailors but at first assumes a blind man couldn't be a threat. He puts out his hand to help him, and then Pew grabs Jim and hurts him.
- With this scene, Jim has a better understanding of what the pirates are after (the sea chest) and that he and his mother are in danger. He makes sense of the captain's arrival in the first scene.
- Jim wonders what he could have done. Should he have spoken up sooner?

4

THE SEA-CHEST

I lost no time, of course, in telling **my mother** all that I knew, and perhaps should have told her long before, and we saw ourselves at once in a difficult and dangerous position. Some of **the man**'s money—if he had any—was certainly due to us, but it was not likely that **our captain's shipmates**, above all the two specimens seen by me, **Black Dog** and **the blind beggar**, would be inclined to give up their booty in payment of the dead man's debts. The captain's order to mount at once and ride for **Doctor Livesey** would have left my mother alone and unprotected, which was not to be thought of. Indeed, it seemed impossible for either of us to remain much longer in the house; the fall of coals in the kitchen grate, the very ticking of the clock, filled us with alarms. The neighbourhood, to our ears, seemed haunted by approaching footsteps; and what between the dead body of the captain on the parlour floor and the thought of that detestable blind beggar hovering near at hand and ready to return, there were moments when, as the saying goes, I jumped in my skin for terror. Something must speedily be resolved upon, and it occurred to us at last to go forth together and seek help in **the neighbouring hamlet.** No sooner said than done. Bare-headed as we were, we ran out at once in the gathering evening and the frosty fog.

The hamlet lay not many hundred yards away, though out of view, on the other side of the next cove; and what greatly encouraged me, it was in an opposite direction from that whence the blind man had made his appearance and whither he had presumably returned. We were not many minutes on the road, though we sometimes stopped to lay hold of each other and hearken. But there was no unusual sound—nothing but the low wash of the ripple and the croaking of the inmates of the wood.

It was already candle-light when we reached the hamlet, and I shall never forget how much I was cheered to see the yellow shine in doors and windows; but that, as it proved, was the best of the help we were likely to get in that quarter. For—you would have thought men would have been ashamed of themselves—no soul would consent to return with us to the Admiral Benbow. The more we told of our troubles, the more—**man, woman, and child**—they clung to the shelter of their houses. The name of **Captain Flint**, though it was strange to me, was well enough known to some there and carried a great weight of terror. **Some of the men who had been to field-work** on the far side of the Admiral Benbow remembered, besides, to have seen **several strangers** on the road, and taking them to be **smugglers**, to have bolted away; and **one at least** had seen a little lugger in what we called Kitt's Hole. For that matter, anyone who was **a comrade of the captain's** was enough to frighten them to death. And the short and the long of the matter was, that while we could get several who were willing enough to ride to Dr. Livesey's, which lay in another direction, not one would help us to defend the inn.

They say cowardice is infectious; but then argument is, on the other hand, a great emboldener; and so when each had said his say, my mother made them a speech. She would not, she declared, lose money that belonged to her fatherless boy; "If none of the rest of you dare," she said, "Jim and I dare. Back we will go, the way we came, and small thanks to you **big, hulking, chicken-hearted men**. We'll have that chest open, if we die for it. And I'll thank you for that bag, **Mrs. Crossley**, to bring back our lawful money in."

Of course I said I would go with my mother, and of course they all cried out at our foolhardiness, but even then not a man would go along with us. All they would do was to give me a loaded pistol lest we were attacked, and to promise to have horses ready saddled in case we were pursued on our return, while **one lad** was to ride forward to the doctor's in search of armed assistance.

My heart was beating finely when we two set forth in the cold night upon this dangerous venture. A full moon was beginning to rise and peered redly through the upper edges of the fog, and this increased our haste, for it was plain, before we came forth again, that all would be as bright as day, and our departure exposed to the eyes of any watchers. We slipped along the hedges, noiseless and swift, nor did we see or hear anything to increase our terrors, till, to our relief, the door of the Admiral Benbow had closed behind us.

I slipped the bolt at once, and we stood and panted for a moment in the dark, alone in the house with the dead captain's body. Then my mother got a candle in the bar, and holding each other's hands, we advanced into the parlour. He lay as we had left him, on his back, with his eyes open and one arm stretched out.

"Draw down the blind, Jim," whispered my mother; "they might come and watch outside. And now," said she when I had done so, "we have to get the key off *that*; and who's to touch it, I should like to know!" and she gave a kind of sob as she said the words.

I went down on my knees at once. On the floor close to his hand there was a little round of paper, blackened on the one side. I could not doubt that this was the *black spot*; and taking it up, I found written on the other side, in a very good, clear hand, this short message: "You have **till ten tonight**."

"He had till ten, Mother," said I; and just as I said it, our old clock began striking. This sudden noise startled us shockingly; but the news was good, **for it was only six**. [*Jim is assuming the pirates will do what they said*.]

"Now, Jim," she said, "that key."

I felt in his pockets, one after another. A few small coins, a thimble, and some thread and big needles, a piece of pigtail tobacco bitten away at the end, his gully with the crooked handle, a pocket compass, and a tinder box were all that they contained, and I began to despair.

"Perhaps it's round his neck," suggested my mother.

Overcoming a strong repugnance, I tore open his shirt at the neck, and there, sure enough, hanging to a bit of tarry string, which I cut with his own gully, we found the key. At this triumph we were filled with hope and hurried upstairs without delay to the little room where he had slept so long and where his box had stood since the day of his arrival.

It was like any other seaman's chest on the outside, the initial "B" burned on the top of it with a hot iron, and the corners somewhat smashed and broken as by long, rough usage.

"Give me the key," said my mother; and though the lock was very stiff, she had turned it and thrown back the lid in a twinkling.

A strong smell of tobacco and tar rose from the interior, but nothing was to be seen on the top except a suit of very good clothes, carefully brushed and folded. They had never been worn, my mother said. Under that, the miscellany began—a quadrant, a tin canikin, several sticks of tobacco, two brace of very handsome pistols, a piece of bar silver, an old Spanish watch and some other trinkets of little value and mostly of foreign make, a pair of compasses mounted with brass, and five or six curious West Indian shells. I have often wondered since why he should have carried about these shells with him in his wandering, guilty, and hunted life.

In the meantime, we had found nothing of any value but the silver and the trinkets, and neither of these were in our way. Underneath there was an old boat-cloak, whitened with sea-salt on many a harbour-bar. My mother pulled it up with impatience, and there lay before us, the last things in the chest, a bundle tied up in oilcloth, and looking like papers, and a canvas bag that gave forth, at a touch, the jingle of gold.

"I'll show these rogues that I'm an honest woman," said my mother. "I'll have my dues, and not a farthing over. Hold Mrs. Crossley's bag." And she began to count over the amount of the captain's score from the sailor's bag into the one that I was holding.

It was a long, difficult business, for the coins were of all countries and sizes—doubloons, and louis d'ors, and guineas, and pieces of eight, and I know not what besides, all shaken together at random. The guineas, too, were about the scarcest, and it was with these only that my mother knew how to make her count.

When we were about half-way through, I suddenly put my hand upon her arm, for I had heard in the silent frosty air a sound that brought my heart into my mouth—the tap-tapping of **the blind man**'s stick upon the frozen road. It drew nearer and nearer, while we sat holding our breath. Then it struck sharp on the inn door, and then we could hear the handle being turned and the bolt rattling as the wretched being tried to enter; and then there was a long time of silence both within and without. At last the tapping recommenced, and, to our indescribable joy and gratitude, died slowly away again until it ceased to be heard.

"Mother," said I, "take the whole and let's be going," for I was sure the bolted door must have seemed suspicious and would bring the whole hornet's nest about our ears, though how thankful I was that I had bolted it, none could tell who had never met that terrible blind man.

But my mother, frightened as she was, would not consent to take a fraction more than was due to her and was obstinately unwilling to be content with less. **It was not yet seven**, she said, by a long way; she knew her rights and she would have them; and she was still arguing with me when a little low whistle sounded a good way off upon the hill. That was enough, and more than enough, for both of us.

"I'll take what I have," she said, jumping to her feet.

"And I'll take this to square the count," said I, picking up the oilskin packet. [*What does Jim think this is?*]

Next moment we were both groping downstairs, leaving the candle by the empty chest; and the next we had opened the door and were in full retreat. We had not started a moment too soon. The fog was rapidly dispersing; already the moon shone quite clear on the high ground on either side; and it was only in the exact bottom of the dell and round the tavern door that a thin veil still hung unbroken to conceal the first steps of our escape. Far less than half-way to the hamlet, very little beyond the bottom of the hill, we must come forth into the moonlight. Nor was this all, for the sound of **several footsteps** running came already to our ears, and as we looked back in their direction, a light tossing to and fro and still rapidly advancing showed that one of the newcomers carried a lantern.

"My dear," said my mother suddenly, "take the money and run on. I am going to faint."

This was certainly the end for both of us, I thought. How I cursed the cowardice of the neighbours; how I blamed my poor mother for her honesty and her greed, for her past foolhardiness and present weakness! We were just at **the little bridge**, by good fortune; and I helped her, tottering as she was, to the edge of the bank, where, sure enough, she gave a sigh and fell on my shoulder. I do not know how I found the strength to do it at all, and I am afraid it was roughly done, but I managed to drag her down the bank and a little way under the arch. Farther I could not move her, for the bridge was too low to let me do more than crawl below it. So there we had to stay—my mother almost entirely exposed and both of us within earshot of the inn.

• ANALYZING THE SCENE •

STORY EVENT

A Story Event is an active change of a universal human value for one or more characters as a result of conflict (one character's desires clash with another's, or an environmental shift changes the value positively or negatively).

A Working Scene contains at least one Story Event. To determine a scene's Story Event, answer these four Socratic questions:

1. What are the characters literally doing—that is, what are their micro on-the-surface actions?

Jim and Mrs. Hawkins ask their neighbors in the hamlet for help, but they refuse to get involved. Jim and his mother return to the inn where they search the captain's sea chest as the pirates approach.

2. What is the essential tactic of the characters—that is, what above-the-surface macro behaviors are they employing that are linked to a universal human value?

Mrs. Hawkins is trying to get what she is owed, and Jim wants to protect his mother. The neighbors are avoiding trouble by laying low. They are willing to help in ways that don't involve risk to themselves like offering horses and sending someone to fetch Livesey.

3. What beyond-the-surface universal human values have changed for one or more characters in the scene? Which one of those value changes is most important and should be included in the Story Grid Spreadsheet?

The pirates are coming back to the inn, and Jim and his mother were hopeful of help from their neighbors. The people of the hamlet have heard of the pirates and won't help except to send a rider for Livesey. Jim and his mother secure payment and Jim takes the captain's papers. But the most important change here is that Jim and his mother choose to further endanger themselves by returning to the inn.

Threat of Danger to Danger Realized

4. The Scene Event Synthesis: What Story Event sums up the scene's on-the-surface, above-the-surface, and beyond-the-surface change? We will enter that event in the Story Grid Spreadsheet.

After the neighbors refuse to help, Jim and Mrs. Hawkins return to the inn and search the chest. They get out and hide just as a gang of pirates approaches the inn.

HOW THE SCENE ABIDES BY THE FIVE COMMANDMENTS OF STORYTELLING

Inciting Incident: Causal. Jim informs Mrs. Hawkins that the pirates will be coming in six hours.

Turning Point Progressive Complication: Active. The neighbors refuse to help them.

Crisis: Best bad choice. If they let the pirates have the contents of the chest, they won't be compensated for the captain's stay, but if they return to the inn to get the money, they put themselves in direct danger.

Climax: Mrs. Hawkins refuses to give up the money, and Jim goes with her to the inn.

Resolution: The pirates return before the deadline, and Jim grabs the captain's papers before he and his mother hide beneath a bridge.

NOTES

- Jim has strong criticism for his mother and recognizes she is ridiculous for worrying about taking no more than she is due. What could it matter to the pirates? She's risking their lives and denying reality.
- Jim curses the neighbors for their cowardice, but they recognize the danger involved in the situation. Jim and his mother are naïve about the pirates.
- It's naïve of Jim to believe the pirates will honor their deadline.
- Jim tells his mother about Bones and Pew right away, but he doesn't insist on going to the authorities as Bones had asked.

5

THE LAST OF THE BLIND MAN

My curiosity in a sense, was stronger than my fear, for I could not remain where I was, but crept back to **the bank** again, whence, sheltering my head behind a bush of broom, I might command the road before our door. I was scarcely in position ere my enemies began to arrive, **seven or eight of them**, running hard, their feet beating out of time along the road and **the man with the lantern** some paces in front. **Three men** ran together, hand in hand; and I made out, even through the mist, that the middle man of this trio was the **blind beggar**. The next moment his voice showed me that I was right.

"Down with the door!" he cried.

"Aye, aye, sir!" answered two or three; and a rush was made upon the **Admiral Benbow**, the lantern-bearer following; and then I could see them pause, and hear speeches passed in a lower key, as if they were surprised to find the door open. But the pause was brief, for the blind man again issued his commands. His voice sounded louder and higher, as if he were afire with eagerness and rage.

"In, in, in!" he shouted, and cursed them for their delay.

Four or five of them obeyed at once, two remaining on the road with the formidable beggar. There was a pause, then a cry of surprise, and then a voice shouting from the house, "**Bill's** dead."

But the blind man swore at them again for their delay.

43

"Search him, some of you shirking lubbers, and the rest of you aloft and get the chest," he cried.

I could hear their feet rattling up our old stairs, so that the house must have shook with it. Promptly afterwards, fresh sounds of astonishment arose; the window of the captain's room was thrown open with a slam and a jingle of broken glass, and **a man** leaned out into the moonlight, head and shoulders, and addressed the blind beggar on the road below him.

"**Pew**," he cried, "they've been before us. Someone's turned the chest out alow and aloft."

"Is it there?" roared Pew.

"The money's there."

The blind man cursed the money.

"Flint's fist, I mean," he cried. [*Readers haven't been told or shown what this is yet.*]

"We don't see it here nohow," returned the man.

"Here, you below there, is it on Bill?" cried the blind man again.

At that another fellow, probably him who had remained below to search the captain's body, came to the door of the inn. "Bill's been overhauled a'ready," said he; "nothin' left."

"It's these people of the inn—it's that boy. I wish I had put his eyes out!" cried the blind man, Pew. "There were no time ago—they had the door bolted when I tried it. Scatter, lads, and find 'em."

"Sure enough, they left their glim here," said the fellow from the window.

"Scatter and find 'em! Rout the house out!" reiterated Pew, striking with his stick upon the road.

Then there followed a great to-do through all our old inn, heavy feet pounding to and fro, furniture thrown over, doors kicked in, until the very rocks re-echoed and the men came out again, one after another, on the road and declared that we were nowhere to be found. And just the same whistle that had alarmed my mother and myself over the dead captain's money was once more clearly audible through the night, but this time twice repeated. I had thought it to be the blind man's trumpet, so to speak, summoning his crew to the assault, but I now found that it was a signal from the hillside towards the hamlet, and from its effect upon the buccaneers, a signal to warn them of approaching danger.

"There's **Dirk** again," said one. "Twice! We'll have to budge, mates."

"Budge, you skulk!" cried Pew. "Dirk was a fool and a coward from the first--you wouldn't mind him. They must be close by; they can't be far; you have your hands on it. Scatter and look for them, dogs! Oh, shiver my soul," he cried, "if I had eyes!"

This appeal seemed to produce some effect, for two of the fellows began to look here and there among the lumber, but half-heartedly, I thought, and with half an eye to their own danger all the time, while the rest stood irresolute on the road.

"You have your hands on thousands, you fools, and you hang a leg! You'd be as rich as kings if you could find it, and you know it's here, and you stand there skulking. There wasn't one of you dared face Bill, and I did it--a blind man! And I'm to lose my chance for you! I'm to be a poor, crawling beggar, sponging for rum, when I might be rolling in a coach! If you had the pluck of a weevil in a biscuit you would catch them still."

"Hang it, Pew, we've got the doubloons!" grumbled one.

"They might have hid the blessed thing," said another. "Take the Georges, Pew, and don't stand here squalling."

Squalling was the word for it; Pew's anger rose so high at these objections till at last, his passion completely taking the upper hand, he struck at them right and left in his blindness and his stick sounded heavily on more than one.

These, in their turn, cursed back at the blind miscreant, threatened him in horrid terms, and tried in vain to catch the stick and wrest it from his grasp.

This quarrel was the saving of us, for while it was still raging, another sound came from the top of the hill on the side of the hamlet-- the tramp of horses galloping. Almost at the same time a pistol-shot, flash and report, came from the hedge side. And that was plainly the last signal of danger, for the buccaneers turned at once and ran, separating in every direction, one seaward along the cove, one slant across the hill, and so on, so that in half a minute not a sign of them remained but Pew. Him they had deserted, whether in sheer panic or out of revenge for his ill words and blows I know not; but there he remained behind, tapping up and down the road in a frenzy, and groping and calling for his comrades. Finally he took a wrong turn and ran a few steps past me, towards the hamlet, crying, "**Johnny, Black Dog**, Dirk," and other names, "you won't leave old Pew, mates—not old Pew!"

Just then the noise of horses topped the rise, and **four or five riders** came in sight in the moonlight and swept at full gallop down the slope.

At this Pew saw his error, turned with a scream, and ran straight for the ditch, into which he rolled. But he was on his feet again in a second and made another dash, now utterly bewildered, right under the nearest of the coming horses.

The rider tried to save him, but in vain. Down went Pew with a cry that rang high into the night; and the four hoofs trampled and spurned him and passed by. He fell on his side, then gently collapsed upon his face and moved no more.

I leaped to my feet and hailed the riders. They were pulling up, at any rate, horrified at the accident; and I soon saw what they were. One, tailing out behind the rest, was **a lad** that had gone from the hamlet to **Dr. Livesey**'s; the rest were **revenue officers**, whom he had met by the way, and with whom he had had the intelligence to return at once. Some news of the lugger in Kitt's Hole had found its way to **Supervisor Dance** and set him forth that night in our direction, and to that circumstance **my mother** and I owed our preservation from death.

Pew was dead, stone dead. As for my mother, when we had carried her up to **the hamlet**, a little cold water and salts and that soon brought her back again, and she was none the worse for her terror, though she still continued to deplore the balance of the money. In the meantime the supervisor rode on, as fast as he could, to Kitt's Hole; but his men had to dismount and grope down the dingle, leading, and sometimes supporting, their horses, and in continual fear of ambushes; so it was no great matter for surprise that when they got down to the Hole the lugger was already under way, though still close in. He hailed her. A voice replied, telling him to keep out of the moonlight or he would get some lead in him, and at the same time a bullet whistled close by his arm. Soon after, the lugger doubled the point and disappeared. Mr. Dance stood there, as he said, "like a fish out of water," and all he could do was to dispatch a man to B— to warn the cutter. "And that," said he, "is just about as good as nothing. They've got off clean, and there's an end. Only," he added, "I'm glad I trod on Master Pew's corns," for by this time he had heard my story.

I went back with him to the **Admiral Benbow**, and you cannot imagine a house in such a state of smash; the very clock had been thrown down by these fellows in their furious hunt after **my mother** and myself; and though nothing had actually been taken away except the captain's money-bag and a little silver from the till, I could see at once that we were ruined. Mr. Dance could make nothing of the scene.

"They got the money, you say? Well, then, Hawkins, what in fortune were they after? More money, I suppose?"

"No, sir; not money, I think," replied I. "In fact, sir, I believe I have the thing in my breast pocket; and to tell you the truth, I should like to get it put in safety."

"To be sure, boy; quite right," said he. "I'll take it, if you like."

"I thought perhaps Dr. Livesey—" I began.

"Perfectly right," he interrupted very cheerily, "perfectly right—a **gentleman** and **a magistrate**. And, now I come to think of it, I might as well ride round there myself and report to him or **squire**. Master Pew's dead, when all's done; not that I regret it, but he's dead, you see, and people will make it out against **an officer of his Majesty's revenue**, if make it out they can. Now, I'll tell you, Hawkins, if you like, I'll take you along."

I thanked him heartily for the offer, and we walked back to the hamlet where the horses were. By the time I had told mother of my purpose they were all in the saddle.

"**Dogger**," said Mr. Dance, "you have a good horse; take up this lad behind you."

As soon as I was mounted, holding on to Dogger's belt, the supervisor gave the word, and the party struck out at a bouncing trot on the road to Dr. Livesey's house.

STORY EVENT

A Story Event is an active change of a universal human value for one or more characters as a result of conflict (one character's desires clash with another's, or an environmental shift changes the value positively or negatively).

A Working Scene contains at least one Story Event. To determine a scene's Story Event, answer these four Socratic questions:

1. What are the characters literally doing—that is, what are their micro on-the-surface actions?

Jim and his mother hide while the pirates search and ransack the inn. The revenue men ride up and accidentally kill Pew while he stumbles in the road. The other pirates escape. Jim leaves his mother in the hamlet and rides with Dance and the other revenue men to find Livesey.

2. What is the essential tactic of the characters—that is, what above-the-surface macro behaviors are they employing that are linked to a universal human value?

Jim's mother hides while he observes the pirates and hopes for help. Pew wants to find "Flint's fist." The other pirates want this too but are afraid of getting caught.

3. What beyond-the-surface universal human values have changed for one or more characters in the scene? Which one of those value changes is most important and should be included in the Story Grid Spreadsheet?

Jim and his mother begin in imminent danger of death because given time the pirates will find them. But the arrival of Dance and the other revenue men (thanks to a rider from the hamlet) interrupt the pirates. Pew is trampled in the road, but the other pirates escape. Jim and his mother are safe for now, but the inn is destroyed.

Imminent Death to Safe but Ruined

4. The Scene Event Synthesis: What Story Event sums up the scene's on-the-surface, above-the-surface, and beyond-the-surface change? We will enter that event in the Story Grid Spreadsheet.

The pirates wreck the inn while searching for the map, but the revenue men interrupt them and kill Pew while the other pirates escape. Jim asks Dance to take him to Livesey.

HOW THE SCENE ABIDES BY THE FIVE COMMANDMENTS OF STORYTELLING

Inciting Incident: Causal. Pew and the other pirates enter the inn seeking the treasure map.

Turning Point Progressive Complication: Active. Jim and his mom are safe, but the pirates destroy the inn.

Crisis: Best bad choice. Does Jim tell Dance about the papers and risk losing them, or does he attempt to hold on to them until he can meet Livesey?

Climax: Jim tells Dance he has what the pirates were looking for and that he'd like to take it to Livesey himself.

Resolution: Dance agrees to take Jim, and they leave the hamlet.

NOTES

- Jim is more curious than scared at the beginning of the scene. Although he has some sense of the danger he's in, it's not enough dampen his excitement.
- Notice the commentary Jim shares that comes from his perspective in the future.
- This is the first time Jim tells someone he has something of value.

6

THE CAPTAIN'S PAPERS

We rode hard all the way till we drew up before **Dr. Livesey's door**. The house was all dark to the front.

Mr. Dance told me to jump down and knock, and **Dogger** gave me a stirrup to descend by. The door was opened almost at once by **the maid**.

"Is Dr. Livesey in?" I asked.

No, she said, he had come home in the afternoon but had gone up to **the hall** to dine and pass the evening with **the squire**.

"So there we go, boys," said Mr. Dance.

This time, as the distance was short, I did not mount, but ran with Dogger's stirrup-leather to the lodge gates and up the long, leafless, moonlit avenue to where the white line of the hall buildings looked on either hand on great old gardens. Here Mr. Dance dismounted, and taking me along with him, was admitted at a word into the house.

The servant led us down a matted passage and showed us at the end into a great library, all lined with bookcases and busts upon the top of them, where the squire and **Dr. Livesey** sat, pipe in hand, on either side of a bright fire.

I had never seen the squire so near at hand. He was a tall man, over six feet high, and broad in proportion, and he had a bluff, rough-and-ready face, all roughened and reddened and lined in his long travels.

His eyebrows were very black, and moved readily, and this gave him a look of some temper, not bad, you would say, but quick and high.

"Come in, Mr. Dance," says he, very stately and condescending.

"Good evening, Dance," says the doctor with a nod. "And good evening to you, friend Jim. What good wind brings you here?"

The supervisor stood up straight and stiff and told his story like a lesson; and you should have seen how the two gentlemen leaned forward and looked at each other, and forgot to smoke in their surprise and interest. When they heard how **my mother** went back to the inn, Dr. Livesey fairly slapped his thigh, and the squire cried "Bravo!" and broke his long pipe against the grate. Long before it was done, **Mr. Trelawney** (that, you will remember, was the squire's name) had got up from his seat and was striding about the room, and the doctor, as if to hear the better, had taken off his powdered wig and sat there looking very strange indeed with his own close-cropped black poll.

At last Mr. Dance finished the story.

"Mr. Dance," said the squire, "you are a very noble fellow. And as for riding down that black, **atrocious miscreant**, I regard it as an act of virtue, sir, like stamping on a cockroach. [*Trelawney is expressing a strong worldview here. Some people are less than human.*] This lad Hawkins is a trump, I perceive. Hawkins, will you ring that bell? Mr. Dance must have some ale."

"And so, Jim," said the doctor, "you have the thing that they were after, have you?"

"Here it is, sir," said I, and gave him the oilskin packet.

The doctor looked it all over, as if his fingers were itching to open it; but instead of doing that, he put it quietly in the pocket of his coat.

"Squire," said he, "when Dance has had his ale he must, of course, be off on **his Majesty**'s service; but I mean to keep **Jim Hawkins** here to sleep at my house, and with your permission, I propose we should have up the cold pie and let him sup."

"As you will, Livesey," said the squire; "Hawkins has earned better than cold pie."

So a big pigeon pie was brought in and put on a sidetable, and I made a hearty supper, for I was as hungry as a hawk, while Mr. Dance was further complimented and at last dismissed.

"And now, squire," said the doctor.

"And now, Livesey," said the squire in the same breath.

"One at a time, one at a time," laughed Dr. Livesey. "You have heard of this **Flint**, I suppose?"

"Heard of him!" cried the squire. "Heard of him, you say! He was the bloodthirstiest buccaneer that sailed. **Blackbeard** was a child to Flint. **The Spaniards** were so prodigiously afraid of him that, I tell you, sir, I was sometimes proud he was **an Englishman**. I've seen his top-sails with these eyes, **off Trinidad**, and the cowardly son of a rum-puncheon that I sailed with put back—put back, sir, into **Port of Spain**." [*Trelawney's opinion about pirates is inconsistent. Is it because Flint is at the top of his social hierarchy?*]

"Well, I've heard of him myself, in **England**," said the doctor. "But the point is, had he money?"

"Money!" cried the squire. "Have you heard the story? What were these villains after but money? What do they care for but money? For what would they risk their rascal carcasses but money?"

"That we shall soon know," replied the doctor. "But you are so confoundedly hot-headed and exclamatory that I cannot get a word in. What I want to know is this: Supposing that I have here in my pocket some clue to where Flint buried his treasure, will that treasure amount to much?"

"Amount, sir!" cried the squire. "It will amount to this: If we have the clue you talk about, I fit out a ship in **Bristol dock**, and take you and Hawkins here along, and I'll have that treasure if I search a year."

"Very well," said the doctor. "Now, then, if Jim is agreeable, we'll open the packet"; and he laid it before him on the table. [*Jim as narrator doesn't indicate whether he responded.*]

The bundle was sewn together, and the doctor had to get out his instrument case and cut the stitches with his medical scissors. It contained two things—a book and a sealed paper. [*Now we know the contents of the oilskin packet.*]

"First of all we'll try the book," observed the doctor.

The squire and I were both peering over his shoulder as he opened it, for Dr. Livesey had kindly motioned me to come round from the side-table, where I had been eating, to enjoy the sport of the search. On the first page there were only some scraps of writing, such as a man with a pen in his hand might make for idleness or practice. One was the same as the tattoo mark, "**Billy Bones** his fancy"; then there was "**Mr. W. Bones**, mate," "No more rum," "Off Palm Key he got itt," and some other snatches, mostly single words and unintelligible. I could not help wondering who it was that had "got itt," and what "itt" was that he got. A knife in his back as like as not.

"Not much instruction there," said Dr. Livesey as he passed on.

The next ten or twelve pages were filled with a curious series of entries. There was a date at one end of the line and at the other a sum of money, as in common account-books, but instead of explanatory writing, only a varying number of crosses between the two. On the **12th of June, 1745**, for instance, a sum of seventy pounds had plainly become due to **someone**, and there was nothing but six crosses to explain the cause. In a few cases, to be sure, the name of a place would be added, as "**Offe Caraccas**," or a mere entry of latitude and longitude, as "620 17' 20", 190 2' 40"."

The record lasted over nearly **twenty years**, the amount of the separate entries growing larger as time went on, and at the end a grand total had been made out after five or six wrong additions, and these words appended, "**Bones**, his pile."

"I can't make head or tail of this," said Dr. Livesey.

"The thing is as clear as noonday," cried the squire. "This is the black-hearted hound's account-book. These crosses stand for the names of ships or towns that they sank or plundered. The sums are the scoundrel's share, and where he feared an ambiguity, you see he added something clearer. 'Offe Caraccas,' now; you see, here was some unhappy vessel boarded off that coast. God help the **poor souls that manned her**—coral long ago."

"Right!" said the doctor. "See what it is to be **a traveller**. Right! And the amounts increase, you see, as he rose in rank."

There was little else in the volume but a few bearings of places noted in the blank leaves towards the end and a table for reducing French, English, and Spanish moneys to a common value.

"Thrifty man!" cried the doctor. "He wasn't the one to be cheated."

"And now," said the squire, "for the other."

The paper had been sealed in several places with a thimble by way of seal; the very thimble, perhaps, that I had found in **the captain's** pocket. The doctor opened the seals with great care, and there fell out the map of an island, with latitude and longitude, soundings, names of hills and bays and inlets, and every particular that would be needed to bring a ship to a safe anchorage upon its shores. [*This is the first time Jim tells us it's a map.*] It was about nine miles long and five across, shaped, you might say, like a fat dragon standing up, and had two fine land-locked harbours, and a hill in the centre part marked "The Spy-glass." There were several additions of a later date, but above all, three crosses of red ink—two on the north part of the island, one in the southwest—and beside this last, in the same red ink, and in a small, neat hand, very different from the captain's tottery characters, these words: "Bulk of treasure here."

Over on the back the same hand had written this further information:

Tall tree, Spy-glass shoulder, bearing a point to the N. of N.N.E.

Skeleton Island E.S.E. and by E.

Ten feet.

The bar silver is in the north cache; you can find it by the trend of the east hummock, ten fathoms south of the black crag with the face on it.

The arms are easy found, in the sand-hill, N. point of north inlet cape, bearing E. and a quarter N.

J.F.

That was all; but brief as it was, and to me incomprehensible, it filled the squire and Dr. Livesey with delight.

"Livesey," said the squire, "you will give up this wretched practice at once. Tomorrow I start for Bristol. In three weeks' time—three weeks! —two weeks—ten days—we'll have the best ship, sir, and the choicest crew in England. Hawkins shall come as **cabin-boy**. You'll make a famous cabin-boy, Hawkins. [*The decision is made for Jim, but it seems unlikely he would decline.*] You, Livesey, are **ship's doctor**; I am **admiral**. We'll take **Redruth**, **Joyce**, and **Hunter**. We'll have favourable winds, a quick passage, and not the least difficulty in finding the spot, and money to eat, to roll in, to play duck and drake with ever after."

"Trelawney," said the doctor, "I'll go with you; and I'll go bail for it, so will Jim, and be a credit to the undertaking. There's only one man I'm afraid of."

"And who's that?" cried the squire. "Name the dog, sir!"

"You," replied the doctor; "for you cannot hold your tongue. We are not the only men who know of this paper. **These fellows** who attacked the inn tonight—bold, desperate blades, for sure—and **the rest who stayed aboard that lugger**, and more, I dare say, not far off, are, one and all, through thick and thin, bound that they'll get that money. We must none of us go alone till we get to sea. Jim and I shall stick together in the meanwhile; you'll take Joyce and Hunter when you ride to Bristol, and from first to last, not one of us must breathe a word of what we've found."

"Livesey," returned the squire, "you are always in the right of it. I'll be as silent as the grave."

• ANALYZING THE SCENE •

STORY EVENT

A Story Event is an active change of a universal human value for one or more characters as a result of conflict (one character's desires clash with another's, or an environmental shift changes the value positively or negatively).

A Working Scene contains at least one Story Event. To determine a scene's Story Event, answer these four Socratic questions:

1. **What are the characters literally doing—that is, what are their micro on-the-surface actions?**

Dance and Jim go in search of Livesey. Dance reports on the happenings and is fed and dismissed. Livesey, Jim, and Trelawney open the packet and find the map and instructions to locate the treasure. They agree to go after it.

2. **What is the essential tactic of the characters—that is, what above-the-surface macro behaviors are they employing that are linked to a universal human value?**

Dance seeks reassurance that he won't get in trouble for Pew's death. Jim wants to get the packet to safety. Livesey and Trelawney want to know what's in the documents Jim found in the captain's sea chest.

3. **What beyond-the-surface universal human values have changed for one or more characters in the scene? Which one of those value changes is most important and should be included in the Story Grid Spreadsheet?**

Dance is anxious about having killed Pew but is relieved when Trelawney tells him it's not a problem. Jim, Livesey, and Trelawney are unaware of the contents of the package at first. Once they find the map and instructions, they are amateurs who agree to pursue a sea voyage knowing that a crew of violent men are also interested. They are temporarily safe, but they agree to take a big risk that will put their lives in danger.

Temporary Safety to Taking a Risk

4. **The Scene Event Synthesis: What Story Event sums up the**

scene's on-the-surface, above-the-surface, and beyond-the-surface change? We will enter that event in the Story Grid Spreadsheet.

Jim, Livesey, and Trelawney examine the captain's papers, and when they find the map and instructions, they agree to seek the treasure.

HOW THE SCENE ABIDES BY THE FIVE COMMANDMENTS OF STORYTELLING

Inciting Incident: Causal. Jim and Dance seek Livesey.

Turning Point Progressive Complication: Revelatory. The captain's papers contain a map and specific instructions to find Flint's treasure.

Crisis: Best bad choice. If they seek the treasure, they'll be in great danger, but if they turn over the documents to the authorities, they won't get the treasure or the adventure.

Climax: They decide to keep the documents secret and agree to seek the treasure together.

Resolution: Livesey stresses the importance of keeping their adventure a secret.

NOTES

- Jim's problem isn't that he fails to notice clues and red flags. He pays close attention to the people, their appearance, expressions, and voices. His challenge is in how he interprets what he observes. He makes assumptions about friends and foes on the basis of people's manners and the way they look.
- Trelawney expresses his negative belief about pirates, saying they are only after money. "For what do they care or risk their carcasses but money." But he and Livesey are no different from the pirates in this respect. The treasure doesn't belong to them, and they understand there could be danger. They are willing to risk their lives for the treasure too.
- Trelawney also expresses admiration for Flint as a fellow citizen of England, though. There is a clue here that they

aren't taking the risk for the money alone but for the adventure and glory.

- Notice that Jim makes no real decision in this scene. He hands over the packet of papers, and he relies on the adults to decide what should be done with it.
- Livesey and Trelawney mistakenly believe they can handle this mission in which they will be out of their depth. They are taken in by the romance of adventure just as Jim was when the captain arrived at the inn.
- The title of this chapter reveals that the oilskin packet contains papers. Later in the scene, we find out that a map is among the papers. As narrator, Jim could have revealed this at any time. The officials who asked for the account would already be aware. Notice how Stevenson is generating intrigue through his use of the narrative drive of mystery.

PART TWO: THE SEA-COOK

7

I GO TO BRISTOL

It was longer than **the squire** imagined ere we were ready for the sea, and none of our first plans—not even **Dr. Livesey**'s, of keeping me beside him—could be carried out as we intended. The doctor had to go to London for **a physician** to take charge of his practice; the squire was hard at work at Bristol; and I lived on at **the hall** under the charge of old **Redruth**, the gamekeeper, almost a prisoner, but full of sea-dreams and the most charming anticipations of strange islands and adventures. I brooded by the hour together over the map, all the details of which I well remembered. Sitting by the fire in the housekeeper's room, I approached that island in my fancy from every possible direction; I explored every acre of its surface; I climbed a thousand times to that tall hill they call the Spy-glass, and from the top enjoyed the most wonderful and changing prospects. Sometimes the isle was thick with **savages**, with whom we fought, sometimes full of dangerous animals that hunted us, but in all my fancies nothing occurred to me so strange and tragic as our actual adventures.

So the weeks passed on, till one fine day there came a letter addressed to Dr. Livesey, with this addition, "To be opened, in the case of his absence, by Tom Redruth or young **Hawkins**." Obeying this order, we found, or rather I found—for the gamekeeper was a poor hand at reading anything but print—the following important news:

Old Anchor Inn, Bristol, March 1, 17—

Dear Livesey—As I do not know whether you are at the hall or still in London, I send this in double to both places.

The ship is bought and fitted. She lies at anchor, ready for sea. You never imagined a sweeter schooner—a child might sail her—two hundred tons; name, Hispaniola.

*I got her through my old friend, **Blandly**, who has proved himself throughout the most surprising rump. The admirable fellow literally slaved in my interest, and so, I may say, did everyone in Bristol, as soon as they got wind of the port we sailed for—treasure, I mean.*

"Redruth," said I, interrupting the letter, "Dr. Livesey will not like that. The squire has been talking, after all."

"Well, who's a better right?" growled the gamekeeper. "A pretty rum go if squire ain't to talk for Dr. Livesey, I should think." [*Status matters more than good sense.*]

At that I gave up all attempts at commentary and read straight on:

Blandly himself found the Hispaniola, *and by the most admirable management got her for the merest trifle. There is **a class of men in Bristol** monstrously prejudiced against Blandly. They go the length of declaring that this honest creature would do anything for money, that the Hispaniola belonged to him, and that he sold it me absurdly high—the most transparent calumnies. None of them dare, however, to deny the merits of the ship.*

*So far there was not a hitch. The **workpeople**, to be sure—**riggers and what not**—were most annoyingly slow; but time cured that. It was **the crew** that troubled me.*

*I wished a round score of men—in case of **natives, buccaneers,** or the odious **French**—and I had the worry of the deuce itself to find so much as half a dozen, till the most remarkable stroke of fortune brought me the very man that I required.*

I was standing on the dock, when, by the merest accident, I fell in talk with him. I found he was an old sailor, kept a public-house, knew all the seafaring men in Bristol, had lost his health ashore, and wanted a good berth as cook to get to sea again. He had hobbled down there that morning, he said, to get a smell of the salt.

*I was monstrously touched—so would you have been—and, out of pure pity, I engaged him on the spot to be ship's cook. **Long John Silver**, he is called,*

64

*and has lost a leg; but that I regarded as a recommendation, since he lost it in his country's service, under the immortal **Hawke**. He has no pension, Livesey. Imagine the abominable age we live in!*

*Well, sir, I thought I had only found a cook, but it was a crew I had discovered. Between Silver and myself we got together in a few days a company of **the toughest old salts imaginable**—not pretty to look at, but fellows, by their faces, of the most indomitable spirit. I declare we could fight a frigate.*

*Long John even got rid of **two out of the six or seven** I had already engaged. He showed me in a moment that they were just the sort of **freshwater swabs** we had to fear in an adventure of importance.*

I am in the most magnificent health and spirits, eating like a bull, sleeping like a tree, yet I shall not enjoy a moment till I hear my old tarpaulins tramping round the capstan. Seaward, ho! Hang the treasure! It's the glory of the sea that has turned my head. So now, Livesey, come post; do not lose an hour, if you respect me.

*Let young Hawkins go at once to see **his mother**, with Redruth for a guard; and then both come full speed to Bristol.*

John Trelawney

*Postscript—I did not tell you that Blandly, who, by the way, is to send **a consort** after us if we don't turn up by the end of August, had found an admirable fellow for **sailing master**—a stiff man, which I regret, but in all other respects a treasure. Long John Silver unearthed a very competent man for **a mate**, a man named **Arrow**. I have a **boatswain** who pipes, Livesey; so things shall go man-o'-war fashion on board the good ship Hispaniola.*

*I forgot to tell you that Silver is a man of substance; I know of my own knowledge that he has a banker's account, which has never been overdrawn. He leaves **his wife** to manage the inn; and as she is **a woman of colour**, a pair of old bachelors like you and I may be excused for guessing that it is the wife, quite as much as the health, that sends him back to roving.*

J. T.

P.P.S.—Hawkins may stay one night with his mother.

J. T.

You can fancy the excitement into which that letter put me. I was half beside myself with glee; and if ever I despised a man, it was old Tom Redruth, who could do nothing but grumble and lament. Any of the **under-gamekeepers** would gladly have changed places with him; but such was not the squire's pleasure, and the squire's pleasure was like law among them all. Nobody but old Redruth would have dared so much as even to grumble.

The next morning he and I set out on foot for **the Admiral Benbow**, and there I found **my mother** in good health and spirits. **The captain,** who had so long been a cause of so much discomfort, was gone where the wicked cease from troubling. The squire had had everything repaired, and the public rooms and the sign repainted, and had added some furniture—above all a beautiful armchair for mother in the bar. He had found her **a boy as an apprentice** also so that she should not want help while I was gone.

It was on seeing that boy that I understood, for the first time, my situation. I had thought up to that moment of the adventures before me, not at all of the home that I was leaving; and now, at sight of this clumsy stranger, who was to stay here in my place beside my mother, I had my first attack of tears. I am afraid I led that boy a dog's life, for as he was new to the work, I had a hundred opportunities of setting him right and putting him down, and I was not slow to profit by them.

The night passed, and the next day, after dinner, Redruth and I were afoot again and on the road. I said good-bye to Mother and the cove where I had lived since I was born, and the dear old Admiral Benbow—since he was repainted, no longer quite so dear. One of my last thoughts was of the captain, who had so often strode along the beach with his cocked hat, his sabre-cut cheek, and his old brass telescope. Next moment we had turned the corner and my home was out of sight.

The mail picked us up about dusk at the **Royal George** on the heath. I was wedged in between Redruth and **a stout old gentleman,** and in spite of the swift motion and the cold night air, I must have dozed a great deal from the very first, and then slept like a log up hill and down dale through stage after stage, for when I was awakened at last it was by a punch in the ribs, and I opened my eyes to find that we were standing still before a large building in a city street and that the day had already broken a long time.

"Where are we?" I asked.

"**Bristol**," said Tom. "Get down."

Mr. Trelawney had taken up his residence at **an inn far down the docks** to superintend the work upon the schooner. Thither we had now to walk, and our way, to my great delight, lay along the quays and beside the great multitude of ships of all sizes and rigs and nations. In one, **sailors** were singing at their work, in another there were **men aloft**, high over my head, hanging to threads that seemed no thicker than a spider's. Though I had lived by the shore all my life, I seemed never to have been near the sea till then. The smell of tar and salt was something new. I saw the most wonderful figureheads, that had all been far over the ocean. I saw, besides, **many old sailors**, with rings in their ears, and whiskers curled in ringlets, and tarry pigtails, and their swaggering, clumsy sea-walk; and if I had seen as many **kings** or **archbishops** I could not have been more delighted.

And I was going to sea myself, to sea in a schooner, with **a piping boatswain** and **pig-tailed singing seamen**, to sea, bound for an unknown island, and to seek for buried treasure!

While I was still in this delightful dream, we came suddenly in front of a large inn and met **Squire Trelawney**, all dressed out like a sea-officer, in stout blue cloth, coming out of the door with a smile on his face and a capital imitation of a sailor's walk.

"Here you are," he cried, "and the doctor came last night from London. Bravo! The ship's company complete!"

"Oh, sir," cried I, "when do we sail?"

"Sail!" says he. "We sail tomorrow!"

• ANALYZING THE SCENE •

STORY EVENT

A Story Event is an active change of a universal human value for one or more characters as a result of conflict (one character's desires clash with another's, or an environmental shift changes the value positively or negatively).

A Working Scene contains at least one Story Event. To determine a scene's Story Event, answer these four Socratic questions:

1. What are the characters literally doing—that is, what are their micro on-the-surface actions?

Jim waits for weeks with Redruth for his summons. He spends that time pouring over the treasure map and fantasizing about the adventure to come. Trelawney's letter arrives, and Jim visits his mother before leaving for Bristol. He criticizes the boy who stays at the inn to help his mother. Redruth and Jim make their way to Bristol by mail coach.

2. What is the essential tactic of the characters—that is, what above-the-surface macro behaviors are they employing that are linked to a universal human value?

Jim is dreaming of adventure. Trelawney and Livesey are making preparations to leave. Long John Silver has inveigled his way onto the crew of the *Hispaniola*.

3. What beyond-the-surface universal human values have changed for one or more characters in the scene? Which one of those value changes is most important and should be included in the Story Grid Spreadsheet?

While waiting to travel, Jim is caught up in the excitement but returning to the inn gives him mixed feelings. The fantasy version of his trip gives way to reality. It's not pleasant for him, but he is becoming more aware of what it means to leave home.

Fantasy to Reality

4. The Scene Event Synthesis: What Story Event sums up the scene's on-the-surface, above-the-surface, and beyond-the-surface change? We will enter that event in the Story Grid Spreadsheet.

Jim fills his head with fantasies about his adventure, but before leaving the inn, he remembers the old captain.

HOW THE SCENE ABIDES BY THE FIVE COMMANDMENTS OF STORYTELLING

Inciting Incident: Causal. Jim is staying at Trelawney's hall while the adults prepare for the voyage.

Turning Point Progressive Complication: Revelatory. Jim returns home for a night and for the first time thinks of what he's giving up at home. He realizes he can't have his cake and eat it too.

Crisis: Best bad choice. Jim could stay home where he is safe and give up the chance of adventure or leave and risk never returning.

Climax: He chooses to leave home, but he is mean to the boy who will take his place and help his mother.

Resolution: Far from the adventures he imagined, Jim rides to Bristol in the mail carriage, squashed between Redruth and another man. He sleeps most of the way to Bristol. He arrives and Trelawney tells them they will set sail the next day.

NOTES

- The line "a child might sail her" foreshadows Jim's sea adventure later.
- This scene sets up how Jim is still immature. He remembers the captain, but only in a romantic way, not his terrible end in fear and pain. He moves here from fantasy to reality, but the lesson doesn't stay with him.
- In terms of the narrative device, Jim does not present himself in a favorable light here. This lends him credibility.
- Men in Bristol accuse Blandly of doing anything for money, which was Trelawney's statement about pirates in scene 6. It doesn't occur to him that Blandly might be connected with the pirates or might reveal sensitive information. Trelawney is also blinded by his romantic feeling about the adventure.
- Jim doesn't mention concerns about the seafaring man with

one leg here. He is so observant he couldn't help but notice, but between the lines, we realize he must come up with what he believes is a rational explanation.

- Redruth is the only person who doesn't want to go on the voyage, probably because he understands it will be dangerous. He is similar to the people in the hamlet in this way, but he's willing to stick by Trelawney.
- Part of crossing the threshold can be a review of what we're leaving behind, and this scene covers this transition effectively.

8

AT THE SIGN OF THE SPY-GLASS

When **I** had done breakfasting **the squire** gave me a note addressed to **John Silver**, at the sign of the Spy-glass, and told me I should easily find the place by following the line of the docks and keeping a bright lookout for a little tavern with a large brass telescope for sign. I set off, overjoyed at this opportunity to see some more of the ships and **seamen**, and picked my way among **a great crowd of people** and carts and bales, for the dock was now at its busiest, until I found the tavern in question.

It was a bright enough little place of entertainment. The sign was newly painted; the windows had neat red curtains; the floor was cleanly sanded. There was a street on each side and an open door on both, which made the large, low room pretty clear to see in, in spite of clouds of tobacco smoke.

The customers were mostly **seafaring men**, and they talked so loudly that I hung at the door, almost afraid to enter.

As I was waiting, a man came out of a side room, and at a glance I was sure he must be **Long John**. His left leg was cut off close by the hip, and under the left shoulder he carried a crutch, which he managed with wonderful dexterity, hopping about upon it like a bird. He was very tall and strong, with a face as big as a ham—plain and pale, but intelligent and smiling. Indeed, he seemed in the most cheerful spirits, whistling as he moved about among the tables, with a merry word or a slap on the shoulder for the more favoured of his guests.

Now, to tell you the truth, from the very first mention of Long John in Squire Trelawney's letter I had taken a fear in my mind that he might prove to be the very one-legged sailor whom I had watched for so long at the old Benbow. But one look at the man before me was enough. I had seen the captain, and Black Dog, and the blind man, Pew, and I thought I knew what a buccaneer was like—a very different creature, according to me, from this clean and pleasant-tempered landlord.

I plucked up courage at once, crossed the threshold, and walked right up to the man where he stood, propped on his crutch, talking to a customer.

"Mr. Silver, sir?" I asked, holding out the note.

"Yes, my lad," said he; "such is my name, to be sure. And who may you be?" And then as he saw the squire's letter, he seemed to me to give something almost like a start.

"Oh!" said he, quite loud, and offering his hand. "I see. You are our new **cabin-boy**; pleased I am to see you."

And he took my hand in his large firm grasp.

Just then one of the customers at the far side rose suddenly and made for the door. It was close by him, and he was out in the street in a moment. But his hurry had attracted my notice, and I recognized him at glance. It was **the tallow-faced man**, wanting two fingers, who had come first to the Admiral Benbow.

"Oh," I cried, "stop him! It's **Black Dog!**"

"I don't care two coppers who he is," cried Silver. "But he hasn't paid his score. **Harry**, run and catch him."

One of the others who was nearest the door leaped up and started in pursuit.

"If he were **Admiral Hawke** he shall pay his score," cried Silver; and then, relinquishing my hand, "Who did you say he was?" he asked. "Black what?"

"Dog, sir," said I. "Has Mr. Trelawney not told you of **the buccaneers**? He was one of them."

"So?" cried Silver. "In my house! **Ben**, run and help Harry. One of those swabs, was he? Was that you drinking with him, **Morgan**? Step up here."

The man whom he called Morgan—an old, grey-haired, mahogany-faced sailor—came forward pretty sheepishly, rolling his quid.

"Now, Morgan," said Long John very sternly, "you never clapped your eyes on that Black—Black Dog before, did you, now?" [*Notice how Silver is "leading the witness."*]

"Not I, sir," said Morgan with a salute.

"You didn't know his name, did you?"

"No, sir."

"By the powers, Tom Morgan, it's as good for you!" exclaimed the landlord. "If you had been mixed up with the like of that, you would never have put another foot in my house, you may lay to that. And what was he saying to you?"

"I don't rightly know, sir," answered Morgan.

"Do you call that a head on your shoulders, or a blessed dead-eye?" cried Long John. "Don't rightly know, don't you! Perhaps you don't happen to rightly know who you was speaking to, perhaps? Come, now, what was he jawing—v'yages, cap'ns, ships? Pipe up! What was it?"

"We was a-talkin' of keel-hauling," answered Morgan.

"Keel-hauling, was you? And a mighty suitable thing, too, and you may lay to that. Get back to your place for a lubber, Tom."

And then, as Morgan rolled back to his seat, Silver added to me in a confidential whisper that was very flattering, as I thought, "He's quite an honest man, Tom Morgan, on'y stupid. And now," he ran on again, aloud, "let's see—Black Dog? No, I don't know the name, not I. Yet I kind of think I've—yes, I've seen the swab. He used to come here with a blind beggar, he used."

"That he did, you may be sure," said I. "I knew that blind man too. His name was **Pew**."

"It was!" cried Silver, now quite excited. "Pew! That were his name for certain. Ah, he looked a shark, he did! If we run down this Black Dog, now, there'll be news for Cap'n Trelawney! Ben's a good runner; few seamen run better than Ben. He should run him down, hand over hand, by the powers! He talked o' keel-hauling, did he? I'LL keel-haul him!"

73

All the time he was jerking out these phrases he was stumping up and down the tavern on his crutch, slapping tables with his hand, and giving such a show of excitement as would have convinced an **Old Bailey judge** or a **Bow Street runner** (early British police officers). My suspicions had been thoroughly reawakened on finding Black Dog at the Spy-glass, and I watched the cook narrowly. But he was too deep, and too ready, and too clever for me, and by the time the two men had come back out of breath and confessed that they had lost the track in a crowd, and been scolded like thieves, I would have gone bail for the innocence of Long John Silver.

"See here, now, Hawkins," said he, "here's a blessed hard thing on a man like me, now, ain't it? There's Cap'n Trelawney—what's he to think? Here I have this confounded **son of a Dutchman** sitting in my own house drinking of my own rum! Here you comes and tells me of it plain; and here I let him give us all the slip before my blessed deadlights! Now, Hawkins, you do me justice with the cap'n. You're a lad, you are, but you're as smart as paint. I see that when you first come in. Now, here it is: What could I do, with this old timber I hobble on? When I was an **A B master mariner** I'd have come up alongside of him, hand over hand, and broached him to in a brace of old shakes, I would; but now—"

And then, all of a sudden, he stopped, and his jaw dropped as though he had remembered something.

"The score!" he burst out. "Three goes o' rum! Why, shiver my timbers, if I hadn't forgotten my score!"

And falling on a bench, he laughed until the tears ran down his cheeks. I could not help joining, and we laughed together, peal after peal, until the tavern rang again.

"Why, what a precious **old sea-calf** [*I talk too much.*] I am!" he said at last, wiping his cheeks. "You and me should get on well, Hawkins, for I'll take my davy [*swear an oath*] I should be rated ship's boy. But come now, stand by to go about. This won't do. Dooty is dooty, messmates. I'll put on my old cockerel hat, and step along of you to Cap'n Trelawney, and report this here affair. For mind you, it's serious, young Hawkins; and neither you nor me's come out of it with what I should make so bold as to call credit. Nor you neither, says you; not smart—none of the pair of us smart. But dash my buttons! That was a good un about my score."

And he began to laugh again, and that so heartily, that though I did not see the joke as he did, I was again obliged to join him in his mirth.

On our little walk along the quays, he made himself the most interesting companion, telling me about the different ships that we passed by, their rig, tonnage, and nationality, explaining the work that was going forward—how one was discharging, another taking in cargo, and a third making ready for sea—and every now and then telling me some little anecdote of ships or seamen or repeating a nautical phrase till I had learned it perfectly. I began to see that here was one of the best of possible shipmates.

When we got to the inn, the squire and **Dr. Livesey** were seated together, finishing a quart of ale with a toast in it, before they should go aboard the schooner on a visit of inspection.

Long John told the story from first to last, with a great deal of spirit and the most perfect truth. "That was how it were, now, weren't it, Hawkins?" he would say, now and again, and I could always bear him entirely out.

The two gentlemen regretted that Black Dog had got away, but we all agreed there was nothing to be done, and after he had been complimented, Long John took up his crutch and departed.

"All hands aboard by four this afternoon," shouted the squire after him.

"Aye, aye, sir," cried the cook, in the passage.

"Well, squire," said Dr. Livesey, "I don't put much faith in your discoveries, as a general thing; but I will say this, John Silver suits me."

"The man's a perfect trump," declared the squire.

"And now," added the doctor, "Jim may come on board with us, may he not?"

"To be sure he may," says squire. "Take your hat, Hawkins, and we'll see the ship."

• ANALYZING THE SCENE •

STORY EVENT

A Story Event is an active change of a universal human value for one or more characters as a result of conflict (one character's desires clash with another's, or an environmental shift changes the value positively or negatively).

A Working Scene contains at least one Story Event. To determine a scene's Story Event, answer these four Socratic questions:

1. What are the characters literally doing—that is, what are their micro on-the-surface actions?

Jim takes a letter from Trelawney to Silver and decides he can't be the man with the wooden leg Bones warned him about. While at the Spy-glass, he spots Black Dog leaving, and Silver sends men to chase him. Silver and Jim meet Trelawney and Livesey and tell them the tale.

2. What is the essential tactic of the characters—that is, what above-the-surface macro behaviors are they employing that are linked to a universal human value?

Jim is taking the measure of Silver, who is steering Jim away from the truth. Jim is so charmed by Silver, he can't see what's wrong.

3. What beyond-the-surface universal human values have changed for one or more characters in the scene? Which one of those value changes is most important and should be included in the Story Grid Spreadsheet?

Jim is wary when he goes to the pub, because he's had some concern about the seafaring man with one leg, but Silver wins him over with his charm and appearance. Jim is still naïve because he believes he can accurately judge people by their manner and appearance. This moves him and his friends into danger because he dismisses any concerns he had about Silver.

Wary to Trusting

4. The Scene Event Synthesis: What Story Event sums up the scene's on-the-surface, above-the-surface, and beyond-the-surface change? We will enter that event in the Story Grid Spreadsheet.

Silver charms Jim, who fails to mention the seafaring man with one leg Bones told him about.

HOW THE SCENE ABIDES BY THE FIVE COMMANDMENTS OF STORYTELLING

Inciting Incident: Causal. Trelawney sends Jim to deliver a message to Silver.

Turning Point Progressive Complication: Active. Silver asks Jim to "do him justice" with Trelawney, meaning back up his account of the Black Dog incident.

Crisis: Irreconcilable goods choice. If Jim reveals the captain's warning to Trelawney and Livesey, he'll be acting responsibly for the safety of his friends and him, but it might look bad for Silver, a charming man who has been kind to him.

Climax: Jim fails to speak up and confirms Silver's account of the incident with Black Dog.

Resolution: They all agree nothing could have been done about Black Dog and that Silver is an asset to the crew. They take Jim to see the ship.

NOTES

- Jim believes he can trust Silver and that he's not the seafaring man with one leg he was warned about. This seems to be a result of Silver's appearance and probably also the condition of his establishment. This is a guideline, most likely passed down to Jim from his parents (collective cultural grammar), that would have served him well in most circumstances at the Admiral Benbow inn. But in the wider world, it won't. Part of maturation is realizing that the rules of one domain don't necessarily apply to all domains.
- The letter in the prior scene described Silver, but Jim didn't mention it. It's possible that Jim reserves judgment until he sees Silver perhaps because he believes he's a good judge of character or because Silver keeps an establishment like his

father did. But notice that Jim the narrator is choosing when to reveal information.

- The language of sailors along with the sights and sounds let us know we've dropped into a whole new world.
- Long John Silver plays the role of threshold guardian here. He's introducing Jim to the extraordinary world. He's not trying to discourage Jim but telling him how things are. His goal is to steer Jim away from the truth and make him an ally.
- Jim must have noticed the connection between the name of Silver's pub and the name of the hill on Treasure Island since he has studied the map so closely, but he doesn't mention it.

9

POWDER AND ARMS

The *Hispaniola* lay some way out, and we went under the figureheads and round the sterns of many other ships, and their cables sometimes grated underneath our keel, and sometimes swung above us. At last, however, we got alongside, and were met and saluted as we stepped aboard by the mate, **Mr. Arrow**, a brown old sailor with earrings in his ears and a squint. He and the squire were very thick and friendly, but I soon observed that things were not the same between **Mr. Trelawney** and the captain.

This last was a sharp-looking man who seemed angry with everything on board and was soon to tell us why, for we had hardly got down into the cabin when **a sailor** followed us.

"**Captain Smollett**, sir, axing to speak with you," said he.

"I am always at the captain's orders. Show him in," said the squire.

The captain, who was close behind his messenger, entered at once and shut the door behind him.

"Well, Captain Smollett, what have you to say? All well, I hope; all shipshape and seaworthy?"

"Well, sir," said the captain, "better speak plain, I believe, even at the risk of offence. I don't like this cruise; I don't like **the men**; and I don't like **my officer**. That's short and sweet."

"Perhaps, sir, you don't like the ship?" inquired the squire, very angry, as I could see.

"I can't speak as to that, sir, not having seen her tried," said the captain. "She seems a clever craft; more I can't say."

"Possibly, sir, you may not like **your employer**, either?" says the squire.

But here **Dr. Livesey** cut in.

"Stay a bit," said he, "stay a bit. No use of such questions as that but to produce ill feeling. The captain has said too much or he has said too little, and I'm bound to say that I require an explanation of his words. You don't, you say, like this cruise. Now, why?"

"I was engaged, sir, on what we call sealed orders, to sail this ship for that gentleman where he should bid me," said the captain. "So far so good. But now I find that **every man before the mast** knows more than I do. I don't call that fair, now, do you?"

"No," said Dr. Livesey, "I don't."

"Next," said the captain, "I learn we are going after treasure— hear it from **my own hands**, mind you. Now, treasure is ticklish work; I don't like treasure voyages on any account, and I don't like them, above all, when they are secret and when (begging your pardon, Mr. Trelawney) the secret has been told to the parrot."

"**Silver's** parrot?" asked the squire.

"It's a way of speaking," said the captain. "Blabbed, I mean. It's my belief neither of you gentlemen know what you are about, but I'll tell you my way of it—life or death, and a close run."

"That is all clear, and, I dare say, true enough," replied Dr. Livesey. "We take the risk, but we are not so ignorant as you believe us. Next, you say you don't like the crew. Are they not **good seamen**?"

"I don't like them, sir," returned Captain Smollett. "And I think I should have had the choosing of my own hands, if you go to that." [*It's customary for captains to choose their own mate and crew.*]

"Perhaps you should," replied the doctor. "My friend should, perhaps, have taken you along with him; but the slight, if there be one, was unintentional. And you don't like **Mr. Arrow**?"

"I don't, sir. I believe he's a good seaman, but he's too free with the crew to be a good officer. **A mate** should keep himself to himself—shouldn't drink with the men before the mast!"

"Do you mean he drinks?" cried the squire.

"No, sir," replied the captain, "only that he's too familiar."

"Well, now, and the short and long of it, captain?" asked the doctor. "Tell us what you want."

"Well, gentlemen, are you determined to go on this cruise?"

"Like iron," answered the squire.

"Very good," said the captain. "Then, as you've heard me very patiently, saying things that I could not prove, hear me a few words more. They are putting the powder and the arms in the fore hold. Now, you have a good place under the cabin; why not put them there?—first point. Then, you are bringing **four of your own people** with you, and they tell me some of them are to be berthed forward. Why not give them the berths here beside the cabin?—second point."

"Any more?" asked Mr. Trelawney.

"One more," said the captain. "There's been too much blabbing already."

"Far too much," agreed the doctor.

"I'll tell you what I've heard myself," continued Captain Smollett: "that you have a map of an island, that there's crosses on the map to show where treasure is, and that the island lies—" And then he named the latitude and longitude exactly.

"I never told that," cried the squire, "to a soul!"

"The hands know it, sir," returned the captain.

"Livesey, that must have been you or **Hawkins**," cried the squire.

"It doesn't much matter who it was," replied the doctor. And I could see that neither he nor the captain paid much regard to Mr. Trelawney's protestations. Neither did I, to be sure, he was so loose a talker; yet in this case I believe he was really right and that nobody had told the situation of the island.

"Well, gentlemen," continued the captain, "I don't know who has this map; but I make it a point, it shall be kept secret even from me and Mr. Arrow. Otherwise I would ask you to let me resign."

"I see," said the doctor. "You wish us to keep this matter dark and to make a garrison of the stern part of the ship, manned with my friend's own people, and provided with all the arms and powder on board. **In other words, you fear a mutiny.**"

"Sir," said Captain Smollett, "with no intention to take offence, I deny your right to put words into my mouth. No captain, sir, would be justified in going to sea at all if he had ground enough to say that. As for Mr. Arrow, I believe him thoroughly honest; some of the men are the same; all may be for what I know. But I am responsible for the ship's safety and the life of **every man Jack** [*each and every person*] aboard of her. I see things going, as I think, not quite right. And I ask you to take certain precautions or let me resign my berth. And that's all."

"Captain Smollett," began the doctor with a smile, "did ever you hear the fable of the mountain and the mouse? You'll excuse me, I dare say, but you remind me of that fable. When you came in here, I'll stake my wig, you meant more than this."

"Doctor," said the captain, "you are smart. When I came in here I meant to get discharged. I had no thought that Mr. Trelawney would hear a word."

"No more I would," cried the squire. "Had Livesey not been here I should have seen you to the deuce. As it is, I have heard you. I will do as you desire, but I think the worse of you."

"That's as you please, sir," said the captain. "You'll find I do my duty."

And with that he took his leave.

"Trelawney," said the doctor, "contrary to all my notions, I believed you have managed to get two honest men on board with you—that man and John Silver."

"Silver, if you like," cried the squire; "but as for that intolerable humbug, I declare I think his conduct unmanly, unsailorly, and downright un-English."

"Well," says the doctor, "we shall see." [*Livesey is reserving judgment.*]

When we came on deck, the men had begun already to take out the arms and powder, yo-ho-ing at their work, while the captain and Mr. Arrow stood by superintending.

The new arrangement was quite to my liking. The whole schooner had been overhauled; six berths had been made astern out of what had been the after-part of the main hold; and this set of cabins was only joined to the galley and forecastle by a sparred passage on the port side. It had been originally meant that the captain, Mr. Arrow, **Hunter**, **Joyce**, the doctor, and the squire were to occupy these six berths. Now **Redruth** and I were to get two of them and Mr. Arrow and the captain were to sleep on deck in the companion, which had been enlarged on each side till you might almost have called it a round-house. Very low it was still, of course; but there was room to swing two hammocks, and even the mate seemed pleased with the arrangement. Even he, perhaps, had been doubtful as to the crew, but that is only guess, for as you shall hear, we had not long the benefit of his opinion.

We were all hard at work, changing the powder and the berths, when the last man or two, and **Long John** along with them, came off in a shore-boat.

The cook came up the side like a monkey for cleverness, and as soon as he saw what was doing, "So ho, mates!" says he. "What's this?"

"We're a-changing of the powder, Jack," answers one.

"Why, by the powers," cried Long John, "if we do, we'll miss the morning tide!"

"My orders!" said the captain shortly. "You may go below, my man. Hands will want supper."

"Aye, aye, sir," answered the cook, and touching his forelock, he disappeared at once in the direction of his galley.

"That's a good man, captain," said the doctor.

"Very likely, sir," replied Captain Smollett. "Easy with that, men—easy," he ran on, to the fellows who were shifting the powder; and then suddenly observing me examining the swivel we carried amidships, a long brass nine, "Here you, ship's boy," he cried, "out o' that! Off with you to the cook and get some work."

And then as I was hurrying off I heard him say, quite loudly, to the doctor, "I'll have no favourites on my ship."

I assure you I was quite of the squire's way of thinking, and hated the captain deeply.

• ANALYZING THE SCENE •

STORY EVENT

A Story Event is an active change of a universal human value for one or more characters as a result of conflict (one character's desires clash with another's, or an environmental shift changes the value positively or negatively).

A Working Scene contains at least one Story Event. To determine a scene's Story Event, answer these four Socratic questions:

1. What are the characters literally doing—that is, what are their micro on-the-surface actions?

The crew is preparing to set sail when Smollett asks to speak with Trelawney and Livesey. He tells them of the problems he sees with the mission and crew. He demands be able to take precautions or be relieved of the job. Trelawney agrees but is grumpy about it, and Jim begins to dislike Smollett too.

2. What is the essential tactic of the characters—that is, what above-the-surface macro behaviors are they employing that are linked to a universal human value?

Smollett believes Trelawney and Livesey don't know what they are doing. He wants them to heed his warning or let him out of the trip. Trelawney thinks Smollett isn't showing him proper respect. Livesey wants to understand Smollett's concerns. Silver wants to get the lay of the land and find out why conditions are changing.

3. What beyond-the-surface universal human values have changed for one or more characters in the scene? Which one of those value changes is most important and should be included in the Story Grid Spreadsheet?

Smollett alerts Trelawney and Livesey to a problem and gives them an ultimatum to move the ammunition and powder and change the sleeping arrangements. Trelawney doesn't like it, but without Smollett their voyage will be further delayed. They aren't safe because there are still pirates aboard, but the voyage is a little safer because Smollett speaks up and allows them to make reasonable adjustments.

Danger to Less Danger

4. The Scene Event Synthesis: What Story Event sums up the scene's on-the-surface, above-the-surface, and beyond-the-surface change? We will enter that event in the Story Grid Spreadsheet.

Trelawney agrees to address Smollett's concerns by moving the garrison, but he and Jim begin to dislike Smollett.

HOW THE SCENE ABIDES BY THE FIVE COMMANDMENTS OF STORYTELLING

Inciting Incident: Causal. Smollett asks to speak with Trelawney and Livesey.

Turning Point Progressive Complication: Active. Smollett gives an ultimatum. Move the garrison to the stern where it can be guarded by Trelawney's own men, or he will leave.

Crisis: Best bad choice. If Trelawney and Livesey don't do what Smollett asks, they'll lose their captain, but if they agree to his conditions, Trelawney fears he's being disrespected.

Climax: Trelawney agrees because of Livesey, but he thinks less of Smollett.

Resolution: Smollett and Arrow supervise the moving of the garrison items. The ship is remodeled. Silver shows interest in the rearrangement and seems concerned they'll miss the morning tide. Jim and Trelawney dislike Smollett.

NOTE

• As the scene opens, Jim, Livesey, and Trelawney are excited about the mission and believe everything is in order. They have been fortunate. Even though Black Dog was spotted, the *Hispaniola* will leave before he can cause mischief. But Smollett tells them about problems and gives them an ultimatum, which Trelawney doesn't appreciate. Trelawney reacts immaturely here. It's Smollett's responsibility to keep everyone safe, so he's doing the job he was hired to do. Livesey is more reasonable, but he is still unwilling to stop the mission. Jim and the adults he relies on still can't see the real problem.

10

THE VOYAGE

All that night we were in a great bustle getting things stowed in their place, and boatfuls of **the squire's friends, Mr. Blandly** and the like, coming off to wish him a good voyage and a safe return. We never had a night at the Admiral Benbow when I had half the work; and I was dog-tired when, a little before dawn, **the boatswain** sounded his pipe and **the crew** began to man the capstan-bars. I might have been twice as weary, yet I would not have left **the deck**, all was so new and interesting to me—the brief commands, the shrill note of the whistle, the men bustling to their places in the glimmer of the ship's lanterns.

"Now, **Barbecue**, tip us a stave," cried **one voice**.

"The old one," cried another.

"Aye, aye, mates," said Long John, who was standing by, with his crutch under his arm, and at once broke out in the air and words I knew so well:

"Fifteen men on the dead man's chest—"

And then the whole crew bore chorus:—

"Yo-ho-ho, and a bottle of rum!"

And at the third "Ho!" drove the bars before them with a will.

Even at that exciting moment it carried me back to the old Admiral Benbow in a second, and I seemed to hear the voice of **the captain** piping in the chorus. But soon the anchor was short up; soon it was hanging dripping at the bows; soon the sails began to draw, and the land and shipping to flit by on either side; and before I could lie down to snatch an hour of slumber the *Hispaniola* had begun her voyage to the **Isle of Treasure.**

I am not going to relate that voyage in detail. It was fairly prosperous. The ship proved to be a good ship, the crew were **capable seamen,** and the captain thoroughly understood his business. But before we came the length of Treasure Island, two or three things had happened which require to be known.

Mr. Arrow, first of all, turned out even worse than **the captain** had feared. He had no command among the men, and people did what they pleased with him. But that was by no means the worst of it, for after a day or two at sea he began to appear on deck with hazy eye, red cheeks, stuttering tongue, and other marks of drunkenness. Time after time he was ordered below in disgrace. Sometimes he fell and cut himself; sometimes he lay all day long in his little bunk at one side of the companion; sometimes for a day or two he would be almost sober and attend to his work at least passably.

In the meantime, we could never make out where he got the drink. That was the ship's mystery. Watch him as we pleased, we could do nothing to solve it; and when we asked him to his face, he would only laugh if he were drunk, and if he were sober deny solemnly that he ever tasted anything but water.

He was not only useless as **an officer** and a bad influence amongst the men, but it was plain that at this rate he must soon kill himself outright, so nobody was much surprised, nor very sorry, when one dark night, with a head sea, he disappeared entirely and was seen no more.

"Overboard!" said the captain. "Well, gentlemen, that saves the trouble of putting him in irons."

But there we were, without **a mate**; and it was necessary, of course, to advance one of the men. The boatswain, **Job Anderson,** was the likeliest man aboard, and though he kept his old title, he served in a way as mate. **Mr. Trelawney** had followed the sea, and his knowledge made him very useful, for he often took a watch himself in easy weather. And the **coxswain, Israel Hands,** was a careful, wily, old, experienced seaman who could be trusted at a pinch with almost anything.

He was a great confidant of Long John Silver, and so the mention of his name leads me on to speak of our ship's cook, Barbecue, as the men called him.

Aboard ship he carried his crutch by a lanyard round his neck, to have both hands as free as possible. It was something to see him wedge the foot of the crutch against a bulkhead, and propped against it, yielding to every movement of the ship, get on with his cooking like someone safe ashore. Still more strange was it to see him in the heaviest of weather cross the deck. He had a line or two rigged up to help him across the widest spaces—Long John's earrings, they were called; and he would hand himself from one place to another, now using the crutch, now trailing it alongside by the lanyard, as quickly as another man could walk. Yet some of the men who had sailed with him before expressed their pity to see him so reduced.

"He's **no common man**, Barbecue," said the coxswain to me. "He had good schooling in his young days and can speak like a book when so minded; and brave—a lion's nothing alongside of Long John! I seen him grapple four and knock their heads together—him unarmed."

All the crew respected and even obeyed him. He had a way of talking to each and doing everybody some particular service. To me he was unweariedly kind, and always glad to see me in **the galley**, which he kept as clean as a new pin, the dishes hanging up burnished and his parrot in a cage in one corner.

"Come away, **Hawkins**," he would say; "come and have a yarn with John. Nobody more welcome than yourself, my son. Sit you down and hear the news. Here's **Cap'n Flint**—I calls my parrot **Cap'n Flint**, after **the famous buccaneer**—here's Cap'n Flint predicting success to our v'yage. Wasn't you, cap'n?"

And the parrot would say, with great rapidity, "Pieces of eight! Pieces of eight! Pieces of eight!" till you wondered that it was not out of breath, or till John threw his handkerchief over the cage.

"Now, that bird," he would say, "is, maybe, two hundred years old, Hawkins—they live forever mostly; and if anybody's seen more wickedness, it must be **the devil himself**. She's sailed with England, the

great Cap'n England, the pirate. She's been at Madagascar, and at Malabar, and Surinam, and Providence, and Portobello. She was at the fishing up of the wrecked plate ships. It's there she learned 'Pieces of eight,' and little wonder; three hundred and fifty thousand of 'em, Hawkins! She was at the boarding of the viceroy of the Indies out of Goa, she was; and to look at her you would think she was a babby. But you smelt powder—didn't you, cap'n?"

"Stand by to go about," the parrot would scream.

"Ah, she's a handsome craft, she is," the cook would say, and give her sugar from his pocket, and then the bird would peck at the bars and swear straight on, passing belief for wickedness. "There," John would add, "you can't touch pitch and not be mucked, lad. Here's this poor old innocent bird o' mine swearing blue fire, and none the wiser, you may lay to that. She would swear the same, in a manner of speaking, before **chaplain.**" And John would touch his forelock with a solemn way he had that made me think he was the best of men. [*Jim has no doubts about Silver.*]

In the meantime, the squire and **Captain Smollett** were still on pretty distant terms with one another. The squire made no bones about the matter; he despised the captain. The captain, on his part, never spoke but when he was spoken to, and then sharp and short and dry, and not a word wasted. He owned, when driven into a corner, that he seemed to have been wrong about the crew, that some of them were as brisk as he wanted to see and all had behaved fairly well. As for the ship, he had taken a downright fancy to her. "She'll lie a point nearer the wind than a man has a right to expect of **his own married wife**, sir. But," he would add, "all I say is, we're not home again, and I don't like the cruise."

The squire, at this, would turn away and march up and down the deck, chin in air.

"A trifle more of that man," he would say, "and I shall explode."

We had some heavy weather, which only proved the qualities of the *Hispaniola*. Every man on board seemed well content, and they must have been hard to please if they had been otherwise, for it is my belief there was never a ship's company so spoiled since **Noah** put to sea. Double grog was going on the least excuse; there was duff on odd days, as, for instance, if the squire heard it was any man's birthday, and always a barrel of apples standing broached in the waist for anyone to help himself that had a fancy.

"Never knew good come of it yet," the captain said to Dr. Livesey. "Spoil **forecastle hands**, make **devils**. That's my belief."

But good did come of the apple barrel, as you shall hear, for if it had not been for that, we should have had no note of warning and might all have perished by the hand of treachery.

This was how it came about.

We had run up the trades to get the wind of the island we were after —I am not allowed to be more plain—and now we were running down for it with a bright lookout day and night. It was about the last day of our outward voyage by the largest computation; some time that night, or at latest before noon of the morrow, we should sight the Treasure Island. We were heading S.S.W. and had a steady breeze abeam and a quiet sea. The *Hispaniola* rolled steadily, dipping her bowsprit now and then with a whiff of spray. All was drawing alow and aloft; everyone was in the bravest spirits because we were now so near an end of the first part of our adventure.

Now, **just after sundown**, when all my work was over and I was on my way to my berth, it occurred to me that I should like an apple. I ran on deck. **The watch** was all forward looking out for the island. **The man at the helm** was watching the luff of the sail and whistling away gently to himself, and that was the only sound excepting the swish of the sea against the bows and around the sides of the ship.

In I got bodily into the apple barrel, and found there was scarce an apple left; but sitting down there in the dark, what with the sound of the waters and the rocking movement of the ship, I had either fallen asleep or was on the point of doing so when **a heavy man** sat down with rather a clash close by. The barrel shook as he leaned his shoulders against it, and I was just about to jump up when the man began to speak. It was Silver's voice, and before I had heard a dozen words, I would not have shown myself for all the world, but lay there, trembling and listening, in the extreme of fear and curiosity, for from these dozen words I understood that the lives of **all the honest men aboard** depended upon me alone.

• ANALYZING THE SCENE •

STORY EVENT

A Story Event is an active change of a universal human value for one or more characters as a result of conflict (one character's desires clash with another's, or an environmental shift changes the value positively or negatively).

A Working Scene contains at least one Story Event. To determine a scene's Story Event, answer these four Socratic questions:

1. What are the characters literally doing—that is, what are their micro on-the-surface actions?

The crew of the *Hispaniola* sets sail, they lose Arrow, and pick up trade winds for the island. One day when they are close, Jim innocently goes looking for an apple and, while hiding in the barrel, overhears Silver.

2. What is the essential tactic of the characters—that is, what above-the-surface macro behaviors are they employing that are linked to a universal human value?

Jim as narrator is conveying the facts. As the luminary agent, Jim is enjoying the adventure. The pirates are biding their time and eliminating threats. Smollett continues to make his views known.

3. What beyond-the-surface universal human values have changed for one or more characters in the scene? Which one of those value changes is most important and should be included in the Story Grid Spreadsheet?

Arrow begins to act strangely and then disappears and is presumed to have fallen overboard. In the last moment of this scene, Jim realizes the danger he and his friends are in and that he is the only one who knows. Up to this point, he's been a kind of sidekick. The adults have let him come along. He must grow up very quickly now.

Blissful Ignorance to Knowledge of Danger

4. The Scene Event Synthesis: What Story Event sums up the scene's on-the-surface, above-the-surface, and beyond-the-surface change? We will enter that event in the Story Grid Spreadsheet.

Jim explains how he missed several clues before he overhears that the lives of all the honest people aboard are at risk.

HOW THE SCENE ABIDES BY THE FIVE COMMANDMENTS OF STORYTELLING

Inciting Incident: Causal. The ship departs from Bristol.

Turning Point Progressive Complication: Active. After falling into an apple barrel, Jim hears Silver's voice nearby.

Crisis: Best bad choice. Should Jim announce his presence or stay silent?

Climax: Jim stays silent.

Resolution: He learns that the lives of all honest people aboard are at risk.

NOTE

- Even though Jim dismisses clues that should tell him that not all is as it seems (the song Bones used to sing, Silver's parrot named Captain Flint, the name of his pub, and Arrow's disappearance) his subconscious mind is working it out, and in retrospect, he can see how he was misled.

11

WHAT I HEARD IN THE APPLE BARREL

"No, not I," said **Silver**. "**Flint** was cap'n; I was **quartermaster**, along of my timber leg. The same broadside I lost my leg, **old Pew** lost his deadlights. It was **a master surgeon**, him that ampytated me—out of college and all—Latin by the bucket, and what not; but he was hanged **like a dog**, and sun-dried like the rest, at **Corso Castle**. That was **Roberts' men**, that was, and comed of changing names to their ships —*Royal Fortune* and so on. Now, what a ship was christened, so let her stay, I says. So it was with the *Cassandra*, as brought us all safe home from **Malabar**, after **England** took the **viceroy of the Indies**; so it was with the old *Walrus*, Flint's old ship, as I've seen amuck with the red blood and fit to sink with gold."

"Ah!" cried another voice, that of **the youngest hand on board**, and evidently full of admiration. "He was the flower of the flock, was Flint!"

"**Davis** was a man too, by all accounts," said Silver. "I never sailed along of him; first with England, then with Flint, that's my story; and now here on my own account, in a manner of speaking. I laid by nine hundred safe, from England, and two thousand after Flint. That ain't bad for a man before the mast—all safe in bank. 'Tain't earning now, it's saving does it, you may lay to that. Where's all **England's men** now? I dunno. Where's **Flint's**? Why, most on 'em aboard here, and glad to get the duff—been begging before that, some on 'em. Old Pew, as had lost his sight, and might have thought shame, spends twelve hundred pound in a year, like **a lord in Parliament.** Where is he now? Well, he's dead now and under hatches; but for two year before that, shiver my timbers, the man was starving! He begged, and he stole, and he cut throats, and starved at that, by the powers!"

"Well, it ain't much use, after all," said the young seaman.

"'Tain't much use for fools, you may lay to it—that, nor nothing," cried Silver. "But now, you look here: you're young, you are, but you're as smart as paint. I see that when I set my eyes on you, and I'll talk to you like a man."

You may imagine how I felt when I heard this abominable old rogue addressing another in the very same words of flattery as he had used to myself. I think, if I had been able, that I would have killed him through the barrel. Meantime, he ran on, little supposing he was overheard. [*RLS is drawing attention to the parallels in case the reader missed it. This is a hard but necessary lesson for Jim.*]

"Here it is about **gentlemen of fortune.** They lives rough, and they risk swinging, but they eat and drink like fighting-cocks, and when a cruise is done, why, it's hundreds of pounds instead of hundreds of farthings in their pockets. Now, the most goes for rum and a good fling, and to sea again in their shirts. But that's not the course I lay. I puts it all away, some here, some there, and none too much anywheres, by reason of suspicion. I'm fifty, mark you; once back from this cruise, I set up gentleman in earnest. Time enough too, says you. Ah, but I've lived easy in the meantime, never denied myself o' nothing heart desires, and slep' soft and ate dainty all my days but when at sea. And how did I begin? Before the mast, like you!"

"Well," said the other, "but all the other money's gone now, ain't it? You daren't show face in Bristol after this."

"Why, where might you suppose it was?" asked Silver derisively.

"At Bristol, in banks and places," answered his companion.

"It were," said the cook; "it were when we weighed anchor. But **my old missis** has it all by now. [*Contrary to Trelawney's thoughts on Silver's relationship with his wife, they are a team.*] And the Spy-glass is sold, lease and goodwill and rigging; and the old girl's off to meet me. I would tell you where, for I trust you, but it'd make jealousy among **the mates.**"

[He's not just clever and charming. He's a great strategist playing the long game.]

"And can you trust your missis?" asked the other.

"Gentlemen of fortune," returned the cook, "usually trusts little among themselves, and right they are, you may lay to it. But I have a way with me, I have. When a mate brings a slip on his cable—one as knows me, I mean—it won't be in the same world with old John. There was some that was feared of Pew, and some that was feared of Flint; but Flint his own self was feared of me. Feared he was, and proud. They was the roughest crew afloat, was Flint's; the **devil himself** would have been feared to go to sea with them. Well now, I tell you, I'm not a boasting man, and you seen yourself how easy I keep company, but when I was quartermaster, *lambs* wasn't the word for **Flint's old buccaneers**. Ah, you may be sure of yourself in old John's ship."

"Well, I tell you now," replied the lad, "I didn't half a quarter like the job till I had this talk with you, John; but there's my hand on it now."

"And a brave lad you were, and smart too," answered Silver, shaking hands so heartily that all the barrel shook, "and a finer figurehead for a gentleman of fortune I never clapped my eyes on."

By this time I had begun to understand the meaning of their terms. By a "gentleman of fortune" they plainly meant neither more nor less than a common pirate, and the little scene that I had overheard was the last act in the corruption of one of the honest hands—perhaps of the last one left aboard. But on this point I was soon to be relieved, for Silver giving a little whistle, a third man strolled up and sat down by the party. *[Jim the narrator is serving as a herald to provide information and context for the uninitiated. Much of our modern ideas about pirates come from this story.]*

"**Dick's** square," said Silver.

"Oh, I know'd Dick was square," returned the voice of **the coxswain, Israel Hands**. "He's no fool, is Dick." And he turned his quid and spat. "But look here," he went on, "here's what I want to know, **Barbecue:** how long are we a-going to stand off and on like a blessed bumboat? I've had a'most enough o' **Cap'n Smollett**; he's hazed me long enough, by thunder! I want to go into that cabin, I do. I want their pickles and wines, and that."

"Israel," said Silver, "your head ain't much account, nor ever was. But you're able to hear, I reckon; leastways, your ears is big enough. Now, here's what I say: you'll berth forward, and you'll live hard, and you'll speak soft, and you'll keep sober till I give the word; and you may lay to that, my son."

"Well, I don't say no, do I?" growled the coxswain. "What I say is, when? That's what I say."

"When! By the powers!" cried Silver. "Well now, if you want to know, I'll tell you when. The last moment I can manage, and that's when. Here's **a first-rate seaman**, Cap'n Smollett, sails the blessed ship for us. Here's this **squire** and **doctor** with a map and such—I don't know where it is, do I? No more do you, says you. Well then, I mean this squire and doctor shall find the stuff, and help us to get it aboard, by the powers. Then we'll see. If I was sure of you all, **sons of double Dutchmen**, I'd have Cap'n Smollett navigate us half-way back again before I struck."

"Why, we're all seamen aboard here, I should think," said the lad Dick.

"We're all **forecastle hands**, you mean," snapped Silver. "We can steer a course, but who's to set one? That's what all you gentlemen split on, first and last. If I had my way, I'd have Cap'n Smollett work us back into the trades at least; then we'd have no blessed miscalculations and a spoonful of water a day. But I know the sort you are. I'll finish with 'em at the island, as soon's the blunt's on board, and a pity it is. But you're never happy till you're drunk. Split my sides, I've a sick heart to sail with the likes of you!"

"Easy all, Long John," cried Israel. "Who's a-crossin' of you?"

"Why, how many tall ships, think ye, now, have I seen laid aboard? And how many **brisk lads** drying in the sun at **Execution Dock**?" cried Silver. "And all for this same hurry and hurry and hurry. You hear me? I seen a thing or two at sea, I have. If you would on'y lay your course, and a p'int to windward, you would ride in carriages, you would. But not you! I know you. You'll have your mouthful of rum tomorrow, and go hang."

"Everybody knowed you was a kind of a chapling, John; but there's others as could hand and steer as well as you," said Israel. "They liked a bit o' fun, they did. They wasn't so high and dry, nohow, but took their fling, like jolly companions every one."

"So?" says Silver. "Well, and where are they now? Pew was that sort, and he died a beggar-man. Flint was, and he died of rum at Savannah. Ah, they was a sweet crew, they was! On'y, where are they?"

"But," asked Dick, "when we do lay 'em athwart, what are we to do with 'em, anyhow?"

"There's the man for me!" cried the cook admiringly. "That's what I call business. Well, what would you think? Put 'em ashore like **maroons**? That would have been England's way. Or cut 'em down like that much pork? That would have been Flint's, or **Billy Bones's**."

"Billy was the man for that," said Israel. "'**Dead men** don't bite,' says he. Well, he's dead now hisself; he knows the long and short on it now; and if ever a rough hand come to port, it was Billy."

"Right you are," said Silver; "rough and ready. But mark you here, I'm an easy man—I'm quite the gentleman, says you; but this time it's serious. Dooty is dooty, mates. I give my vote—death. When I'm in Parlyment and riding in my coach, I don't want none of these **sea-lawyers** in the cabin a-coming home, unlooked for, like the devil at prayers. Wait is what I say; but when the time comes, why, let her rip!"

"John," cries the coxswain, "you're a man!"

"You'll say so, Israel when you see," said Silver. "Only one thing I claim—I claim Trelawney. I'll wring his calf's head off his body with these hands, Dick!" he added, breaking off. "You just jump up, like a sweet lad, and get me an apple, to wet my pipe like."

You may fancy the terror I was in! I should have leaped out and run for it if I had found the strength, but my limbs and heart alike misgave me. I heard Dick begin to rise, and then someone seemingly stopped him, and the voice of Hands exclaimed, "Oh, stow that! Don't you get sucking of that bilge, John. Let's have a go of the rum."

"Dick," said Silver, "I trust you. I've a gauge on the keg, mind. There's the key; you fill a pannikin and bring it up."

Terrified as I was, I could not help thinking to myself that this must have been how **Mr. Arrow** got the strong waters that destroyed him. [*In case Jim had any doubts about the threat, learning how they probably did away with Arrow makes it clear.*]

Dick was gone but a little while, and during his absence Israel spoke straight on in the cook's ear. It was but a word or two that I could catch, and yet I gathered some important news, for besides other scraps that tended to the same purpose, this whole clause was audible: "Not another man of them'll jine." Hence there were still faithful men on board.

When Dick returned, one after another of the trio took the pannikin and drank—one "To luck," another with a "Here's to old Flint," and Silver himself saying, in a kind of song, "Here's to ourselves, and hold your luff, plenty of prizes and plenty of duff."

Just then a sort of brightness fell upon me in the barrel, and looking up, I found the moon had risen and was silvering the mizzen-top and shining white on the luff of the fore-sail; and almost at the same time the voice of **the lookout** shouted, "Land ho!"

STORY EVENT

A Story Event is an active change of a universal human value for one or more characters as a result of conflict (one character's desires clash with another's, or an environmental shift changes the value positively or negatively).

A Working Scene contains at least one Story Event. To determine a scene's Story Event, answer these four Socratic questions:

1. What are the characters literally doing—that is, what are their micro on-the-surface actions?

While hiding in the apple barrel, Jim overhears Silver talk with Dick and Hands about their plans.

2. What is the essential tactic of the characters—that is, what above-the-surface macro behaviors are they employing that are linked to a universal human value?

Jim is accepting a hard truth and gathering intelligence about Silver's plan. Silver is managing the mission by recruiting a new member and reassuring an existing one.

3. What beyond-the-surface universal human values have changed for one or more characters in the scene? Which one of those value changes is most important and should be included in the Story Grid Spreadsheet?

Jim learns that he, Trelawney, Livesey, and Smollett are in danger and that some members of the crew are still loyal to them. This is an important moment in the global story, but at the level of the scene, Silver's quick action to reassure Hands and convince him to wait really moves the global value. If the pirates were to spring their trap right away, Jim's friends would be caught unaware without time to form their own plan.

Risk of Imminent Death to Temporary Reprieve

4. The Scene Event Synthesis: What Story Event sums up the scene's on-the-surface, above-the-surface, and beyond-the-surface change? We will enter that event in the Story Grid Spreadsheet.

Jim overhears Silver explain the pirates' plan to kill the faithful party and convince Hands to wait to implement it.

HOW THE SCENE ABIDES BY THE FIVE COMMANDMENTS OF STORYTELLING

Inciting Incident: Silver reveals information that lets Jim know he was the sailor Bones warned him about.

Turning Point Progressive Complication: Hands challenges Silver about how long they must wait to take over the ship.

Crisis: Best bad choice. If Silver makes the pirates wait, he risks losing control of them, but if he allows the other pirates to kill the honest members of the crew, they may not have enough people with the right skills to leave the island.

Climax: Silver tells Hands they must wait.

Resolution: Hands agrees to wait. Jim learns why Arrow was behaving so strangely. The lookout calls out, "Land ho!"

NOTES

- Jim has to accept a hard truth here. In the beginning hook, he is on the lookout for the seafaring man with one leg and has nightmares about encountering him. In this sequence, his dreams are full of fantasies. He forgot or ignored much of what he learned from Bones because he was so charmed by Silver. Instead of warning Trelawney and Livesey about his suspicions, he allowed himself to be hoodwinked.
- This is another installment of the *speech in praise of the shadow agent or villain*, a convention of the Action Story. Silver's speech is more informative than the captain's speech earlier. Not all pirates, or "gentlemen of fortune" are the same. Some, like Black Dog and Pew, look dangerous, but others, like Silver, are shapeshifters who seem friendly and trustworthy.
- What's interesting about this speech is we can't deny Silver is a sensible man. His choices if made within a legal

economy would be applauded. We can understand his need for security—even as he's attempting to corrupt an honest member of the crew. This highlights an important aspect of the speech in praise of the shadow agent. It should show the power divide between the shadow and luminary agents, but it should also show us the shadow agent has a point. When people are not able to improve their circumstances through conventional or legal means, they sometimes choose to do so through illegal avenues in a parallel economy.

- "Gentlemen of fortune" is an interesting choice of words to describe pirates. Positions are very important in the culture of the story's setting and Stevenson's time. In conventional society at the time, we would describe Livesey and Trelawney as gentlemen because of their positions in society. But they are engaged in pirate's work on this voyage, even though they try to avoid taking lives.

- Despite the similarities here, it's important to note that an aspect of the power divide between the shadow and luminary agents is in what they are willing to do to get what they want. The luminary agent must be willing to kill to preserve life, but they are constrained and should not take life without a dire need. This is a disadvantage when facing the shadow agent who is not limited. This is part of how we define luminary and shadow agents.

- This scene sets up another *deadline* or *ticking clock*, another convention of the Action Story. We need this pressure to progressively complicate the conflict. This scene establishes clear life and death stakes on both sides, which guarantees a fight to the death. If one of the parties could simply wait out the other or walk away, life truly wouldn't be at stake. Here Jim learns the pirates will kill the faithful party once they secure the treasure. Jim and his friends must defeat them before the pirates have no incentive to keep them alive.

- Placing Jim in the barrel is a clever way to give us Silver's perspective without changing the narrative device. Livesey's narrative in coming scenes makes sense, but we couldn't get Silver's perspective in the same way.

- It's seems odd that we still have a romantic view of pirates and celebrate "Talk Like a Pirate Day." They killed many innocent people. Why do we celebrate them? They make excellent shadow agents because they are powerful individuals who operate outside of society's rules. And while we empathize with Jim and his friends, we might appreciate the power the pirates wield. They pursue what they want without concern for the rules.

12

COUNCIL OF WAR

There was a great rush of feet across the deck. I could hear people tumbling up from the cabin and the forecastle, and slipping in an instant outside my barrel, I dived behind the fore-sail, made a double towards the stern, and came out upon the open deck in time to join **Hunter** and **Dr. Livesey** in the rush for the weather bow.

There **all hands** were already congregated. A belt of fog had lifted almost simultaneously with the appearance of the moon. Away to the south-west of us we saw two low hills, about a couple of miles apart, and rising behind one of them a third and higher hill, whose peak was still buried in the fog. All three seemed sharp and conical in figure.

So much I saw, almost in a dream, for I had not yet recovered from my horrid fear of a minute or two before. And then I heard the voice of **Captain Smollett** issuing orders. The *Hispaniola* was laid a couple of points nearer the wind and now sailed a course that would just clear the island on the east.

"And now, men," said the captain, when all was sheeted home, "has any one of you ever seen that land ahead?"

"I have, sir," said **Silver**. "I've watered there with a trader I was cook in."

"The anchorage is on the south, behind an islet, I fancy?" asked the captain.

"Yes, sir; **Skeleton Island** they calls it. It were a main place for pirates once, and a hand we had on board knowed all their names for it. That hill to the nor'ard they calls the Fore-mast Hill; there are three hills in a row running south'ard—fore, main, and mizzen, sir. But the main—that's the big un, with the cloud on it—they usually calls the Spy-glass [*same name as Silver's establishment*], by reason of a lookout they kept when they was in the anchorage cleaning, for it's there they cleaned their ships, sir, asking your pardon."

"I have a chart here," says Captain Smollett. "See if that's the place."

Long John's eyes burned in his head as he took the chart, but by the fresh look of the paper I knew he was doomed to disappointment. This was not the map we found in **Billy Bones**'s chest, but an accurate copy, complete in all things—names and heights and soundings—with the single exception of the red crosses and the written notes. [*This copy was made for Captain Smollett at his request not to be made aware of the location of the treasure.*] Sharp as must have been his annoyance, Silver had the strength of mind to hide it.

"Yes, sir," said he, "this is the spot, to be sure, and very prettily drawn out. Who might have done that, I wonder? The pirates were too ignorant, I reckon. Aye, here it is: '**Capt. Kidd**'s Anchorage'—just the name my shipmate called it. There's a strong current runs along the south, and then away nor'ard up the west coast. Right you was, sir," says he, "to haul your wind and keep the weather of the island. Leastways, if such was your intention as to enter and careen, and there ain't no better place for that in these waters."

"Thank you, my man," says Captain Smollett. "I'll ask you later on to give us a help. You may go."

I was surprised at the coolness with which John avowed his knowledge of the island, and I own I was half-frightened when I saw him drawing nearer to myself. He did not know, to be sure, that I had overheard his council from the apple barrel, and yet I had by this time taken such a horror of his cruelty, duplicity, and power that I could scarce conceal a shudder when he laid his hand upon my arm.

"Ah," says he, "this here is a sweet spot, this island—a sweet spot for a lad to get ashore on. You'll bathe, and you'll climb trees, and you'll hunt goats, you will; and you'll get aloft on them hills like a goat yourself. Why, it makes me young again. I was going to forget my timber leg, I was. It's a pleasant thing to be young and have ten toes, and you may lay to that. When you want to go a bit of exploring, you just ask old John, and he'll put up a snack for you to take along."

And clapping me in the friendliest way upon the shoulder, he hobbled off forward and went below.

Captain Smollett, the **squire**, and Dr. Livesey were talking together on the quarter-deck, and anxious as I was to tell them my story, I durst not interrupt them openly. While I was still casting about in my thoughts to find some probable excuse, Dr. Livesey called me to his side. He had left his pipe below, and being a slave to tobacco, had meant that I should fetch it; but as soon as I was near enough to speak and not to be overheard, I broke immediately, "Doctor, let me speak. Get the captain and squire down to the cabin, and then make some pretence to send for me. I have terrible news."

The doctor changed countenance a little, but next moment he was master of himself.

"Thank you, Jim," said he quite loudly, "that was all I wanted to know," as if he had asked me a question.

And with that he turned on his heel and rejoined the other two. They spoke together for a little, and though none of them started, or raised his voice, or so much as whistled, it was plain enough that Dr. Livesey had communicated my request, for the next thing that I heard was the captain giving an order to **Job Anderson**, and all hands were piped on deck.

"My lads," said Captain Smollett, "I've a word to say to you. This land that we have sighted is the place we have been sailing for. Mr. Trelawney, being a very open-handed gentleman, as we all know, has just asked me a word or two, and as I was able to tell him that every man on board had done his duty, alow and aloft, as I never ask to see it done better, why, he and I and the doctor are going below to the cabin to drink *your* health and luck, and you'll have grog served out for you to drink *our* health and luck. I'll tell you what I think of this: I think it handsome. And if you think as I do, you'll give a good sea-cheer for the gentleman that does it."

The cheer followed—that was a matter of course; but it rang out so full and hearty that I confess I could hardly believe these same men were plotting for our blood.

"One more cheer for Cap'n Smollett," cried Long John when the first had subsided.

And this also was given with a will.

On the top of that **the three gentlemen** went below, and not long after, word was sent forward that Jim Hawkins was wanted in the cabin. I found them all three seated round the table, a bottle of Spanish wine and some raisins before them, and the doctor smoking away, with his wig on his lap, and that, I knew, was a sign that he was agitated. The stern window was open, for it was a warm night, and you could see the moon shining behind on the ship's wake.

"Now, Hawkins," said the squire, "you have something to say. Speak up."

I did as I was bid, and as short as I could make it, told the whole details of Silver's conversation. Nobody interrupted me till I was done, nor did any one of the three of them make so much as a movement, but they kept their eyes upon my face from first to last.

"Jim," said Dr. Livesey, "take a seat."

And they made me sit down at table beside them, poured me out a glass of wine, filled my hands with raisins, and all three, one after the other, and each with a bow, drank my good health, and their service to me, for my luck and courage. [*They're treating Jim as an equal here.*]

"Now, captain," said the squire, "you were right, and I was wrong. I own myself an ass, and I await your orders." [*Trelawney immediately apologizes.*]

"No more an ass than I, sir," returned the captain. "I never heard of a crew that meant to mutiny but what showed signs before, for any man that had an eye in his head to see the mischief and take steps according. But this crew," he added, "beats me."

"Captain," said the doctor, "with your permission, that's Silver. A very remarkable man."

"He'd look remarkably well from a yard-arm, sir," returned the captain. "But this is talk; this don't lead to anything. I see three or four points, and with Mr. Trelawney's permission, I'll name them."

"You, sir, are the captain. It is for you to speak," says Mr. Trelawney grandly.

"First point," began Mr. Smollett. [*Captain Smollett acts as a herald here.*] "We must go on, because we can't turn back. If I gave the word to go about, they would rise at once. Second point, we have time before us —at least until this treasure's found. Third point, there are **faithful hands**. Now, sir, it's got to come to blows sooner or later, and what I propose is to take time by the forelock [*seize the opportunity*], as the saying is, and come to blows some fine day when they least expect it. We can count, I take it, on **your own home servants**, Mr. Trelawney?"

"As upon myself," declared the squire.

"Three," reckoned the captain; "ourselves make seven, counting Hawkins here. Now, about the honest hands?"

"Most likely Trelawney's own men," said the doctor; "those he had picked up for himself before he lit on Silver."

"Nay," replied the squire. "**Hands** was one of mine."

"I did think I could have trusted Hands," added the captain.

"And to think that they're all **Englishmen**!" broke out the squire. "Sir, I could find it in my heart to blow the ship up." [*Compare this statement with his one statement that he is proud that Flint was an Englishman.*]

"Well, gentlemen," said the captain, "the best that I can say is not much. We must lay to, if you please, and keep a bright lookout. It's trying on a man, I know. It would be pleasanter to come to blows. But there's no help for it till we know our men. Lay to, and whistle for a wind, that's my view."

"Jim here," said the doctor, "can help us more than anyone. The men are not shy with him, and Jim is a noticing lad."

"Hawkins, I put prodigious faith in you," added the squire.

I began to feel pretty desperate at this, for I felt altogether helpless; and yet, by an odd train of circumstances, it was indeed through me that safety came. In the meantime, talk as we pleased, there were only seven out of the twenty-six on whom we knew we could rely; and out of these seven one was a boy, so that the grown men on our side were six to their nineteen.

• ANALYZING THE SCENE •

STORY EVENT

A Story Event is an active change of a universal human value for one or more characters as a result of conflict (one character's desires clash with another's, or an environmental shift changes the value positively or negatively).

A Working Scene contains at least one Story Event. To determine a scene's Story Event, answer these four Socratic questions:

1. What are the characters literally doing—that is, what are their micro on-the-surface actions?

Jim delivers the bad news to Livesey, Trelawney, and Smollett that the bulk of the crew plans to mutiny and kill the honest members of the crew. The leaders discuss the problem while the crew members are given an extra ration of grog.

2. What is the essential tactic of the characters—that is, what above-the-surface macro behaviors are they employing that are linked to a universal human value?

Jim needs to warn Livesey, Trelawney, and Smollett of the danger they face. They need to come up with a plan if they are going to stay alive for the immediate future.

3. What beyond-the-surface universal human values have changed for one or more characters in the scene? Which one of those value changes is most important and should be included in the Story Grid Spreadsheet?

The adults become aware of the danger they are in. This is similar to Jim's adjustment in the prior scene. In their eyes, Jim goes from being an errand boy to an asset counted among the adults.

Unaware to Aware with a Plan

4. The Scene Event Synthesis: What Story Event sums up the scene's on-the-surface, above-the-surface, and beyond-the-surface change? We will enter that event in the Story Grid Spreadsheet.

Jim breaks his habit of not speaking up to inform Livesey, Smollett, and Trelawney about the danger. As a group they decide to follow Smollett's advice to lay low and allow Jim to gather more intelligence.

. . .

HOW THE SCENE ABIDES BY THE FIVE COMMANDMENTS OF STORYTELLING

Inciting Incident: Causal. Jim makes his way on deck.

Turning Point Progressive Complication: Active. Without calling attention to their meeting, Jim tells Livesey, Trelawney, and Smollett about Silver's plans.

Crisis: Best bad choice. Smollett lays out a plan. They can't turn back without raising suspicions, so do they act right away or bide their time?

Climax: They will wait and gather intelligence. They have an advantage because Silver doesn't know they're aware. This gives them time to figure out who the faithful members of the crew are.

Resolution: Everyone agrees to the plan, and Jim feels uncertain of his ability to do his part.

NOTES

- Before this scene, Jim doesn't count himself as one of the adults. They begin treating him as an equal and don't doubt his account at all. Compare how the adults treat him here to the way Jim was sent away with no role in preparing for the voyage (scene 7). Jim remains concerned, though. He was wrong in his assessment of Silver, yet the adults are looking to him as someone who can gather information.
- Notice how the crisis in this scene is similar to one Silver faces in scene 11. Strike right away or wait? Both leaders conclude it is best to wait.
- Trelawney is naïve for an adult of his position and experience, and it's interesting that he and Jim have similar feelings toward Smollett until this point in the story. Trelawney understands he should trust the captain, but he still has no useful guide for telling friend from foe in the current situation.

PART THREE: MY SHORE ADVENTURE

13

HOW MY SHORE ADVENTURE BEGAN

The appearance of the island when I came on deck next morning was altogether changed. Although the breeze had now utterly ceased, we had made a great deal of way during the night and were now lying becalmed about half a mile to the south-east of the low eastern coast. Grey-coloured woods covered a large part of the surface. This even tint was indeed broken up by streaks of yellow sand-break in the lower lands, and by many tall trees of the pine family, out-topping the others —some singly, some in clumps; but the general colouring was uniform and sad. The hills ran up clear above the vegetation in spires of naked rock. All were strangely shaped, and the Spy-glass, which was by three or four hundred feet the tallest on the island, was likewise the strangest in configuration, running up sheer from almost every side and then suddenly cut off at the top like a pedestal to put a statue on.

The *Hispaniola* was rolling scuppers under in the ocean swell. The booms were tearing at the blocks, the rudder was banging to and fro, and the whole ship creaking, groaning, and jumping like a manufactory. I had to cling tight to the backstay, and the world turned giddily before my eyes, for though I was a good enough sailor when there was way on, this standing still and being rolled about like a bottle was a thing I never learned to stand without a qualm or so, above all in the morning, on an empty stomach.

Perhaps it was this—perhaps it was the look of the island, with its grey, melancholy woods, and wild stone spires, and the surf that **we** could both see and hear foaming and thundering on the steep beach—at least, although the sun shone bright and hot, and the shore birds were fishing and crying all around us, and you would have thought anyone would have been glad to get to land after being so long at sea, my heart sank, as the saying is, into my boots; and from the first look onward, I hated the very thought of Treasure Island.

We had a dreary morning's work before us, for there was no sign of any wind, and the boats had to be got out and manned, and the ship warped three or four miles round the corner of the island and up the narrow passage to the haven behind **Skeleton Island**. I volunteered for one of the boats, where I had, of course, no business. The heat was sweltering, and the men grumbled fiercely over their work. **Anderson** was in command of my boat, and instead of keeping the crew in order, he grumbled as loud as the worst.

"Well," he said with an oath, "it's not forever."

I thought this was a very bad sign, for up to that day the men had gone briskly and willingly about their business; but the very sight of the island had relaxed the cords of discipline.

All the way in, **Long John** stood by the **steersman** and conned the ship. He knew the passage like the palm of his hand, and though the man in the chains got everywhere more water than was down in the chart, John never hesitated once.

"There's a strong scour with the ebb," he said, "and this here passage has been dug out, in a manner of speaking, with a spade."

We brought up just where the anchor was in the chart, about a third of a mile from each shore, the mainland on one side and Skeleton Island on the other. The bottom was clean sand. The plunge of our anchor sent up clouds of birds wheeling and crying over the woods, but in less than a minute they were down again and all was once more silent.

The place was entirely land-locked, buried in woods, the trees coming right down to high-water mark, the shores mostly flat, and the hilltops standing round at a distance in a sort of amphitheatre, one here, one there. Two little rivers, or rather two swamps, emptied out into this pond, as you might call it; and the foliage round that part of the shore had a kind of poisonous brightness. From the ship we could see nothing of the house or stockade, for they were quite buried among trees; and if it had not been for the chart on the companion, we might have been the first that had ever anchored there since the island arose out of the seas.

There was not a breath of air moving, nor a sound but that of the surf booming half a mile away along the beaches and against the rocks outside. A peculiar stagnant smell hung over the anchorage—a smell of sodden leaves and rotting tree trunks. I observed the doctor sniffing and sniffing, like someone tasting a bad egg.

"I don't know about treasure," he said, "but I'll stake my wig there's fever here."

If the conduct of **the men** had been alarming in the boat, it became truly threatening when they had come aboard. They lay about the deck growling together in talk. The slightest order was received with a black look and grudgingly and carelessly obeyed. Even **the honest hands** must have caught the infection, for there was not one man aboard to mend another. Mutiny, it was plain, hung over us like a thunder-cloud.

And it was not only we of the **cabin party** who perceived the danger. Long John was hard at work going from group to group, spending himself in good advice, and as for example no man could have shown a better. He fairly outstripped himself in willingness and civility; he was all smiles to everyone. If an order were given, John would be on his crutch in an instant, with the cheeriest "Aye, aye, sir!" in the world; and when there was nothing else to do, he kept up one song after another, as if to conceal the discontent of the rest.

Of all the gloomy features of that gloomy afternoon, this obvious anxiety on the part of Long John appeared the worst.

We held a council in the cabin.

"Sir," said **the captain**, "if I risk another order, the whole ship'll come about our ears by the run. You see, sir, here it is. I get a rough answer, do I not? Well, if I speak back, pikes will be going in two shakes; if I don't, Silver will see there's something under that, and the game's up. Now, we've only one man to rely on."

"And who is that?" asked the squire.

"Silver, sir," returned the captain; "he's as anxious as you and I to smother things up. This is a tiff; he'd soon talk 'em out of it if he had the chance, and **what I propose to do is to give him the chance. Let's allow the men an afternoon ashore.** If they all go, why we'll fight the ship. If they none of them go, well then, we hold the cabin, and God defend the right. If some go, you mark my words, sir, Silver'll bring 'em aboard again as mild as lambs."

It was so decided; loaded pistols were served out to all the sure men; **Hunter, Joyce,** and **Redruth** were taken into our confidence and received the news with less surprise and a better spirit than we had looked for, and then the captain went on deck and addressed the crew.

"My lads," said he, "we've had a hot day and are all tired and out of sorts. A turn ashore'll hurt nobody—the boats are still in the water; you can take the gigs, and as many as please may go ashore for the afternoon. I'll fire a gun half an hour before sundown."

I believe the silly fellows must have thought they would break their shins over treasure as soon as they were landed, for they all came out of their sulks in a moment and gave a cheer that started the echo in a faraway hill and sent the birds once more flying and squalling round the anchorage.

The captain was too bright to be in the way. He whipped out of sight in a moment, leaving Silver to arrange the party, and I fancy it was as well he did so. Had he been on deck, he could no longer so much as have pretended not to understand the situation. It was as plain as day. Silver was the captain, and a mighty rebellious crew he had of it. **The honest hands**—and I was soon to see it proved that there were such on board—must have been very stupid fellows. Or rather, I suppose the truth was this, that all hands were disaffected by the example of the ringleaders—only some more, some less; and **a few,** being good fellows in the main, could neither be led nor driven any further. It is one thing to be idle and skulk and quite another to take a ship and murder a number of **innocent men.**

At last, however, the party was made up. **Six fellows** were to stay on board, and the remaining thirteen, including Silver, began to embark.

Then it was that there came into my head the first of the mad notions that contributed so much to save our lives. If six men were left by Silver, it was plain our party could not take and fight the ship; and since only six were left, it was equally plain that the cabin party had no present need of my assistance. It occurred to me at once to go ashore. In a jiffy I had slipped over the side and curled up in the fore-sheets of the nearest boat, and almost at the same moment she shoved off.

No one took notice of me, only the bow oar saying, "Is that you, Jim? Keep your head down." But Silver, from the other boat, looked sharply over and called out to know if that were me; and from that moment I began to regret what I had done.

The crews raced for the beach, but the boat I was in, having some start and being at once the lighter and the better manned, shot far ahead of her consort, and the bow had struck among the shore-side trees and I had caught a branch and swung myself out and plunged into the nearest thicket while Silver and the rest were still a hundred yards behind.

"Jim, Jim!" I heard him shouting.

But you may suppose I paid no heed; jumping, ducking, and breaking through, I ran straight before my nose till I could run no longer.

STORY EVENT

A Story Event is an active change of a universal human value for one or more characters as a result of conflict (one character's desires clash with another's, or an environmental shift changes the value positively or negatively).

A Working Scene contains at least one Story Event. To determine a scene's Story Event, answer these four Socratic questions:

1. What are the characters literally doing—that is, what are their micro on-the-surface actions?

Some crew members tow the ship with row boats to reach to the anchorage. Another council is held where it's decided to let Silver take the men ashore and get them back under control. Jim jumps into one of the boats. Silver notices Jim and shouts for him. But Jim escapes inland as soon as he can.

2. What is the essential tactic of the characters—that is, what above-the-surface macro behaviors are they employing that are linked to a universal human value?

Smollett and Silver want to keep the crew members calm. The crew members are impatient to get to the treasure. Jim wants to figure out how he can be of help.

3. What beyond-the-surface universal human values have changed for one or more characters in the scene? Which one of those value changes is most important and should be included in the Story Grid Spreadsheet?

The crew is about to revolt because they want to take action. The faithful party is at risk of being exposed or inciting an immediate attack. Smollett lets the crew go on shore, which calms the situation for the moment.

Attack Imminent to Attack Delayed

4. The Scene Event Synthesis: What Story Event sums up the scene's on-the-surface, above-the-surface, and beyond-the-surface change? We will enter that event in the Story Grid Spreadsheet.

The crew is on the verge of revolting when Smollett allows them to go ashore. Jim goes in a boat with them but runs when they reach the shore.

HOW THE SCENE ABIDES BY THE FIVE COMMANDMENTS OF STORYTELLING

Inciting Incident: Causal. The crew must tow the ship to where they can drop anchor and go ashore.

Turning Point Progressive Complication: Revelatory. Smollett realizes he has almost no control of the crew, but Silver also has an interest in keeping the crew in line.

Crisis: Best bad choice. Should Smollett crack down on the crew and risk immediate mutiny or let them get away with insubordination and let Silver know the leadership is on to them?

Climax: Smollett decides to let the crew go ashore to give Silver privacy to get the crew back in line.

Resolution: Silver notices that Jim is going ashore and tries to get his attention, but Jim runs into the thicket.

NOTES

- At the level of the scene, Smollett's decision is the climax, but Jim's quick thinking in the resolution of the scene ends up helping the faithful party the most.
- Notice the difference between the island of Jim's fantasies before leaving for Bristol and the reality. Even as he remembers these events for his narrative, his experience at the time influences the way he talks about what happens. This supports the authenticity of the narrative device. Stevenson's writing effectively simulates the reality of a narrative.

14

THE FIRST BLOW

I was so pleased at having given the slip to **Long John** that I began to enjoy myself and look around me with some interest on the strange land that I was in.

I had crossed a marshy tract full of willows, bulrushes, and odd, outlandish, swampy trees; and I had now come out upon the skirts of an open piece of undulating, sandy country, about a mile long, dotted with a few pines and a great number of contorted trees, not unlike the oak in growth, but pale in the foliage, like willows. On the far side of the open stood one of the hills, with two quaint, craggy peaks shining vividly in the sun.

I now felt for the first time the joy of exploration. The isle was uninhabited; **my shipmates** I had left behind, and nothing lived in front of me but dumb brutes and fowls. I turned hither and thither among the trees. Here and there were flowering plants, unknown to me; here and there I saw snakes, and one raised his head from a ledge of rock and hissed at me with a noise not unlike the spinning of a top. Little did I suppose that he was a deadly enemy and that the noise was the famous rattle. [*Jim also can't tell which plants and animals may be dangerous to him. He's in an unfamiliar environment where the rules are different.*]

Then I came to a long thicket of these oaklike trees—live, or evergreen, oaks, I heard afterwards they should be called—which grew low along the sand like brambles, the boughs curiously twisted, the foliage compact, like thatch. The thicket stretched down from the top of one of the sandy knolls, spreading and growing taller as it went, until it reached the margin of the broad, reedy fen, through which the nearest of the little rivers soaked its way into the anchorage. The marsh was steaming in the strong sun, and the outline of the Spy-glass trembled through the haze.

All at once there began to go a sort of bustle among the bulrushes; a wild duck flew up with a quack, another followed, and soon over the whole surface of the marsh a great cloud of birds hung screaming and circling in the air. I judged at once that some of my shipmates must be drawing near along the borders of the fen. Nor was I deceived, for soon I heard the very distant and low tones of a human voice, which, as I continued to give ear, grew steadily louder and nearer. This put me in a great fear, and I crawled under cover of the nearest live-oak and squatted there, hearkening, as silent as a mouse.

Another voice answered, and then the first voice, which I now recognized to be Silver's, once more took up the story and ran on for a long while in a stream, only now and again interrupted by the other. By the sound they must have been talking earnestly, and almost fiercely; but no distinct word came to my hearing.

At last **the speakers** seemed to have paused and perhaps to have sat down, for not only did they cease to draw any nearer, but the birds themselves began to grow more quiet and to settle again to their places in the swamp.

And now I began to feel that I was neglecting my business, that since I had been so foolhardy as to come ashore with these desperadoes, the least I could do was to overhear them at their councils, and that my plain and obvious duty was to draw as close as I could manage, under the favourable ambush of the crouching trees.

I could tell the direction of the speakers pretty exactly, not only by the sound of their voices but by the behaviour of the few birds that still hung in alarm above the heads of the intruders. Crawling on all fours, I made steadily but slowly towards them, till at last, raising my head to an aperture among the leaves, I could see clear down into a little green dell beside the marsh, and closely set about with trees, where Long John Silver and another of the crew stood face to face in conversation.

The sun beat full upon them. Silver had thrown his hat beside him on the ground, and his great, smooth, blond face, all shining with heat, was lifted to the other man's in a kind of appeal.

"Mate," he was saying, "it's because I thinks gold dust of you—gold dust, and you may lay to that! If I hadn't took to you like pitch, do you think I'd have been here a-warning of you? All's up—you can't make nor mend; it's to save your neck that I'm a-speaking, and if one of the wild uns knew it, where'd I be, **Tom**—now, tell me, where'd I be?"

"Silver," said the other man—and I observed he was not only red in the face, but spoke as hoarse as a crow, and his voice shook too, like a taut rope—"Silver," says he, "you're old, and you're honest, or has the name for it; and you've money too, which lots of poor sailors hasn't; and you're brave, or I'm mistook. And will you tell me you'll let yourself be led away with that kind of a mess of **swabs**? Not you! As sure as **God** sees me, I'd sooner lose my hand. If I turn agin my dooty—"

And then all of a sudden he was interrupted by a noise. I had found one of the honest hands—well, here, at that same moment, came news of another. Far away out in the marsh there arose, all of a sudden, a sound like the cry of anger, then another on the back of it; and then one horrid, long-drawn scream. The rocks of the Spy-glass re-echoed it a score of times; the whole troop of marsh-birds rose again, darkening heaven, with a simultaneous whirr; and long after that death yell was still ringing in my brain, silence had re-established its empire, and only the rustle of the redescending birds and the boom of the distant surges disturbed the languor of the afternoon.

Tom had leaped at the sound, like a horse at the spur, but Silver had not winked an eye. He stood where he was, resting lightly on his crutch, watching his companion like a snake about to spring.

"John!" said **the sailor**, stretching out his hand.

"Hands off!" cried Silver, leaping back a yard, as it seemed to me, with the speed and security of a trained gymnast. [*Sometimes Silver seems to be limited by his injury. Other times he seems quite capable of getting around as he wishes. Changing his appearance is one of many tactics he uses to pursue his goals.*]

"Hands off, if you like, John Silver," said the other. "It's a black conscience that can make you feared of me. But in heaven's name, tell me, what was that?"

"That?" returned Silver, smiling away, but warier than ever, his eye a mere pin-point in his big face, but gleaming like a crumb of glass. "That? Oh, I reckon that'll be **Alan**."

And at this point Tom flashed out like a hero.

"Alan!" he cried. "Then rest his soul for a true seaman! And as for you, John Silver, long you've been a mate of mine, but you're mate of mine no more. If I die like a dog, I'll die in my dooty. You've killed Alan, have you? Kill me too, if you can. But I defies you."

And with that, this brave fellow turned his back directly on the cook and set off walking for the beach. But he was not destined to go far. With a cry John seized the branch of a tree, whipped the crutch out of his armpit, and sent that uncouth missile hurtling through the air. It struck poor Tom, point foremost, and with stunning violence, right between the shoulders in the middle of his back. His hands flew up, he gave a sort of gasp, and fell.

Whether he were injured much or little, none could ever tell. Like enough, to judge from the sound, his back was broken on the spot. But he had no time given him to recover. Silver, agile as a monkey even without leg or crutch, was on the top of him next moment and had twice buried his knife up to the hilt in that defenceless body. From my place of ambush, I could hear him pant aloud as he struck the blows.

I do not know what it rightly is to faint, but I do know that for the next little while the whole world swam away from before me in a whirling mist; Silver and the birds, and the tall Spy-glass hilltop, going round and round and topsy-turvy before my eyes, and all manner of bells ringing and distant voices shouting in my ear.

When I came again to myself the monster had pulled himself together, his crutch under his arm, his hat upon his head. Just before him Tom lay motionless upon the sward; but the murderer minded him not a whit, cleansing his blood-stained knife the while upon a wisp of grass. Everything else was unchanged, the sun still shining mercilessly on the steaming marsh and the tall pinnacle of the mountain, and I could scarce persuade myself that murder had been actually done and a human life cruelly cut short a moment since before my eyes.

But now John put his hand into his pocket, brought out a whistle, and blew upon it several modulated blasts that rang far across the heated air. [*This is similar to what happened the night when the men attacked the inn.*] I could not tell, of course, the meaning of the signal, but it instantly awoke my fears. More men would be coming. I might be discovered. They had already slain two of the honest people; after Tom and Alan, might not I come next?

Instantly I began to extricate myself and crawl back again, with what speed and silence I could manage, to the more open portion of the wood. As I did so, I could hear hails coming and going between the old buccaneer and his comrades, and this sound of danger lent me wings. As soon as I was clear of the thicket, I ran as I never ran before, scarce minding the direction of my flight, so long as it led me from the murderers; and as I ran, fear grew and grew upon me until it turned into a kind of frenzy.

Indeed, could anyone be more entirely lost than I? When the gun fired, how should I dare to go down to the boats among those fiends, still smoking from their crime? Would not the first of them who saw me wring my neck like a snipe's? Would not my absence itself be an evidence to them of my alarm, and therefore of my fatal knowledge? It was all over, I thought. Good-bye to the *Hispaniola*; good-bye to **the squire, the doctor,** and **the captain**! There was nothing left for me but death by starvation or death by the hands of the mutineers.

All this while, as I say, I was still running, and without taking any notice, I had drawn near to the foot of the little hill with the two peaks and had got into a part of the island where the live-oaks grew more widely apart and seemed more like forest trees in their bearing and dimensions. Mingled with these were a few scattered pines, some fifty, some nearer seventy, feet high. The air too smelt more freshly than down beside the marsh.

And here a fresh alarm brought me to a standstill with a thumping heart.

• ANALYZING THE SCENE •

STORY EVENT

A Story Event is an active change of a universal human value for one or more characters as a result of conflict (one character's desires clash with another's, or an environmental shift changes the value positively or negatively).

A Working Scene contains at least one Story Event. To determine a scene's Story Event, answer these four Socratic questions:

1. What are the characters literally doing—that is, what are their micro on-the-surface actions?

Jim explores the island while the pirates isolate and murder two honest hands who wouldn't join them.

2. What is the essential tactic of the characters—that is, what above-the-surface macro behaviors are they employing that are linked to a universal human value?

Jim wants to elude the pirates while the pirates seek to eliminate the honest crew members.

3. What beyond-the-surface universal human values have changed for one or more characters in the scene? Which one of those value changes is most important and should be included in the Story Grid Spreadsheet?

In this scene, Tom and Alan are killed and Jim believes there is no way for him to rejoin Livesey and Trelawney. He assumes he'll be killed by the pirates or left to starve on the island.

Life to Death

4. The Scene Event Synthesis: What Story Event sums up the scene's on-the-surface, above-the-surface, and beyond-the-surface change? We will enter that event in the Story Grid Spreadsheet.

Jim flees and explores the island. He spies on Silver who kills Tom after Alan is killed by the other pirates. Jim runs and believes he's stuck on the island.

. . .

HOW THE SCENE ABIDES BY THE FIVE COMMANDMENTS OF STORYTELLING

Inciting Incident: Causal. Jim explores the island.

Turning Point Progressive Complication: Active. Silver blows a whistle to call the rest of the pirates to him, possibly because Jim ran from him.

Crisis: Irreconcilable goods choice. Jim can hide or go try to figure out what the pirates are up to.

Climax: Feeling it's his duty to gather intelligence, he moves close enough to observe Silver.

Resolution: Two honest crew members, Tom and Alan, are killed. Jim concludes he won't be able to get back to the ship, and then he encounters something alarming at the foot of the little hill with two peaks.

NOTES

- This is an important moment in the story—a point of no return on multiple levels. Jim heard what Silver and the other pirates planned before, but it fully registers here when he sees Silver kill Tom.
- At the end of scene 13, Jim reacts in a way Silver doesn't expect. And this must alert the pirate that something is up. Silver can't ignore the threat. Jim now realizes even though Silver seemed to like him, the pirate might kill him.
- The crew was sent on shore in hopes that Silver could get them under control again. Alan's death shows us that Silver has lost control. This forces his hand so he must kill Tom. A violent group of pirates not following their leader is much more dangerous. They stand between Jim and his friends, so his conclusion that his death is inescapable makes sense. He is physically constrained on the island, even though he can still move around.
- Jim has had a major shock. He's learned that his powers of keen observation won't help him if he misreads what he notices. He doesn't know what to do, and he can't go back to

seeing the world through this naïve perspective again. Nothing makes sense and he can't see a way forward. The pirates are dangerous and cunning, and knowing who they are doesn't matter. Jim can't defeat them yet.

- Notice how Jim's observations are full of wonder for a few moments during this scene. He won't be able to maintain this innocence if he's going to survive the trials to come. He must face the horrible truth that a person he liked and trusted is willing to kill him.

15

THE MAN OF THE ISLAND

From the side of the hill, which was here steep and stony, a spout of gravel was dislodged and fell rattling and bounding through the trees. My eyes turned instinctively in that direction, and I saw a figure leap with great rapidity behind the trunk of a pine. What it was, whether bear or man or monkey, I could in no wise tell. It seemed dark and shaggy; more I knew not. But the terror of this new apparition brought me to a stand.

I was now, it seemed, cut off upon both sides; behind me the **murderers**, before me this lurking nondescript. And immediately I began to prefer the dangers that I knew to those I knew not. **Silver** himself appeared less terrible in contrast with this creature of the woods, and I turned on my heel, and looking sharply behind me over my shoulder, began to retrace my steps in the direction of the boats.

Instantly the figure reappeared, and making a wide circuit, began to head me off. I was tired, at any rate; but had I been as fresh as when I rose, I could see it was in vain for me to contend in speed with such an adversary. From trunk to trunk the creature flitted like a deer, running manlike on two legs, but unlike any man that I had ever seen, stooping almost double as it ran. Yet a man it was, I could no longer be in doubt about that.

I began to recall what I had heard of **cannibals**. I was within an ace of calling for help. But the mere fact that he was a man, however wild, had somewhat reassured me, and my fear of Silver began to revive in proportion. I stood still, therefore, and cast about for some method of escape; and as I was so thinking, the recollection of my pistol flashed into my mind. As soon as I remembered I was not defenceless, courage glowed again in my heart and I set my face resolutely for this man of the island and walked briskly towards him.

He was concealed by this time behind another tree trunk; but he must have been watching me closely, for as soon as I began to move in his direction he reappeared and took a step to meet me. Then he hesitated, drew back, came forward again, and at last, to my wonder and confusion, threw himself on his knees and held out his clasped hands in supplication.

At that I once more stopped.

"Who are you?" I asked.

"**Ben Gunn**," he answered, and his voice sounded hoarse and awkward, like a rusty lock. "I'm poor Ben Gunn, I am; and I haven't spoke with **a Christian** these three years."

I could now see that he was **a white man** like myself and that his features were even pleasing. His skin, wherever it was exposed, was burnt by the sun; even his lips were black, and his fair eyes looked quite startling in so dark a face. Of all **the beggar-men** that I had seen or fancied, he was the chief for raggedness. He was clothed with tatters of old ship's canvas and old sea-cloth, and this extraordinary patchwork was all held together by a system of the most various and incongruous fastenings, brass buttons, bits of stick, and loops of tarry gaskin. About his waist he wore an old brass-buckled leather belt, which was the one thing solid in his whole accoutrement.

"Three years!" I cried. "Were you shipwrecked?"

"Nay, mate," said he; "marooned."

I had heard the word, and I knew it stood for a horrible kind of punishment common enough among the **buccaneers**, in which the offender is put ashore with a little powder and shot and left behind on some desolate and distant island.

"Marooned three years agone," he continued, "and lived on goats since then, and berries, and oysters. Wherever a man is, says I, a man can do for himself. But, mate, my heart is sore for Christian diet. You mightn't happen to have a piece of cheese about you, now? No? Well, many's the long night I've dreamed of cheese—toasted, mostly—and woke up again, and here I were."

"If ever I can get aboard again," said I, "you shall have cheese by the stone."

All this time he had been feeling the stuff of my jacket, smoothing my hands, looking at my boots, and generally, in the intervals of his speech, showing a childish pleasure in the presence of a fellow creature. But at my last words he perked up into a kind of startled slyness.

"If ever you can get aboard again, says you?" he repeated. "Why, now, who's to hinder you?"

"Not you, I know," was my reply.

"And right you was," he cried. "Now you—what do you call yourself, mate?"

"Jim," I told him.

"Jim, Jim," says he, quite pleased apparently. "Well, now, Jim, I've lived that rough as you'd be ashamed to hear of. Now, for instance, you wouldn't think I had had a pious mother—to look at me?" he asked.

"Why, no, not in particular," I answered.

"Ah, well," said he, "but I had—remarkable pious. And I was a civil, pious boy, and could rattle off my catechism that fast, as you couldn't tell one word from another. And here's what it come to, Jim, and it begun with chuck-farthen on the blessed grave-stones! That's what it begun with, but it went further'n that; and so **my mother** told me, and predicked the whole, she did, the pious woman! But it were Providence that put me here. I've thought it all out in this here lonely island, and I'm back on piety. You don't catch me tasting rum so much, but just a thimbleful for luck, of course, the first chance I have. I'm bound I'll be good, and I see the way to. And, Jim"—looking all round him and lowering his voice to a whisper—"I'm rich."

I now felt sure that the poor fellow had gone crazy in his solitude, and I suppose I must have shown the feeling in my face, for he repeated the statement hotly: "Rich! Rich! I says. And I'll tell you what: I'll make a man of you, Jim. Ah, Jim, you'll bless your stars, you will, you was the first that found me!"

And at this there came suddenly a lowering shadow over his face, and he tightened his grasp upon my hand and raised a forefinger threateningly before my eyes.

"Now, Jim, you tell me true: that ain't **Flint's** ship?" he asked.

At this I had a happy inspiration. I began to believe that I had found **an ally**, and I answered him at once.

"It's not Flint's ship, and Flint is dead; but I'll tell you true, as you ask me—there are some of **Flint's hands** aboard; worse luck for **the rest of us**."

"Not a man—with one—leg?" he gasped.

"Silver?" I asked.

"Ah, Silver!" says he. "That were his name."

"He's the cook, and **the ringleader** too."

He was still holding me by the wrist, and at that he gave it quite a wring. [*Contrast this action with Pew twisting Jim's arm in scene 3*].

"If you was sent by Long John," he said, "I'm as good as pork, and I know it. But where was you, do you suppose?"

I had made my mind up in a moment, and by way of answer told him the whole story of our voyage and the predicament in which we found ourselves. He heard me with the keenest interest, and when I had done he patted me on the head.

"You're **a good lad**, Jim," he said; "and you're all in a clove hitch, ain't you? Well, you just put your trust in Ben Gunn—Ben Gunn's the man to do it. Would you think it likely, now, that **your squire** would prove a liberal-minded one in case of help—him being in a clove hitch, as you remark?"

I told him the squire was the most liberal of men.

"Aye, but you see," returned Ben Gunn, "I didn't mean giving me a gate to keep, and a suit of livery clothes, and such; that's not my mark, Jim. What I mean is, would he be likely to come down to the toon of, say one thousand pounds out of money that's as good as a man's own already?"

"I am sure he would," said I. "As it was, all hands were to share."

"*And* a passage home?" he added with a look of great shrewdness.

"Why," I cried, "the squire's **a gentleman.** And besides, if we got rid of the others, we should want you to help work the vessel home."

"Ah," said he, "so you would." And he seemed very much relieved.

"Now, I'll tell you what," he went on. "So much I'll tell you, and no more. I were in Flint's ship when he buried the treasure; he and six along—**six strong seamen.** They was ashore nigh on a week, and us standing off and on in the old *Walrus.* One fine day up went the signal, and here come Flint by himself in a little boat, and his head done up in a blue scarf. The sun was getting up, and mortal white he looked about the cutwater. But, there he was, you mind, and the six all dead—dead and buried. How he done it, not a man aboard us could make out. It was battle, murder, and sudden death, leastways—him against six. **Billy Bones** was the mate; Long John, he was quartermaster; and they asked him where the treasure was. 'Ah,' says he, 'you can go ashore, if you like, and stay,' he says; 'but as for the ship, she'll beat up for more, by thunder!' That's what he said.

"Well, I was in another ship three years back, and we sighted this island. 'Boys,' said I, 'here's Flint's treasure; let's land and find it.' **The cap'n** was displeased at that, but **my messmates** were all of a mind and landed. Twelve days they looked for it, and every day they had the worse word for me, until one fine morning all hands went aboard. 'As for you, Benjamin Gunn,' says they, 'here's a musket,' they says, 'and a spade, and pick-axe. You can stay here and find Flint's money for yourself,' they says.

"Well, Jim, three years have I been here, and not a bite of Christian diet from that day to this. But now, you look here; look at me. Do I look like **a man before the mast**? No, says you. Nor I weren't, neither, I says."

And with that he winked and pinched me hard.

"Just you mention them words to your squire, Jim," he went on. "Nor he weren't, neither—that's the words. Three years he were the man of this island, light and dark, fair and rain; and sometimes he would maybe think upon a prayer (says you), and sometimes he would maybe think of his old mother, so be as she's alive (you'll say); but the most part of Gunn's time (this is what you'll say)—the most part of his time was took up with another matter. And then you'll give him a nip, like I do."

And he pinched me again in the most confidential manner.

"Then," he continued, "then you'll up, and you'll say this: Gunn is a good man (you'll say), and he puts a precious sight more confidence—a precious sight, mind that—in **a gen'leman born** than in these **gen'leman of fortune**, having been one hisself."

"Well," I said, "I don't understand one word that you've been saying. But that's neither here nor there; for how am I to get on board?"

"Ah," said he, "that's the hitch, for sure. Well, there's my boat, that I made with my two hands. I keep her under the white rock. If the worst come to the worst, we might try that after dark. Hi!" he broke out. "What's that?"

For just then, although the sun had still an hour or two to run, all the echoes of the island awoke and bellowed to the thunder of a cannon.

"They have begun to fight!" I cried. "Follow me."

And I began to run towards the anchorage, my terrors all forgotten, while close at my side the marooned man in his goatskins trotted easily and lightly.

"Left, left," says he; "keep to your left hand, mate Jim! Under the trees with you! Theer's where I killed my first goat. They don't come down here now; they're all mastheaded on them mountings for the fear of Benjamin Gunn. Ah! And there's the cetemery"—cemetery, he must have meant. "You see the mounds? I come here and prayed, nows and thens, when I thought maybe a Sunday would be about doo. It weren't quite a chapel, but it seemed more solemn like; and then, says you, Ben Gunn was short-handed—no **chapling**, nor so much as a Bible and a flag, you says."

So he kept talking as I ran, neither expecting nor receiving any answer.

The cannon-shot was followed after a considerable interval by a volley of small arms.

Another pause, and then, not a quarter of a mile in front of me, I beheld the Union Jack flutter in the air above a wood.

• ANALYZING THE SCENE •

STORY EVENT

A Story Event is an active change of a universal human value for one or more characters as a result of conflict (one character's desires clash with another's, or an environmental shift changes the value positively or negatively).

A Working Scene contains at least one Story Event. To determine a scene's Story Event, answer these four Socratic questions:

1. What are the characters literally doing—that is, what are their micro on-the-surface actions?

Jim learns he and Gunn share a common enemy and that the stranded sailor has a boat. They exchange stories and decide to help one another before cannon and small arms fire break out near the shore.

2. What is the essential tactic of the characters—that is, what above-the-surface macro behaviors are they employing that are linked to a universal human value?

Both Jim and Gunn are sizing each other up and want to escape the island. They must figure out if they can trust one another.

3. What beyond-the-surface universal human values have changed for one or more characters in the scene? Which one of those value changes is most important and should be included in the Story Grid Spreadsheet?

Before encountering Gunn, Jim is alone, afraid, and prepared to accept his fate. When he realizes that he and Gunn have a common enemy, it gives him hope, and he takes a chance. This improves Jim's optimism, but more importantly, it improves his chances of survival. Gunn knows how to find food and avoid disease on the island. He guides Jim back toward the shore.

Despair to Hope

4. The Scene Event Synthesis: What Story Event sums up the scene's on-the-surface, above-the-surface, and beyond-the-surface change? We will enter that event in the Story Grid Spreadsheet.

Jim discovers that Gunn is an ally with a boat, and when they hear the cannon and small-arms fire, Gunn helps Jim make his way back to the anchorage.

HOW THE SCENE ABIDES BY THE FIVE COMMANDMENTS OF STORYTELLING

Inciting Incident: Causal. A figure approaches Jim.

Turning Point Progressive Complication: Revelatory. Gunn knows and is afraid of Silver.

Crisis: Best bad choice. Should Jim be honest with Gunn or not?

Climax: Jim decides to tell the whole story. He can't be sure Gunn won't betray him, but his options are few and a common enemy is a good place to start.

Resolution: Gunn tells Jim about his boat and guides him after fighting breaks out.

NOTES

- Jim is horrified by Gunn at first. He is the opposite of someone he would trust before. But thanks to the point of no return, Jim knows his information processing is not always accurate, and he must look beyond Gunn's appearance.
- In this scene, Jim gets to see a likely future. He could end up stranded like Gunn. (It's interesting how Jim's story mirrors Gunn's own.) Jim doesn't know how to solve his big survival problems yet, but Gunn has managed to survive, so maybe Jim can too, especially with help.
- Jim is starting to talk to others about the danger he's aware of—probably because he sees the benefit of sharing what he knows. His survival instincts have kicked in to oppose the pattern of thought that stopped him from speaking up in the past. He was in flight mode before, and withholding information is a form of flight. He's not fully fighting yet, but he is able to reflect and say what he observes. He's applying

his agency in small ways and receiving validation from the arena.

- Gunn's strong desire for cheese is comical (at a time when we can use a break from intense fear) and helps the reader relate to him. Even if we haven't been without cheese for three years (or don't care for it), we have experienced *really* wanting something we can't have, feeling hope, and then feeling disappointment.
- Remembering the pistol he carries with him affords Jim agency in this situation. Sometimes it's enough to know we have options.

PART FOUR: THE STOCKADE

16

NARRATIVE CONTINUED BY THE DOCTOR: HOW THE SHIP WAS ABANDONED

It was **about half past one**—three bells in the sea phrase—that the two boats went ashore from the *Hispaniola*. **The captain, the squire**, and **I** were talking matters over in the cabin. Had there been a breath of wind, we should have fallen on **the six mutineers** who were left aboard with us, slipped our cable, and away to sea. But the wind was wanting; and to complete our helplessness, down came **Hunter** with the news that **Jim Hawkins** had slipped into a boat and was gone ashore with the rest.

It never occurred to us to doubt Jim Hawkins, but we were alarmed for his safety. With the men in the temper they were in, it seemed an even chance if we should see the lad again. We ran on deck. The pitch was bubbling in the seams; the nasty stench of the place turned me sick; if ever a man smelt fever and dysentery, it was in that abominable anchorage. The six scoundrels were sitting grumbling under a sail in the forecastle; ashore we could see the gigs made fast and a man sitting in each, hard by where the river runs in. One of them was whistling "Lillibullero."

Waiting was a strain, and it was decided that Hunter and I should go ashore with the jolly-boat in quest of information.

The gigs had leaned to their right, but Hunter and I pulled straight in, in the direction of the stockade upon the chart. The two who were left guarding their boats seemed in a bustle at our appearance; "Lillibullero" stopped off, and I could see **the pair** discussing what they ought to do. Had they gone and told **Silver**, all might have turned out differently; but they had their orders, I suppose, and decided to sit quietly where they were and hark back again to "Lillibullero."

There was a slight bend in the coast, and I steered so as to put it between us; even before we landed we had thus lost sight of the gigs. I jumped out and came as near running as I durst, with a big silk handkerchief under my hat for coolness' sake and a brace of pistols ready primed for safety.

I had not gone a hundred yards when I reached **the stockade.**

This was how it was: a spring of clear water rose almost at the top of a knoll. Well, on the knoll, and enclosing the spring, they had clapped a stout loghouse fit to hold two score of people on a pinch and loopholed for musketry on either side. All round this they had cleared a wide space, and then the thing was completed by a paling six feet high, without door or opening, too strong to pull down without time and labour and too open to shelter **the besiegers. The people in the loghouse** had them in every way; they stood quiet in shelter and shot the others like partridges. All they wanted was a good watch and food; for, short of a complete surprise, they might have held the place against **a regiment.**

What particularly took my fancy was the spring. For though we had a good enough place of it in the cabin of the *Hispaniola*, with plenty of arms and ammunition, and things to eat, and excellent wines, there had been one thing overlooked—we had no water. I was thinking this over when there came ringing over the island the cry of a man at the point of death. I was not new to violent death—I have served his Royal Highness the Duke of Cumberland [*British prince and general*], and got a wound myself at Fontenoy [*a 1745 battle in the War of the Austrian Succession*]—but I know my pulse went dot and carry one. "Jim Hawkins is gone," was my first thought.

It is something to have been **an old soldier,** but more still to have been **a doctor.** There is no time to dilly-dally in our work. And so now I made up my mind instantly, and with no time lost returned to the shore and jumped on board the jolly-boat. [*This is an echo of Jim's quick action in leaving the ship at the end of scene 13.*]

By good fortune Hunter pulled a good oar. We made the water fly, and the boat was soon alongside and I aboard the schooner.

I found them all shaken, as was natural. The squire was sitting down, as white as a sheet, thinking of the harm he had led us to, the good soul! And **one of the six forecastle hands** was little better.

"There's a man," says Captain Smollett, nodding towards him, "new to this work. He came nigh-hand fainting, doctor, when he heard the cry. Another touch of the rudder and that man would join us."

I told my plan to the captain, and between us we settled on the details of its accomplishment.

We put **old Redruth** in the gallery between the cabin and the forecastle, with three or four loaded muskets and a mattress for protection. Hunter brought the boat round under the stern-port, and Joyce and I set to work loading her with powder tins, muskets, bags of biscuits, kegs of pork, a cask of cognac, and my invaluable medicine chest.

In the meantime, the squire and the captain stayed on deck, and the latter hailed the **coxswain**, who was **the principal man aboard**.

"**Mr. Hands**," he said, "here are two of us with a brace of pistols each. If any one of you six make a signal of any description, that man's dead."

They were a good deal taken aback, and after a little consultation one and all tumbled down the fore companion, thinking no doubt to take us on the rear. But when they saw Redruth waiting for them in the sparred galley, they went about ship at once, and a head popped out again on deck.

"Down, dog!" cries the captain.

And the head popped back again; and we heard no more, for the time, of these six very faint-hearted seamen.

By this time, tumbling things in as they came, we had the jolly-boat loaded as much as we dared. **Joyce** and I got out through the stern-port, and we made for shore again as fast as oars could take us.

This second trip fairly aroused the watchers along shore. "Lillibullero" was dropped again; and just before we lost sight of them behind the little point, one of them whipped ashore and disappeared. I had half a mind to change my plan and destroy their boats, but I feared that Silver and the others might be close at hand, and all might very well be lost by trying for too much.

We had soon touched land in the same place as before and set to provision the block house. All three made the first journey, heavily laden, and tossed our stores over the palisade. Then, leaving Joyce to guard them—one man, to be sure, but with half a dozen muskets—Hunter and I returned to the jolly-boat and loaded ourselves once more. So we proceeded without pausing to take breath, till the whole cargo was bestowed, when the two servants took up their position in the block house, and I, with all my power, sculled back to the *Hispaniola*.

That we should have risked a second boat load seems more daring than it really was. They had the advantage of numbers, of course, but we had the advantage of arms. Not one of the men ashore had a musket, and before they could get within range for pistol shooting, we flattered ourselves we should be able to give a good account of a half-dozen at least.

The squire was waiting for me at the stern window, all his faintness gone from him. He caught the painter and made it fast, and we fell to loading the boat for our very lives. Pork, powder, and biscuit was the cargo, with only a musket and a cutlass apiece for the squire and me and Redruth and the captain. The rest of the arms and powder we dropped overboard in two fathoms and a half of water, so that we could see the bright steel shining far below us in the sun, on the clean, sandy bottom.

By this time the tide was beginning to ebb, and the ship was swinging round to her anchor. Voices were heard faintly halloaing in the direction of the two gigs; and though this reassured us for Joyce and Hunter, who were well to the eastward, it warned our party to be off.

Redruth retreated from his place in the gallery and dropped into the boat, which we then brought round to the ship's counter, to be handier for Captain Smollett.

"Now, men," said he, "do you hear me?"

There was no answer from the forecastle.

"It's to you, **Abraham Gray**—it's to you I am speaking."

Still no reply.

"Gray," resumed Mr. Smollett, a little louder, "I am leaving this ship, and I order you to follow your captain. I know you are a good man at bottom, and I dare say not one of the lot of you's as bad as he makes out. I have my watch here in my hand; I give you thirty seconds to join me in."

There was a pause.

"Come, my fine fellow," continued the captain; "don't hang so long in stays. I'm risking my life and the lives of these good gentlemen every second."

There was a sudden scuffle, a sound of blows, and out burst Abraham Gray with a knife cut on the side of the cheek, and came running to the captain like a dog to the whistle.

"I'm with you, sir," said he.

And the next moment he and the captain had dropped aboard of us, and we had shoved off and given way.

We were clear out of the ship, but not yet ashore in our stockade.

STORY EVENT

A Story Event is an active change of a universal human value for one or more characters as a result of conflict (one character's desires clash with another's, or an environmental shift changes the value positively or negatively).

A Working Scene contains at least one Story Event. To determine a scene's Story Event, answer these four Socratic questions:

1. **What are the characters literally doing—that is, what are their micro on-the-surface actions?**

Livesey and Hunter row ashore and inspect the stockade and the cabin. When they hear the sound of someone being killed, they return to the ship where Smollett, Trelawney, and those loyal to them abandon ship with provisions and weapons.

2. **What is the essential tactic of the characters—that is, what above-the-surface macro behaviors are they employing that are linked to a universal human value?**

Livesey wants to find the best option of survival for as many honest crew members as possible. When he learns that Jim has gone ashore, he has a reason to go ashore too—to be near in case of danger and to scout out the stockade. When he hears the cry of the man being killed ashore, he assumes Jim has died. He and Trelawney plan their escape to the stockade.

3. **What beyond-the-surface universal human values have changed for one or more characters in the scene? Which one of those value changes is most important and should be included in the Story Grid Spreadsheet?**

In Livesey's mind, Jim has shifted from life to death, but Stevenson would have known this isn't true, and even the reader is pretty sure. Jim hears the man scream in an earlier scene. For the value shift in any scene, we want to look at what we know about the entire story. So we could track Livesey's internal movement because it affects his belief, but we know because of the narrative device that Jim is still alive. The major change that affects everyone's survival is the movement from the ship toward the shore. The innocent members of the crew have left the temporary safety of the ship and are now exposed.

Temporary Safety to Exposed

4. The Scene Event Synthesis: What Story Event sums up the scene's on-the-surface, above-the-surface, and beyond-the-surface change? We will enter that event in the Story Grid Spreadsheet.

Believing Jim to be dead and the pirates openly attacking them, the innocent members of the crew abandon ship and make for the stockade with food and weapons.

HOW THE SCENE ABIDES BY THE FIVE COMMANDMENTS OF STORYTELLING

Inciting Incident: Causal. Livesey learns that Jim went ashore.

Turning Point Progressive Complication: Revelatory. Livesey concludes that Jim has been killed when he hears a man cry out. The pirates are openly attacking.

Crisis: Best bad choice. If they stay on the ship, they could be attacked by the pirates who remain. If they leave the ship, they will be vulnerable to attack on their way to the stockade.

Climax: They begin moving food and weapons to the stockade.

Resolution: Before the last trip, they hear pirates on ship calling to the men guarding the boats on shore. Abraham Gray joins the faithful party.

NOTES

- The reader knows more than Livesey does in this scene, including that Jim is still alive. In addition to the narrative drive of suspense, when we wonder what will happen as Jim runs toward the shore with Gunn, we experience the narrative drive of dramatic irony. Why would Stevenson do this? We get to see Livesey under extreme stress. He behaves differently because he believes Jim is no longer a consideration. He is not emotional about it in the moment, though we know it must pain him. But he's used to acting under pressure and making decisions that affect the lives of others. Notice how Livesey assesses the stockade as an option even before the attack.

- We learn that Livesey has been a soldier, so he has experience in applying his shadow agency, which means he can and will use violence to protect his own life and the lives of those who are innocent.

- It is said that Stevenson dropped in Livesey's point of view because he was stuck while working on the story. These days, it's often not encouraged to switch points of view this deep in the story. It is a little jarring, but it's consistent with the narrative device. At the beginning of the first scene, we're told Jim is preparing his account of the voyage including the arrival of Bones at the inn. Even with an account from the adults, it would be important to hear what Jim knows because he observed things the others didn't see. It makes sense that Livesey would prepare a similar account and that it would include events only he observed.

- Stevenson achieves a different tone and voice in Livesey's narrative. How does he do this? One important way is through the details Livesey notices related to tactical survival that are based on Livesey's knowledge. He's an adult and a veteran. He's become familiar with seagoing terminology and can describe objects and events accurately. Contrast this with Jim's observation of the island in scene 14.

17

NARRATIVE CONTINUED BY THE DOCTOR: THE JOLLY-BOAT'S LAST TRIP

This fifth trip was quite different from any of the others. In the first place, the little gallipot of a boat that we were in was gravely overloaded. Five grown men, and three of them—**Trelawney, Redruth, and the captain**—over six feet high, was already more than she was meant to carry. Add to that the powder, pork, and bread-bags. The gunwale was lipping astern. Several times we shipped a little water, and my breeches and the tails of my coat were all soaking wet before we had gone a hundred yards.

The captain made us trim the boat, and we got her to lie a little more evenly. All the same, we were afraid to breathe.

In the second place, the ebb was now making—a strong rippling current running westward through the basin, and then south'ard and seaward down the straits by which we had entered in the morning. Even the ripples were a danger to our overloaded craft, but the worst of it was that we were swept out of our true course and away from our proper landing-place behind the point. If we let the current have its way we should come ashore beside the gigs, where the pirates might appear at any moment.

"I cannot keep her head for the stockade, sir," said I to the captain. I was steering, while he and Redruth, two fresh men, were at the oars. "The tide keeps washing her down. Could you pull a little stronger?"

"Not without swamping the boat," said he. "You must bear up, sir, if you please—bear up until you see you're gaining."

I tried and found by experiment that the tide kept sweeping us westward until I had laid her head due east, or just about right angles to the way we ought to go.

"We'll never get ashore at this rate," said I.

"If it's the only course that we can lie, sir, we must even lie it," returned the captain. "We must keep upstream. You see, sir," he went on, "if once we dropped to leeward of the landing-place, it's hard to say where we should get ashore, besides the chance of being boarded by the gigs; whereas, the way we go the current must slacken, and then we can dodge back along the shore."

"The current's less a'ready, sir," said the man **Gray**, who was sitting in the fore-sheets; "you can ease her off a bit."

"Thank you, my man," said I, quite as if nothing had happened, for we had all quietly made up our minds to treat him like one of ourselves. Suddenly the captain spoke up again, and I thought his voice was a little changed.

"The gun!" said he.

"I have thought of that," said I, for I made sure he was thinking of a bombardment of the fort. "They could never get the gun ashore, and if they did, they could never haul it through the woods."

"Look astern, doctor," replied the captain.

We had entirely forgotten the long nine; and there, to our horror, were **the five rogues** busy about her, getting off her jacket, as they called the stout tarpaulin cover under which she sailed. Not only that, but it flashed into my mind at the same moment that the round-shot and the powder for the gun had been left behind, and a stroke with an axe would put it all into the possession of the evil ones abroad.

"**Israel** was **Flint**'s gunner," said Gray hoarsely.

At any risk, we put the boat's head direct for the landing-place. By this time we had got so far out of the run of the current that we kept steerage way even at our necessarily gentle rate of rowing, and I could keep her steady for the goal. But the worst of it was that with the course I now held we turned our broadside instead of our stern to the *Hispaniola* and offered a target like a barn door.

152

I could hear as well as see that brandy-faced rascal Israel Hands plumping down a round-shot on the deck.

"Who's the best shot?" asked the captain.

"Mr. Trelawney, out and away," said I.

"Mr. Trelawney, will you please pick me off one of these men, sir? Hands, if possible," said the captain.

Trelawney was as cool as steel. He looked to the priming of his gun.

"Now," cried the captain, "easy with that gun, sir, or you'll swamp the boat. All hands stand by to trim her when he aims."

The squire raised his gun, the rowing ceased, and we leaned over to the other side to keep the balance, and all was so nicely contrived that we did not ship a drop.

They had the gun, by this time, slewed round upon the swivel, and Hands, who was at the muzzle with the rammer, was in consequence the most exposed. However, we had no luck, for just as Trelawney fired, down he stooped, the ball whistled over him, and it was one of the other four who fell.

The cry he gave was echoed not only by his companions on board but by a great number of voices from the shore, and looking in that direction I saw the other pirates trooping out from among the trees and tumbling into their places in the boats.

"Here come the gigs, sir," said I.

"Give way, then," cried the captain. "We mustn't mind if we swamp her now. If we can't get ashore, all's up."

"Only one of the gigs is being manned, sir," I added; "the crew of the other most likely going round by shore to cut us off."

"They'll have a hot run, sir," returned the captain. "Jack ashore, you know. It's not them I mind; it's the round-shot. Carpet bowls! My lady's maid couldn't miss. Tell us, squire, when you see the match, and we'll hold water."

In the meanwhile we had been making headway at a good pace for a boat so overloaded, and we had shipped but little water in the process. We were now close in; thirty or forty strokes and we should beach her, for the ebb had already disclosed a narrow belt of sand below the clustering trees. The gig was no longer to be feared; the little point had already concealed it from our eyes. The ebb-tide, which had so cruelly delayed us, was now making reparation and delaying our assailants. The one source of danger was the gun.

"If I durst," said the captain, "I'd stop and pick off another man."

But it was plain that they meant nothing should delay their shot. They had never so much as looked at their fallen comrade, though he was not dead, and I could see him trying to crawl away.

"Ready!" cried the squire.

"Hold!" cried the captain, quick as an echo.

And he and Redruth backed with a great heave that sent her stern bodily under water. The report fell in at the same instant of time. **This was the first that Jim heard, the sound of the squire's shot not having reached him.** Where the ball passed, not one of us precisely knew, but I fancy it must have been over our heads and that the wind of it may have contributed to our disaster.

At any rate, the boat sank by the stern, quite gently, in three feet of water, leaving the captain and myself, facing each other, on our feet. The other three took complete headers, and came up again drenched and bubbling.

So far there was no great harm. No lives were lost, and we could wade ashore in safety. But there were all our stores at the bottom, and to make things worse, only two guns out of five remained in a state for service. Mine I had snatched from my knees and held over my head, by a sort of instinct. As for the captain, he had carried his over his shoulder by a bandoleer, and like a wise man, lock uppermost. The other three had gone down with the boat.

To add to our concern, we heard voices already drawing near us in the woods along shore, and we had not only the danger of being cut off from the stockade in our half-crippled state but the fear before us whether, if **Hunter** and **Joyce** were attacked by half a dozen, they would have the sense and conduct to stand firm. Hunter was steady, that we knew; Joyce was a doubtful case—a pleasant, polite man for a valet and to brush one's clothes, but not entirely fitted for a man of war.

With all this in our minds, we waded ashore as fast as we could, leaving behind us the poor jolly-boat and a good half of all our powder and provisions.

• ANALYZING THE SCENE •

STORY EVENT

A Story Event is an active change of a universal human value for one or more characters as a result of conflict (one character's desires clash with another's, or an environmental shift changes the value positively or negatively).

A Working Scene contains at least one Story Event. To determine a scene's Story Event, answer these four Socratic questions:

1. What are the characters literally doing—that is, what are their micro on-the-surface actions?

Livesey and the others are crossing from the ship to the stockade in a jolly boat. The pirates left aboard ship train the nine-pound gun to fire on their boat. The pirates on shore split up and send one group in a gig on the water and a party on land to intercept the faithful party. Trelawney fires upon the pirates on the ship.

2. What is the essential tactic of the characters—that is, what above-the-surface macro behaviors are they employing that are linked to a universal human value?

The faithful party is rowing for their lives, trying to get to the safety of the stockade. They are attending to their immediate survival. The pirates are trying to stop them.

3. What beyond-the-surface universal human values have changed for one or more characters in the scene? Which one of those value changes is most important and should be included in the Story Grid Spreadsheet?

One of the pirates dies because Trelawney uses deadly force to survive. But we're looking at the value for the faithful party. Although they all survive this skirmish, they are in bad shape because their boat is now useless. The pirates have the only working boats they know of for returning to the ship. They are short of supplies and face the very real threat of being stranded. In fact, if not for the treasure, the pirates could have left them there right away.

Sufficient Resources to Scarce Resources

4. The Scene Event Synthesis: What Story Event sums up the

scene's on-the-surface, above-the-surface, and beyond-the-surface change? We will enter that event in the Story Grid Spreadsheet.

The pirates attack the faithful party in the jolly boat. Livesey and the others avoid being hit by cannon fire but lose half of their provisions, weapons, and powder.

HOW THE SCENE ABIDES BY THE FIVE COMMANDMENTS OF STORYTELLING

Inciting Incident: Causal. The faithful party has abandoned the ship and is heading for the shore.

Turning Point Progressive Complication: Active. Pirates on the ship turn the cannon on the jolly boat.

Crisis: Best bad choice. Should they go slowly, with broadside facing the long gun on board in an attempt to pick off the men firing the cannon, or should they row quickly for shore and risk swamping the boat? In other words, do they employ shadow agency (destructive force) or not?

Climax: Trelawney (the best shot) fires on the pirates while the faithful party members pause rowing.

Resolution: The cannon fire misses them, but the boat is swamped. They lose some provisions and weapons. They hear voices up by the stockade and don't know the location of the pirates that remained on shore.

NOTES

- When Livesey returns to the ship in the prior scene, he, Trelawney, and Smollett could have used violence to take the ship. Instead, he and the others attempt to escape. They fire only when the pirates begin firing at them. This is an important point because the expectations for the agency deprived and shadow agents are different.
- The reference to the shot Jim heard allows the reader to align the two narratives.
- Notice that Smollett's calculated risk to invite Gray to join

them in scene 16 pays off here. Gray's presence will continue to be an advantage.

- Trelawney proves himself in this scene. He's not just the financier for the voyage, but it turns out he's an excellent shot.

18

NARRATIVE CONTINUED BY THE DOCTOR: END OF THE FIRST DAY'S FIGHTING

We made our best speed across the strip of wood that now divided us from the stockade, and at every step we took the voices of **the buccaneers** rang nearer. Soon we could hear their footfalls as they ran and the cracking of the branches as they breasted across a bit of thicket.

I began to see we should have a brush for it in earnest and looked to my priming.

"**Captain**," said I, "**Trelawney** is the dead shot. Give him your gun; his own is useless."

They exchanged guns, and Trelawney, silent and cool as he had been since the beginning of the bustle, hung a moment on his heel to see that all was fit for service. At the same time, observing **Gray** to be unarmed, I handed him my cutlass. It did all our hearts good to see him spit in his hand, knit his brows, and make the blade sing through the air. It was plain from every line of his body that our new hand was worth his salt.

Forty paces farther we came to the edge of the wood and saw the stockade in front of us. We struck the enclosure about the middle of the south side, and almost at the same time, **seven mutineers—Job Anderson**, the boatswain, at their head—appeared in full cry at the southwestern corner.

They paused as if taken aback, and before they recovered, not only the squire and I, but **Hunter** and **Joyce** from the block house, had time to fire. The four shots came in rather a scattering volley, but they did the business: one of the enemy actually fell, and the rest, without hesitation, turned and plunged into the trees.

After reloading, we walked down the outside of the palisade to see to the fallen enemy. He was stone dead—shot through the heart.

We began to rejoice over our good success when just at that moment a pistol cracked in the bush, a ball whistled close past my ear, and poor **Tom Redruth** stumbled and fell his length on the ground. Both the squire and I returned the shot, but as we had nothing to aim at, it is probable we only wasted powder. Then we reloaded and turned our attention to poor Tom.

The captain and Gray were already examining him, and I saw with half an eye that all was over.

I believe the readiness of our return volley had scattered the mutineers once more, for we were suffered without further molestation to get the poor old gamekeeper hoisted over the stockade and carried, groaning and bleeding, into the log-house.

Poor old fellow, he had not uttered one word of surprise, complaint, fear, or even acquiescence from the very beginning of our troubles till now, when we had laid him down in the log-house to die. He had lain like **a Trojan** behind his mattress in the gallery; he had followed every order silently, doggedly, and well; he was the oldest of our party by a score of years; and now, sullen, old, serviceable servant, it was he that was to die.

The squire dropped down beside him on his knees and kissed his hand, crying like a child.

"Be I going, doctor?" he asked.

"Tom, my man," said I, "you're going home."

"I wish I had had a lick at them with the gun first," he replied.

"Tom," said the squire, "say you forgive me, won't you?"

"Would that be respectful like, from me to you, squire?" was the answer. "Howsoever, so be it, amen!"

After a little while of silence, he said he thought somebody might read a prayer. "It's the custom, sir," he added apologetically. And not long after, without another word, he passed away.

In the meantime the captain, whom I had observed to be wonderfully swollen about the chest and pockets, had turned out a great many various stores—the British colours, a Bible, a coil of stoutish rope, pen, ink, the log-book, and pounds of tobacco. He had found a longish fir-tree lying felled and trimmed in the enclosure, and with the help of Hunter he had set it up at the corner of the log-house where the trunks crossed and made an angle. Then, climbing on the roof, he had with his own hand bent and run up the colours.

This seemed mightily to relieve him. He re-entered the log-house and set about counting up the stores as if nothing else existed. But he had an eye on Tom's passage for all that, and as soon as all was over, came forward with another flag and reverently spread it on the body.

"Don't you take on, sir," he said, shaking the squire's hand. "All's well with him; no fear for a hand that's been shot down in his duty to **captain and owner**. It mayn't be good divinity, but it's a fact."

Then he pulled me aside.

"Dr. Livesey," he said, "in how many weeks do you and squire expect **the consort**?"

I told him it was a question not of weeks but of months, that if we were not back by the end of August **Blandly** was to send to find us, but neither sooner nor later. "You can calculate for yourself," I said.

"Why, yes," returned the captain, scratching his head; "and making a large allowance, sir, for all the gifts of Providence, I should say we were pretty close hauled."

"How do you mean?" I asked.

"It's a pity, sir, we lost that second load. That's what I mean," replied the captain. "As for powder and shot, we'll do. But the rations are short, very short—so short, Dr. Livesey, that we're perhaps as well without that extra mouth."

And he pointed to the dead body under the flag.

Just then, with a roar and a whistle, a round-shot passed high above the roof of the log-house and plumped far beyond us in the wood.

"Oho!" said the captain. "Blaze away! You've little enough powder already, my lads."

At the second trial, the aim was better, and the ball descended inside the stockade, scattering a cloud of sand but doing no further damage.

"Captain," said the squire, "the house is quite invisible from the ship. It must be the flag they are aiming at. Would it not be wiser to take it in?"

"Strike my colours!" cried the captain. "No, sir, not I"; and as soon as he had said the words, I think we all agreed with him. For it was not only a piece of stout, seamanly, good feeling; it was good policy besides and showed our enemies that we despised their cannonade.

All through the evening they kept thundering away. Ball after ball flew over or fell short or kicked up the sand in the enclosure, but they had to fire so high that the shot fell dead and buried itself in the soft sand. We had no ricochet to fear, and though one popped in through the roof of the log-house and out again through the floor, we soon got used to that sort of horse-play and minded it no more than cricket.

"There is one good thing about all this," observed the captain; "the wood in front of us is likely clear. The ebb has made a good while; our stores should be uncovered. Volunteers to go and bring in pork."

Gray and Hunter were the first to come forward. Well armed, they stole out of the stockade, but it proved a useless mission. The mutineers were bolder than we fancied or they put more trust in Israel's gunnery. For four or five of them were busy carrying off our stores and wading out with them to one of the gigs that lay close by, pulling an oar or so to hold her steady against the current. Silver was in the stern-sheets in command; and every man of them was now provided with a musket from some secret magazine of their own.

The captain sat down to his log, and here is the beginning of the entry:

Alexander Smollett, master; David Livesey, ship's doctor; Abraham Gray, carpenter's mate; John Trelawney, owner; John Hunter and Richard Joyce, owner's servants, landsmen—being all that is left faithful of the ship's company—with stores for ten days at short rations, came ashore this day and flew British colours on the log-house in Treasure Island. Thomas Redruth, owner's servant, landsman, shot by the mutineers; James Hawkins, cabin-boy—

And at the same time, I was wondering over poor Jim Hawkins' fate.

A hail on the land side.

"Somebody hailing us," said Hunter, who was on guard.

"Doctor! Squire! Captain! Hullo, Hunter, is that you?" came the cries.

And I ran to the door in time to see Jim Hawkins, safe and sound, come climbing over the stockade.

STORY EVENT

A Story Event is an active change of a universal human value for one or more characters as a result of conflict (one character's desires clash with another's, or an environmental shift changes the value positively or negatively).

A Working Scene contains at least one Story Event. To determine a scene's Story Event, answer these four Socratic questions:

1. What are the characters literally doing—that is, what are their micro on-the-surface actions?

The faithful party runs to the stockade while the pirates fire guns at them. One of the pirates shoots Redruth. Jim's companions take stock of what remains of their provisions and ammunition. Gray and Hunter go toward the shore to recover submerged provisions, but the pirates fire on the stockade and take the salvageable food.

2. What is the essential tactic of the characters—that is, what above-the-surface macro behaviors are they employing that are linked to a universal human value?

At first, members of the faithful party focus on immediate survival by getting to their safe haven. Once they are within the walls of the stockade, Smollett turns his attention to how they will survive long term. The pirates attack and retrieve the abandoned provisions.

3. What beyond-the-surface universal human values have changed for one or more characters in the scene? Which one of those value changes is most important and should be included in the Story Grid Spreadsheet?

The faithful party was exposed and is now sheltered, but Redruth, a faithful and valuable member of the crew, dies. Jim was presumed dead but returns to them alive. They are temporarily safe, but they don't have enough food to survive if they become stranded.

Exposed to Temporarily Safe

4. The Scene Event Synthesis: What Story Event sums up the scene's on-the-surface, above-the-surface, and beyond-the-surface change? We will enter that event in the Story Grid Spreadsheet.

The faithful party reaches the stockade but lose Redruth and are low on provisions.

HOW THE SCENE ABIDES BY THE FIVE COMMANDMENTS OF STORYTELLING

Inciting Incident: Causal. The pirates attack the faithful party as they run for the stockade.

Turning Point Progressive Complication: Revelatory. They don't have enough rations to eat until Blandly's consort shows up.

Crisis: Should they risk a trip to the shore to recover more provisions from the water or not?

Climax: Smollett calls for volunteers, and Gray and Hunter leave the stockade.

Resolution: The pirates have taken the sunken provisions that were salvageable. Jim climbs over the stockade to safety.

NOTES

- This is a great example of a shift in focus from how to survive the next hour to surviving the next month or longer. Different considerations and risks are associated with each situation.
- Can you see how Jim experiences the same shift? He escapes the immediate threat of the pirates (scenes 13 and 14), which leaves him free to consider how to survive if stranded on the island. We're seeing the same process at two different levels, first the individual and then with Jim's closest first-party relationships. Consider how different characters behave differently under similar stress.
- Smollett and Livesey have experienced war, and it's suggested that Trelawney has been in rough situations too. Sometimes challenging experiences that include a loss of innocence reward those who make it through. They gain skills and perspectives that help them in other conflicts. Smollett, Livesey, and Trelawney are able to continue

functioning though they have been attacked and lost people who are dear to them.

- Among other items, Smollett brings the British flag and a Bible from the ship. These were not necessary for their physical survival but would be a reminder of who they are and what they stand for. It is an act of defiance to raise the flag above the stockade. They are not soldiers defending their nation in war, but it's part of their culture. Stevenson didn't have to include these details, but they're a useful way to reveal character. What the characters do is part of who they are. They maintain order. They continue on with their way of life as much as possible.

- The flag gives the faithful party an advantage even though it draws fire. It provides information to Jim in the next scene but also inspires the people within the stockade as a symbol of third-party identity. It causes the pirates to waste ammunition, which may provide cover for Jim on his way to the stockade.

- The value shift is both physical and metaphoric. Jim's friends are exposed. Once within the stockade, they begin to despair. The flag changes their attitude about their circumstances, though. And Jim's appearance seems like a reward from the arena for keeping the faith though things looked grim. They have many obstacles to overcome, but they are not giving into despair.

19

NARRATIVE RESUMED BY JIM HAWKINS: THE GARRISON IN THE STOCKADE

As soon as **Ben Gunn** saw the colours he came to a halt, stopped me by the arm, and sat down.

"Now," said he, "there's **your friends**, sure enough."

"Far more likely it's **the mutineers**," I answered.

"That!" he cried. "Why, in a place like this, where nobody puts in but **gen'lemen of fortune**, **Silver** would fly the Jolly Roger, you don't make no doubt of that. No, that's your friends. There's been blows too, and I reckon your friends has had the best of it; and here they are ashore in the old stockade, as was made years and years ago by **Flint**. Ah, he was the man to have a headpiece, was Flint! Barring rum, his match were never seen. He were afraid of none, not he; on'y Silver—Silver was that genteel."

"Well," said I, "that may be so, and so be it; all the more reason that I should hurry on and join my friends."

"Nay, mate," returned Ben, "not you. You're a good boy, or I'm mistook; but you're on'y a boy, all told. Now, Ben Gunn is fly. Rum wouldn't bring me there, where you're going—not rum wouldn't, till I see your born gen'leman and gets it on his word of honour. And you won't forget my words; 'A precious sight (that's what you'll say), a precious sight more confidence'—and then nips him."

And he pinched me the third time with the same air of cleverness.

"And when Ben Gunn is wanted, you know where to find him, Jim. Just where you found him today. And him that comes is to have a white thing in his hand, and he's to come alone. Oh! And you'll say this: 'Ben Gunn,' says you, 'has reasons of his own.'"

"Well," said I, "I believe I understand. You have something to propose, and you wish to see **the squire** or **the doctor**, and you're to be found where I found you. Is that all?"

"And when? says you," he added. "Why, from about noon observation to about six bells."

"Good," said I, "and now may I go?"

"You won't forget?" he inquired anxiously. "Precious sight, and reasons of his own, says you. Reasons of his own; that's the mainstay; as between man and man. Well, then"—still holding me—"I reckon you can go, Jim. And, Jim, if you was to see Silver, you wouldn't go for to sell Ben Gunn? Wild horses wouldn't draw it from you? No, says you. And if them pirates camp ashore, Jim, what would you say but there'd be widders in the morning?"

Here he was interrupted by a loud report, and a cannonball came tearing through the trees and pitched in the sand not a hundred yards from where we two were talking. The next moment each of us had taken to his heels in a different direction.

For a good hour to come frequent reports shook the island, and balls kept crashing through the woods. I moved from hiding-place to hiding-place, always pursued, or so it seemed to me, by these terrifying missiles. But towards the end of the bombardment, though still I durst not venture in the direction of the stockade, where the balls fell oftenest, I had begun, in a manner, to pluck up my heart again, and after a long detour to the east, crept down among the shore-side trees.

The sun had just set, the sea breeze was rustling and tumbling in the woods and ruffling the grey surface of the anchorage; the tide, too, was far out, and great tracts of sand lay uncovered; the air, after the heat of the day, chilled me through my jacket.

The *Hispaniola* still lay where she had anchored; but, sure enough, there was the Jolly Roger—the black flag of piracy—flying from her peak. Even as I looked, there came another red flash and another report that sent the echoes clattering, and one more round-shot whistled through the air. It was the last of the cannonade.

I lay for some time watching the bustle which succeeded the attack. **Men** were demolishing something with axes on the beach near the stockade—the poor jolly-boat, I afterwards discovered. Away, near the mouth of the river, a great fire was glowing among the trees, and between that point and the ship one of the gigs kept coming and going, **the men**, whom I had seen so gloomy, shouting at the oars like children. But there was a sound in their voices which suggested rum.

At length I thought I might return towards the stockade. I was pretty far down on the low, sandy spit that encloses the anchorage to the east, and is joined at half-water to Skeleton Island; and now, as I rose to my feet, I saw, some distance further down the spit and rising from among low bushes, an isolated rock, pretty high, and peculiarly white in colour. It occurred to me that this might be the white rock of which **Ben Gunn** had spoken and that some day or other a boat might be wanted and I should know where to look for one.

Then I skirted among the woods until I had regained the rear, or shoreward side, of the stockade, and was soon warmly welcomed by **the faithful party.**

I had soon told my story and began to look about me. The log-house was made of unsquared trunks of pine—roof, walls, and floor. The latter stood in several places as much as a foot or a foot and a half above the surface of the sand. There was a porch at the door, and under this porch the little spring welled up into an artificial basin of a rather odd kind—no other than a great ship's kettle of iron, with the bottom knocked out, and sunk "to her bearings," as **the captain** said, among the sand.

Little had been left besides the framework of the house, but in one corner there was a stone slab laid down by way of hearth and an old rusty iron basket to contain the fire.

The slopes of the knoll and all the inside of the stockade had been cleared of timber to build the house, and we could see by the stumps what a fine and lofty grove had been destroyed. Most of the soil had been washed away or buried in drift after the removal of the trees; only where the streamlet ran down from the kettle a thick bed of moss and some ferns and little creeping bushes were still green among the sand. Very close around the stockade—too close for defence, they said—the wood still flourished high and dense, all of fir on the land side, but towards the sea with a large admixture of live-oaks. [*Why does Jim offer these details here? Why not focus on the people and what they tell him? Stevenson knows Livesey can't deliver this because it would have seemed out of place. But this also shows that Jim is beginning to become aware of relevant details within his environment.*]

The cold evening breeze, of which I have spoken, whistled through every chink of the rude building and sprinkled the floor with a continual rain of fine sand. There was sand in our eyes, sand in our teeth, sand in our suppers, sand dancing in the spring at the bottom of the kettle, for all the world like porridge beginning to boil. Our chimney was a square hole in the roof; it was but a little part of the smoke that found its way out, and the rest eddied about the house and kept us coughing and piping the eye. [*Adventure isn't comfortable, but we don't think of these hardships in advance. The details lend support to the change Jim experiences.*]

Add to this that **Gray**, the new man, had his face tied up in a bandage for a cut he had got in breaking away from **the mutineers** and that **poor old Tom Redruth**, still unburied, lay along the wall, stiff and stark, under the Union Jack. [*Jim's opinion of Redruth has changed since scene 7.*]

If we had been allowed to sit idle, we should all have fallen in the blues, but Captain Smollett was never the man for that. All hands were called up before him, and he divided us into watches. **The doctor** and Gray and I for one; **the squire, Hunter**, and **Joyce** upon the other. Tired though we all were, two were sent out for firewood; two more were set to dig a grave for Redruth; the doctor was named cook; I was put sentry at the door; and the captain himself went from one to another, keeping up our spirits and lending a hand wherever it was wanted.

From time to time the doctor came to the door for a little air and to rest his eyes, which were almost smoked out of his head, and whenever he did so, he had a word for me.

"That man Smollett," he said once, "is a better man than I am. And when I say that it means a deal, Jim." [*A mark of maturity is admitting you've been wrong.*]

Another time he came and was silent for a while. Then he put his head on one side, and looked at me.

"Is this Ben Gunn a man?" he asked.

"I do not know, sir," said I. "I am not very sure whether he's sane."

"If there's any doubt about the matter, he is," returned the doctor. "A man who has been three years biting his nails on a desert island, Jim, can't expect to appear as sane as you or me. It doesn't lie in human nature. Was it cheese you said he had a fancy for?"

"Yes, sir, cheese," I answered.

"Well, Jim," says he, "just see the good that comes of being dainty in your food. You've seen my snuff-box, haven't you? And you never saw me take snuff, the reason being that in my snuff-box I carry a piece of Parmesan cheese—a cheese made in Italy, very nutritious. Well, that's for Ben Gunn!" [*This is a nice payoff of the setup in scene 15 when Gunn expressed his love for cheese.*]

Before supper was eaten we buried old Tom in the sand and stood round him for a while bare-headed in the breeze. A good deal of firewood had been got in, but not enough for the captain's fancy, and he shook his head over it and told us we "must get back to this tomorrow rather livelier." [*Smollett is keeping everyone busy but also preparing for uncertain times.*] Then, when we had eaten our pork and each had a good stiff glass of brandy grog, the **three chiefs** got together in a corner to discuss our prospects.

It appears they were at their wits' end what to do, the stores being so low that we must have been starved into surrender long before help came. But our best hope, it was decided, was to kill off the **buccaneers** until they either hauled down their flag or ran away with the *Hispaniola*. **From nineteen they were already reduced to fifteen, two others were wounded, and one at least—the man shot beside the gun—severely wounded, if he were not dead.** Every time we had a crack at them, we were to take it, saving our own lives, with the extremest care. And besides that, we had two able allies—rum and the climate.

As for the first, though we were about half a mile away, we could hear them roaring and singing late into the night; and as for the second, the doctor staked his wig that, camped where they were in the marsh and unprovided with remedies, the half of them would be on their backs before a week.

"So," he added, "if we are not all shot down first they'll be glad to be packing in the schooner. It's always a ship, and they can get to buccaneering again, I suppose."

"First ship that ever I lost," said Captain Smollett. [*He's been maintaining everyone else's morale, and here he allows himself a moment to acknowledge his disappointment.*]

I was dead tired, as you may fancy; and when I got to sleep, which was not till after a great deal of tossing, I slept like a log of wood.

The rest had long been up and had already breakfasted and increased the pile of firewood by about half as much again when I was wakened by a bustle and the sound of voices.

"Flag of truce!" I heard someone say; and then, immediately after, with a cry of surprise, "**Silver** himself!"

And at that, up I jumped, and rubbing my eyes, ran to a loophole in the wall.

• ANALYZING THE SCENE •

STORY EVENT

A Story Event is an active change of a universal human value for one or more characters as a result of conflict (one character's desires clash with another's, or an environmental shift changes the value positively or negatively).

A Working Scene contains at least one Story Event. To determine a scene's Story Event, answer these four Socratic questions:

1. What are the characters literally doing—that is, what are their micro on-the-surface actions?

The pirates stop firing on the stockade, which allows Jim to rejoin his friends. The faithful party continues doing what they can, seeing to Redruth and collecting firewood. Smollett, Trelawney, and Livesey decide on tactics for the immediate future.

2. What is the essential tactic of the characters—that is, what above-the-surface macro behaviors are they employing that are linked to a universal human value?

Gunn wants to make a connection with the faithful party and gives Jim a specific message to deliver. The leaders want to discover the plan that gives them the best chance for survival.

3. What beyond-the-surface universal human values have changed for one or more characters in the scene? Which one of those value changes is most important and should be included in the Story Grid Spreadsheet?

Jim ends up inside the stockade. But the biggest shift is deciding how they will go on. They choose to hold out.

Undecided to Decided

4. The Scene Event Synthesis: What Story Event sums up the scene's on-the-surface, above-the-surface, and beyond-the-surface change? We will enter that event in the Story Grid Spreadsheet.

Jim rejoins his friends, and the leaders decide they will kill the pirates as able without risking their lives and hold out while the rum and climate weaken their foes.

. . .

HOW THE SCENE ABIDES BY THE FIVE COMMANDMENTS OF STORYTELLING

Inciting Incident: Causal. The pirates stop firing on the stockade and log cabin, and Jim rejoins the party.

Turning Point Progressive Complication: Active. The leaders meet to consider options after completing the day's tasks. In other words, they have done all they can do before choosing the way forward.

Crisis: Best bad choice. If they wait too long, they risk dying of starvation, but if they go on the offensive while being outnumbered by the pirates, they risk immediate death.

Climax: They will pick off the pirates when able and wait for rum and climate to undermine them. Above all, they will be careful with their lives.

Resolution: Everyone gets some rest, and the next morning, Silver arrives under a flag of truce.

NOTES

- The conditions are miserable here, and it would be easy to give in to despair. Smollett is mindful of maintaining morale and discipline by keeping everyone active so they will be tired enough to sleep and not dwell on their problems.
- Compare Jim's description of the cabin to his first hours on shore. He's not looking in terror or wonder. He's making tactical assessments and looking for subtext.
- We don't get a closeup view of the pirates' camp, but we hear enough to compare their evening with that of Jim and his friends. The pirates are drinking rum and camping in an area where they can contract yellow fever. They have some distinct advantages in firepower, possession of the ship, and plenty of food. But their lack of discipline and inability to focus on the future are disadvantages.
- The danger of intoxication was set up with Bones in the opening scenes. Livesey said the rum damaged the captain's health, but it also made him less cautious. He spent his

evenings drinking, singing, and telling stories that could easily spread. This is a great example of setting up circumstances that will allow the luminary agent to defeat the shadow agents.

20

SILVER'S EMBASSY

Sure enough, there were two men just outside the stockade, one of them waving a white cloth, the other, no less a person than **Silver** himself, standing placidly by.

It was still quite early, and the coldest morning that I think I ever was abroad in—a chill that pierced into the marrow. The sky was bright and cloudless overhead, and the tops of the trees shone rosily in the sun. But where Silver stood with **his lieutenant**, all was still in shadow, and they waded knee-deep in a low white vapour that had crawled during the night out of the morass. The chill and the vapour taken together told a poor tale of the island. It was plainly a damp, feverish, unhealthy spot.

"Keep indoors, men," said **the captain**. "Ten to one this is a trick."

Then he hailed the buccaneer.

"Who goes? Stand, or we fire."

"Flag of truce," cried Silver.

The captain was in the porch, keeping himself carefully out of the way of a treacherous shot, should any be intended. He turned and spoke to us, "Doctor's watch on the lookout. **Dr. Livesey** take the north side, if you please; **Jim**, the east; **Gray**, west. The watch below, all hands to load muskets. Lively, men, and careful."

And then he turned again to the mutineers.

"And what do you want with your flag of truce?" he cried.

This time it was the other man who replied.

"Cap'n Silver, sir, to come on board and make terms," he shouted.

"Cap'n Silver! Don't know him. Who's he?" cried the captain. And we could hear him adding to himself, "Cap'n, is it? My heart, and here's promotion!"

Long John answered for himself. "Me, sir. These poor lads have chosen me cap'n, after your desertion, sir"—laying a particular emphasis upon the word "desertion." "We're willing to submit, if we can come to terms, and no bones about it. All I ask is your word, Cap'n Smollett, to let me safe and sound out of this here stockade, and one minute to get out o' shot before a gun is fired."

"My man," said Captain Smollett, "I have not the slightest desire to talk to you. If you wish to talk to me, you can come, that's all. If there's any treachery, it'll be on your side, and **the Lord** help you."

"That's enough, cap'n," shouted Long John cheerily. "A word from you's enough. I know **a gentleman**, and you may lay to that."

We could see the man who carried the flag of truce attempting to hold Silver back. Nor was that wonderful, seeing how cavalier had been the captain's answer. But Silver laughed at him aloud and slapped him on the back as if the idea of alarm had been absurd. Then he advanced to the stockade, threw over his crutch, got a leg up, and with great vigour and skill succeeded in surmounting the fence and dropping safely to the other side.

I will confess that I was far too much taken up with what was going on to be of the slightest use as sentry; indeed, I had already deserted my eastern loophole and crept up behind the captain, who had now seated himself on the threshold, with his elbows on his knees, his head in his hands, and his eyes fixed on the water as it bubbled out of the old iron kettle in the sand. [*Once again, Jim is distracted by Silver, as if he were under a spell.*] He was whistling "Come, Lasses and Lads."

Silver had terrible hard work getting up the knoll. What with the steepness of the incline, the thick tree stumps, and the soft sand, he and his crutch were as helpless as a ship in stays. [*Silver appears to be disabled here. He's not moving the way he did in the forest when attacking*]

Tom.] But he stuck to it like a man in silence, and at last arrived before the captain, whom he saluted in the handsomest style. He was tricked out in his best; an immense blue coat, thick with brass buttons, hung as low as to his knees, and a fine laced hat was set on the back of his head.

"Here you are, my man," said the captain, raising his head. "You had better sit down."

"You ain't a-going to let me inside, cap'n?" complained Long John. "It's a main cold morning, to be sure, sir, to sit outside upon the sand."

"Why, Silver," said the captain, "if you had pleased to be an honest man, you might have been sitting in your galley. It's your own doing. You're either **my ship's cook**—and then you were treated handsome—or **Cap'n Silver**, a common mutineer and pirate, and then you can go hang!"

"Well, well, cap'n," returned the sea-cook, sitting down as he was bidden on the sand, "you'll have to give me a hand up again, that's all. A sweet pretty place you have of it here. Ah, there's Jim! The top of the morning to you, Jim. Doctor, here's my service. Why, there you all are together like a happy family, in a manner of speaking."

"If you have anything to say, my man, better say it," said the captain.

"Right you were, Cap'n Smollett," replied Silver. "Dooty is dooty, to be sure. Well now, you look here, that was a good lay of yours last night. I don't deny it was a good lay. Some of you pretty handy with a handspike-end. And I'll not deny neither but what some of my people was shook—maybe all was shook; maybe I was shook myself; maybe that's why I'm here for terms. But you mark me, cap'n, it won't do twice, by thunder! We'll have to do sentry-go and ease off a point or so on the rum. Maybe you think we were all a sheet in the wind's eye. But I'll tell you I was sober; I was on'y dog tired; and if I'd awoke a second sooner, I'd 'a caught you at the act, I would. He wasn't dead when I got round to him, not he."

"Well?" says Captain Smollett as cool as can be.

All that Silver said was a riddle to him, but you would never have guessed it from his tone. As for me, I began to have an inkling. Ben Gunn's last words came back to my mind. I began to suppose that he had paid the buccaneers a visit while they all lay drunk together round their fire, and I reckoned up with glee that we had **only fourteen enemies** to deal with.

"Well, here it is," said Silver. "We want that treasure, and we'll have it—that's our point! You would just as soon save your lives, I reckon; and that's yours. You have a chart, haven't you?" [*This is the first time Silver communicates what the pirates want.*]

"That's as may be," replied the captain.

"Oh, well, you have, I know that," returned Long John. "You needn't be so husky with a man; there ain't a particle of service in that, and you may lay to it. What I mean is, we want your chart. Now, I never meant you no harm, myself."

"That won't do with me, my man," interrupted the captain. "We know exactly what you meant to do, and we don't care, for now, you see, you can't do it."

And the captain looked at him calmly and proceeded to fill a pipe.

"If Abe Gray—" Silver broke out.

"Avast there!" cried Mr. Smollett. "Gray told me nothing, and I asked him nothing; and what's more, I would see you and him and this whole island blown clean out of the water into blazes first. So there's my mind for you, my man, on that."

This little whiff of temper seemed to cool Silver down. He had been growing nettled before, but now he pulled himself together.

"Like enough," said he. "I would set no limits to what gentlemen might consider shipshape, or might not, as the case were. And seein' as how you are about to take a pipe, cap'n, I'll make so free as do likewise." [*The suggestion here is that they are peers.*]

And he filled a pipe and lighted it; and the two men sat silently smoking for quite a while, now looking each other in the face, now stopping their tobacco, now leaning forward to spit. It was as good as the play to see them.

"Now," resumed Silver, "here it is. You give us the chart to get the treasure by, and drop shooting **poor seamen** and stoving of their heads in while asleep. You do that, and we'll offer you a choice. Either you come aboard along of us, once the treasure shipped, and then I'll give you my affy-davy, upon my word of honour, to clap you somewhere safe ashore. Or if that ain't to your fancy, some of my hands being rough and having old scores on account of hazing, then you can stay here, you can. We'll divide stores with you, man for man; and I'll give my affy-davy, as before to speak the first ship I sight, and send 'em here to pick you up. Now, you'll own that's talking. Handsomer you couldn't look to get, now you. And I hope"— raising his voice "that all hands in this here block house will overhaul my words, for what is spoke to one is spoke to all." [*Silver is hedging his bets. If he can't get through to Smollett, maybe someone else will join him.*]

Captain Smollett rose from his seat and knocked out the ashes of his pipe in the palm of his left hand.

"Is that all?" he asked.

"Every last word, by thunder!" answered John. "Refuse that, and you've seen the last of me but musket-balls."

"Very good," said the captain. "Now you'll hear me. If you'll come up one by one, unarmed, I'll engage to clap you all in irons and take you home to **a fair trial in England.** [*A fair trial that results in execution, so it's not really a choice.*] If you won't, my name is Alexander Smollett, I've flown my sovereign's colours, and I'll see you all to **Davy Jones.** You can't find the treasure. You can't sail the ship—there's not a man among you fit to sail the ship. You can't fight us—Gray, there, got away from five of you. Your ship's in irons, Master Silver; you're on a lee shore, and so you'll find. I stand here and tell you so; and they're the last good words you'll get from me, for in the name of heaven, I'll put a bullet in your back when next I meet you. Tramp, my lad. Bundle out of this, please, hand over hand, and double quick."

Silver's face was a picture; his eyes started in his head with wrath. He shook the fire out of his pipe.

"Give me a hand up!" he cried.

"Not I," returned the captain.

"Who'll give me a hand up?" he roared.

Not a man among us moved. Growling the foulest imprecations, he crawled along the sand till he got hold of the porch and could hoist himself again upon his crutch. Then he spat into the spring.

"There!" he cried. "That's what I think of ye. Before an hour's out, I'll stove in your old block house like a rum puncheon. Laugh, by thunder, laugh! Before an hour's out, ye'll laugh upon the other side. Them that die'll be the lucky ones."

And with a dreadful oath he stumbled off, ploughed down the sand, was helped across the stockade, after four or five failures, by the man with the flag of truce, and disappeared in an instant afterwards among the trees.

• ANALYZING THE SCENE •

STORY EVENT

A Story Event is an active change of a universal human value for one or more characters as a result of conflict (one character's desires clash with another's, or an environmental shift changes the value positively or negatively).

A Working Scene contains at least one Story Event. To determine a scene's Story Event, answer these four Socratic questions:

1. What are the characters literally doing—that is, what are their micro on-the-surface actions?

Silver arrives to negotiate with Smollett for the map. Smollett turns him down.

2. What is the essential tactic of the characters—that is, what above-the-surface macro behaviors are they employing that are linked to a universal human value?

Silver is seeking to make a deal with Smollett or at least sway one of the other men inside the stockade to his side. Smollett is acting on the decision of the night before. He wants to put Silver in his place. If Smollett can goad Silver into reckless action, the faithful party may gain an advantage.

3. What beyond-the-surface universal human values have changed for one or more characters in the scene? Which one of those value changes is most important and should be included in the Story Grid Spreadsheet?

The faithful party becomes aware that one of the pirates died, and Jim works out that Gunn was probably behind it. Silver starts out charming and ends by threatening Smollett and the others. The important result is that they have moved from a cease fire to a promised attack.

Cease Fire to Imminent Attack

4. The Scene Event Synthesis: What Story Event sums up the scene's on-the-surface, above-the-surface, and beyond-the-surface change? We will enter that event in the Story Grid Spreadsheet.

Silver promises to attack when Smollett turns down the offer to exchange the map for food and insults the pirate leader.

HOW THE SCENE ABIDES BY THE FIVE COMMANDMENTS OF STORYTELLING

Inciting Incident: Causal. Silver requests permission to enter the stockade and discuss terms.

Turning Point Progressive Complication: Active. Silver offers to spare the faithful party in exchange for the map.

Crisis: Best bad choice. If Smollett doesn't agree to Silver's terms, they risk attack and starvation, but if they agree, they won't be able to trust the pirates.

Climax: Smollett turns Silver down and insults him.

Resolution: Silver goes off in a huff promising to attack within the hour.

21

THE ATTACK

As soon as **Silver** disappeared, **the captain**, who had been closely watching him, turned towards the interior of the house and found not a man of us at his post but **Gray**. It was the first time we had ever seen him angry.

"Quarters!" he roared. And then, as we all slunk back to our places, "Gray," he said, "I'll put your name in the log; you've stood by your duty like a seaman. **Mr. Trelawney**, I'm surprised at you, sir. **Doctor**, I thought you had worn **the king**'s coat! If that was how you served at Fontenoy, sir, you'd have been better in your berth."

The doctor's watch were all back at their loopholes, the rest were busy loading the spare muskets, and everyone with a red face, you may be certain, and a flea in his ear, as the saying is. The captain looked on for a while in silence. Then he spoke.

"My lads," said he, "I've given Silver a broadside. I pitched it in redhot on purpose; and before the hour's out, as he said, we shall be boarded. We're outnumbered, I needn't tell you that, but we fight in shelter; and a minute ago I should have said we fought with discipline. I've no manner of doubt that we can drub them, if you choose."

Then he went the rounds and saw, as he said, that all was clear.

On the two short sides of the house, east and west, there were only two loopholes; on the south side where the porch was, two again; and on the north side, five. There was a round score of muskets for the seven of us; the firewood had been built into four piles—tables, you might say—one about the middle of each side, and on each of these tables some ammunition and four loaded muskets were laid ready to the hand of the defenders. In the middle, the cutlasses lay ranged.

"Toss out the fire," said the captain; "the chill is past, and we mustn't have smoke in our eyes."

The iron fire-basket was carried bodily out by Mr. Trelawney, and the embers smothered among sand.

"Hawkins hasn't had his breakfast. Hawkins, help yourself, and back to your post to eat it," continued Captain Smollett. "Lively, now, my lad; you'll want it before you've done. **Hunter**, serve out a round of brandy to all hands."

And while this was going on, the captain completed, in his own mind, the plan of the defence.

"Doctor, you will take the door," he resumed. "See, and don't expose yourself; keep within, and fire through the porch. Hunter, take the east side, there. **Joyce**, you stand by the west, my man. Mr. Trelawney, you are the best shot—you and Gray will take this long north side, with the five loopholes; it's there the danger is. If they can get up to it and fire in upon us through our own ports, things would begin to look dirty. Hawkins, neither you nor I are much account at the shooting; we'll stand by to load and bear a hand."

As the captain had said, the chill was past. As soon as the sun had climbed above our girdle of trees, it fell with all its force upon the clearing and drank up the vapours at a draught. Soon the sand was baking and the resin melting in the logs of the block house. Jackets and coats were flung aside, shirts thrown open at the neck and rolled up to the shoulders; and we stood there, each at his post, in a fever of heat and anxiety.

An hour passed away.

"Hang them!" said the captain. "This is as dull as the doldrums. Gray, whistle for a wind."

And just at that moment came the first news of the attack.

"If you please, sir," said Joyce, "if I see anyone, am I to fire?"

"I told you so!" cried the captain.

"Thank you, sir," returned Joyce with the same quiet civility.

Nothing followed for a time, but the remark had set us all on the alert, straining ears and eyes—the musketeers with their pieces balanced in their hands, the captain out in the middle of the block house with his mouth very tight and a frown on his face.

So some seconds passed, till suddenly Joyce whipped up his musket and fired. The report had scarcely died away ere it was repeated and repeated from without in a scattering volley, shot behind shot, like a string of geese, from every side of the enclosure. Several bullets struck the log-house, but not one entered; and as the smoke cleared away and vanished, the stockade and the woods around it looked as quiet and empty as before. Not a bough waved, not the gleam of a musket-barrel betrayed the presence of our foes.

"Did you hit your man?" asked the captain.

"No, sir," replied Joyce. "I believe not, sir."

"Next best thing to tell the truth," muttered Captain Smollett. "Load his gun, Hawkins. How many should say there were on your side, doctor?"

"I know precisely," said Dr. Livesey. "Three shots were fired on this side. I saw the three flashes—two close together—one farther to the west."

"Three!" repeated the captain. "And how many on yours, Mr. Trelawney?"

But this was not so easily answered. There had come many from the north—seven by the squire's computation, eight or nine according to Gray. From the east and west only a single shot had been fired. It was plain, therefore, that the attack would be developed from the north and that on the other three sides we were only to be annoyed by a show of hostilities. **But Captain Smollett made no change in his arrangements.** If the mutineers succeeded in crossing the stockade, he argued, they would take possession of any unprotected loophole and shoot us down like rats in our own stronghold.

Nor had we much time left to us for thought. Suddenly, with a loud huzza, a little cloud of pirates leaped from the woods on the north side and ran straight on the stockade. At the same moment, the fire was once more opened from the woods, and a rifle ball sang through the doorway and knocked the doctor's musket into bits.

The boarders swarmed over the fence like monkeys. Squire and Gray fired again and yet again; three men fell, one forwards into the enclosure, two back on the outside. But of these, one was evidently more frightened than hurt, for he was on his feet again in a crack and instantly disappeared among the trees.

Two had bit the dust, one had fled, four had made good their footing inside our defences, while from the shelter of the woods seven or eight men, each evidently supplied with several muskets, kept up a hot though useless fire on the log-house.

The four who had boarded made straight before them for the building, shouting as they ran, and the men among the trees shouted back to encourage them. Several shots were fired, but such was the hurry of the marksmen that not one appears to have taken effect. In a moment, the four pirates had swarmed up the mound and were upon us.

The head of **Job Anderson**, the boatswain, appeared at the middle loophole.

"At 'em, all hands—all hands!" he roared in a voice of thunder.

At the same moment, **another pirate** grasped Hunter's musket by the muzzle, wrenched it from his hands, plucked it through the loophole, and with one stunning blow, laid the poor fellow senseless on the floor. Meanwhile a third, running unharmed all around the house, appeared suddenly in the doorway and fell with his cutlass on the doctor.

Our position was utterly reversed. A moment since we were firing, under cover, at an exposed enemy; now it was we who lay uncovered and could not return a blow.

The log-house was full of smoke, to which we owed our comparative safety. Cries and confusion, the flashes and reports of pistol-shots, and one loud groan rang in my ears.

"Out, lads, out, and fight 'em in the open! Cutlasses!" cried the captain.

I snatched a cutlass from the pile, and someone, at the same time snatching another, gave me a cut across the knuckles which I hardly felt. I dashed out of the door into the clear sunlight. Someone was close behind, I knew not whom. Right in front, the doctor was pursuing his assailant down the hill, and just as my eyes fell upon him, beat down his guard and sent him sprawling on his back with a great slash across the face.

"Round the house, lads! Round the house!" cried the captain; and **even in the hurly-burly, I perceived a change in his voice.**

Mechanically, I obeyed, turned eastwards, and with my cutlass raised, ran round the corner of the house. Next moment I was face to face with **Anderson**. He roared aloud, and his hanger went up above his head, flashing in the sunlight. I had not time to be afraid, but as the blow still hung impending, leaped in a trice upon one side, and missing my foot in the soft sand, rolled headlong down the slope.

When I had first sallied from the door, the other mutineers had been already swarming up the palisade to make an end of us. **One man, in a red night-cap,** with his cutlass in his mouth, had even got upon the top and thrown a leg across. Well, so short had been the interval that when I found my feet again all was in the same posture, the fellow with the red night-cap still half-way over, another still just showing his head above the top of the stockade. **And yet, in this breath of time, the fight was over and the victory was ours.**

Gray, following close behind me, had cut down the **big boatswain** ere he had time to recover from his last blow. Another had been shot at a loophole in the very act of firing into the house and now lay in agony, the pistol still smoking in his hand. A third, as I had seen, the doctor had disposed of at a blow. Of the **four who had scaled the palisade,** one only remained unaccounted for, and he, having left his cutlass on the field, was now clambering out again with the fear of death upon him.

"Fire—fire from the house!" cried the doctor. "And you, lads, back into cover."

But his words were unheeded, no shot was fired, and the **last boarder** made good his escape and disappeared with the rest into the wood. In three seconds nothing remained of the attacking party but the five who had fallen, four on the inside and one on the outside of the palisade.

The doctor and Gray and I ran full speed for shelter. The survivors would soon be back where they had left their muskets, and at any moment the fire might recommence.

The house was by this time somewhat cleared of smoke, and we saw at a glance the price we had paid for victory. Hunter lay beside his loophole, stunned; Joyce by his, shot through the head, never to move again; while right in the centre, the squire was supporting the captain, one as pale as the other.

"The captain's wounded," said Mr. Trelawney.

"Have they run?" asked Mr. Smollett.

"All that could, you may be bound," returned the doctor; "but there's five of them will never run again."

"Five!" cried the captain. "Come, that's better. **Five against three leaves us four to nine.** That's better odds than we had at starting. We were seven to nineteen then, or thought we were, and that's as bad to bear."*

*The mutineers were soon only eight in number, for the man shot by Mr. Trelawney on board the schooner died that same evening of his wound. But this was, of course, not known till after by the faithful party (Stevenson's note).

• ANALYZING THE SCENE •

STORY EVENT

A Story Event is an active change of a universal human value for one or more characters as a result of conflict (one character's desires clash with another's, or an environmental shift changes the value positively or negatively).

A Working Scene contains at least one Story Event. To determine a scene's Story Event, answer these four Socratic questions:

1. **What are the characters literally doing—that is, what are their micro on-the-surface actions?**

Smollett scolds the men in the context of a pep talk. Jim and the others defend themselves and the stockade against the pirates' attack.

2. **What is the essential tactic of the characters—that is, what above-the-surface macro behaviors are they employing that are linked to a universal human value?**

Smollett must remind the others of their key advantages. Discipline is vital. This will help them stay alive while they even the odds. The pirates want to kill the faithful party or force them to surrender the map.

3. **What beyond-the-surface universal human values have changed for one or more characters in the scene? Which one of those value changes is most important and should be included in the Story Grid Spreadsheet?**

The goal of the faithful party was to avoid death and injury. Although they succeed in killing five and chasing off the rest of the pirates, Smollett and Hunter are injured and Joyce is killed.

Healthy to Injured

4. **The Scene Event Synthesis: What Story Event sums up the scene's on-the-surface, above-the-surface, and beyond-the-surface change? We will enter that event in the Story Grid Spreadsheet.**

The pirates attack, and five pirates die, but Smollett and Hunter are injured and Joyce is dead.

. . .

HOW THE SCENE ABIDES BY THE FIVE COMMANDMENTS OF STORYTELLING

Inciting Incident: Causal. Smollett chastises the men for leaving their posts and warns them of the difficulties to come.

Turning Point Progressive Complication: Active. Pirates make it over the fence and attack the cabin.

Crisis: Best bad choice. If they go outside the cabin they'll be exposed, but if they stay inside, they could be trapped.

Climax: Smollett orders the men to grab cutlasses and attack the pirates outside the cabin and inside the fence.

Resolution: Five of the enemy are killed. Smollett is injured, Joyce is killed, and Hunter soon will be dead.

NOTES

- Once the tactical decision is made, the faithful party begins work to even the odds against the pirates. It proves they can adapt and work as a unit instead of working in an unorganized way, like the pirates seem to be doing. The faithful party suffers heavy losses here, but they gain some ground as well.
- Smollett's speech that ends with the line, "I've no manner of doubt that we can drub them, if you choose," is important. He's the leader of the group, but he cannot save them by himself. Everyone must do their part if they are to survive.
- In the final scene of this sequence, Smollett shines. Since he first appears in the narrative, he shows how he doesn't let his guard down, and he doesn't accept anyone letting theirs down either. It would be easy to despair and give up. They could trade the map for safe passage. But how could they trust the pirates now? Smollett understands if they don't maintain discipline now, they will be lost. This is why he offers pep talks and tasks to keep them busy and barks at the suggestion to strike the colors.

PART FIVE: MY SEA ADVENTURE

22

HOW MY SEA ADVENTURE BEGAN

There was no return of **the mutineers**—not so much as another shot out of the woods. They had "got their rations for that day," as **the captain** put it, and we had the place to ourselves and a quiet time to overhaul the wounded and get dinner. **Squire** and I cooked outside in spite of the danger, and even outside we could hardly tell what we were at, for horror of the loud groans that reached us from **the doctor's patients.**

Out of the **eight men who had fallen in the action**, only three still breathed—that **one of the pirates** who had been shot at the loophole, **Hunter**, and Captain Smollett; and of these, the first two were as good as dead; the mutineer indeed died under the **doctor's** knife, and Hunter, do what we could, never recovered consciousness in this world. He lingered all day, breathing loudly like **the old buccaneer** at home in his apoplectic fit, but the bones of his chest had been crushed by the blow and his skull fractured in falling, and some time in the following night, without sign or sound, he went to **his Maker.**

As for the captain, his wounds were grievous indeed, but not dangerous. No organ was fatally injured. **Anderson's** ball—for it was Job that shot him first—had broken his shoulder-blade and touched the lung, not badly; the second had only torn and displaced some muscles in the calf. He was sure to recover, the doctor said, but in the meantime, and for weeks to come, he must not walk nor move his arm, nor so much as speak when he could help it.

My own accidental cut across the knuckles was a flea-bite. Doctor Livesey patched it up with plaster and pulled my ears for me into the bargain.

After dinner the squire and the doctor sat by the captain's side awhile in consultation; and when they had talked to their hearts' content, it being then a little past noon, the doctor took up his hat and pistols, girt on a cutlass, put the chart in his pocket, and with a musket over his shoulder crossed the palisade on the north side and set off briskly through the trees.

Gray and I were sitting together at the far end of the block house, to be out of earshot of our officers consulting; and Gray took his pipe out of his mouth and fairly forgot to put it back again, so thunder-struck he was at this occurrence.

"Why, in the name of **Davy Jones**," said he, "is Dr. Livesey mad?"

"Why no," says I. "He's about the last of this crew for that, I take it."

"Well, shipmate," said Gray, "mad he may not be; but if *he's* not, you mark my words, I am."

"I take it," replied I, "the doctor has his idea; and if I am right, he's going now to see **Ben Gunn**."

I was right, as appeared later; but in the meantime, the house being stifling hot and the little patch of sand inside the palisade ablaze with midday sun, I began to get another thought into my head, which was not by any means so right. What I began to do was to envy the doctor walking in the cool shadow of the woods with the birds about him and the pleasant smell of the pines, while I sat grilling, with my clothes stuck to the hot resin, and so much blood about me and so many poor dead bodies lying all around that I took a disgust of the place that was almost as strong as fear.

All the time I was washing out the block house, and then washing up the things from dinner, this disgust and envy kept growing stronger and stronger, till at last, being near a bread-bag, and no one then observing me, I took the first step towards my escapade and filled both pockets of my coat with biscuit.

I was a fool, if you like, and certainly I was going to do a foolish, over-bold act; but I was determined to do it with all the precautions in my power. These biscuits, should anything befall me, would keep me, at least, from starving till far on in the next day.

The next thing I laid hold of was a brace of pistols, and as I already had a powder-horn and bullets, I felt myself well supplied with arms.

As for the scheme I had in my head, it was not a bad one in itself. I was to go down the sandy spit that divides the anchorage on the east from the open sea, find the white rock I had observed last evening, and ascertain whether it was there or not that Ben Gunn had hidden his boat, a thing quite worth doing, as I still believe. But as I was certain I should not be allowed to leave the enclosure, my only plan was to take French leave, if not and slip out when nobody was watching, and that was so bad a way of doing it as made the thing itself wrong. But I was only a boy, and I had made my mind up. [*Jim the narrator is justifying his actions.*]

Well, as things at last fell out, I found an admirable opportunity. The squire and Gray were busy helping the captain with his bandages, the coast was clear, I made a bolt for it over the stockade and into the thickest of the trees, and before my absence was observed I was out of cry of my companions.

This was my second folly, far worse than the first, as I left but two sound men to guard the house; but like the first, it was a help towards saving all of us. [*This is a reference to jumping into the boat going ashore without telling the others. Meeting Gunn is a significant advantage.*]

I took my way straight for the east coast of the island, for I was determined to go down the sea side of the spit to avoid all chance of observation from the anchorage. It was already late in the afternoon, although still warm and sunny. As I continued to thread the tall woods, I could hear from far before me not only the continuous thunder of the surf, but a certain tossing of foliage and grinding of boughs which showed me the sea breeze had set in higher than usual. Soon cool draughts of air began to reach me, and a few steps farther I came forth into the open borders of the grove, and saw the sea lying blue and sunny to the horizon and the surf tumbling and tossing its foam along the beach.

I have never seen the sea quiet round Treasure Island. The sun might blaze overhead, the air be without a breath, the surface smooth and blue, but still these great rollers would be running along all the external coast, thundering and thundering by day and night; and I scarce believe there is one spot in the island where a man would be out of earshot of their noise.

I walked along beside the surf with great enjoyment, till, thinking I was now got far enough to the south, I took the cover of some thick bushes and crept warily up to the ridge of the spit.

Behind me was the sea, in front the anchorage. The sea breeze, as though it had the sooner blown itself out by its unusual violence, was already at an end; it had been succeeded by light, variable airs from the south and south-east, carrying great banks of fog; and the anchorage, under lee of Skeleton Island, lay still and leaden as when first we entered it. The *Hispaniola*, in that unbroken mirror, was exactly portrayed from the truck to the waterline, the Jolly Roger hanging from her peak.

Alongside lay one of the gigs, **Silver** in the stern-sheets—him I could always recognize—while **a couple of men** were leaning over the stern bulwarks, **one of them with a red cap**—the very rogue that I had seen some hours before stride-legs upon the palisade. Apparently they were talking and laughing, though at that distance—upwards of a mile —I could, of course, hear no word of what was said. All at once there began the most horrid, unearthly screaming, which at first startled me badly, though I had soon remembered the voice of **Captain Flint** and even thought I could make out the bird by her bright plumage as she sat perched upon her master's wrist.

Soon after, the jolly-boat shoved off and pulled for shore, and the man with the red cap and his comrade went below by the cabin companion.

Just about the same time, the sun had gone down behind the Spy-glass, and as the fog was collecting rapidly, it began to grow dark in earnest. I saw I must lose no time if I were to find the boat that evening.

The white rock, visible enough above the brush, was still some eighth of a mile further down the spit, and it took me a goodish while to get up with it, crawling, often on all fours, among the scrub. Night had almost come when I laid my hand on its rough sides. Right below it there was an exceedingly small hollow of green turf, hidden by banks and a thick underwood about knee-deep, that grew there very plentifully; and in the centre of the dell, sure enough, a little tent of goat-skins, like what the gipsies carry about with them in England.

I dropped into the hollow, lifted the side of the tent, and there was Ben Gunn's boat—home-made if ever anything was home-made; a rude, lop-sided framework of tough wood, and stretched upon that a covering of goat-skin, with the hair inside. The thing was extremely small, even for me, and I can hardly imagine that it could have floated with a full-sized man. There was one thwart set as low as possible, a kind of stretcher in the bows, and a double paddle for propulsion.

I had not then seen a coracle, such as the ancient Britons made, but I have seen one since, and I can give you no fairer idea of Ben Gunn's boat than by saying it was like the first and the worst coracle ever made by **man**. But the great advantage of the coracle it certainly possessed, for it was exceedingly light and portable.

Well, now that I had found the boat, you would have thought I had had enough of truantry for once, but in the meantime I had taken another notion and become so obstinately fond of it that I would have carried it out, I believe, in the teeth of **Captain Smollett** himself. This was to slip out under cover of the night, cut the *Hispaniola* adrift, and let her go ashore where she fancied. I had quite made up my mind that **the mutineers**, after their repulse of the morning, had nothing nearer their hearts than to up anchor and away to sea; this, I thought, it would be a fine thing to prevent, and now that I had seen how they left their watchmen unprovided with a boat, I thought it might be done with little risk.

Down I sat to wait for darkness, and made a hearty meal of biscuit. It was a night out of ten thousand for my purpose. The fog had now buried all heaven. As the last rays of daylight dwindled and disappeared, absolute blackness settled down on Treasure Island. And when, at last, I shouldered the coracle and groped my way stumblingly out of the hollow where I had supped, there were but two points visible on the whole anchorage.

One was the great fire on shore, by which the defeated pirates lay carousing in the swamp. The other, a mere blur of light upon the darkness, indicated the position of the anchored ship. She had swung round to the ebb—her bow was now towards me—the only lights on board were in the cabin, and what I saw was merely a reflection on the fog of the strong rays that flowed from the stern window.

The ebb had already run some time, and I had to wade through a long belt of swampy sand, where I sank several times above the ankle, before I came to the edge of the retreating water, and wading a little way in, with some strength and dexterity, set my coracle, keel downwards, on the surface.

• ANALYZING THE SCENE •

STORY EVENT

A Story Event is an active change of a universal human value for one or more characters as a result of conflict (one character's desires clash with another's, or an environmental shift changes the value positively or negatively).

A Working Scene contains at least one Story Event. To determine a scene's Story Event, answer these four Socratic questions:

1. What are the characters literally doing—that is, what are their micro on-the-surface actions?

The faithful party gets to work, seeing to the wounded and preparing meals. Livesey leaves in search of Gunn. Jim leaves the log cabin to find Gunn's coracle. While making his way to the coracle, Jim observes the wind conditions and the pirates. Silver returns to shore after leaving two men on the ship without a boat. Later the pirates are drinking on shore.

2. What is the essential tactic of the characters—that is, what above-the-surface macro behaviors are they employing that are linked to a universal human value?

Jim the narrator is trying to explain his actions, but Jim the luminary agent wants to contribute. He's feeling left out but also wants to seize an opportunity and isn't sure Livesey, Trelawney, and Smollett would go along. The adults don't see that Jim possesses information and perspective they could use. They make plans for Livesey to contact Gunn.

3. What beyond-the-surface universal human values have changed for one or more characters in the scene? Which one of those value changes is most important and should be included in the Story Grid Spreadsheet?

The faithful party is effectively stranded. They don't have access to a boat so they can't get to the ship. The pirates might struggle to manage the ship, but they have access to it, its guns, and the provisions they acquired. Jim's action in this scene gives the faithful party a chance to escape because he obtains a working boat and notices the ship is not well guarded.

Stranded to Chance of Escape

4. The Scene Event Synthesis: What Story Event sums up the scene's on-the-surface, above-the-surface, and beyond-the-surface change? We will enter that event in the Story Grid Spreadsheet.

After Livesey leaves to find Gunn, Jim leaves to find Gunn's coracle and decides to use it to cut the ship loose.

HOW THE SCENE ABIDES BY THE FIVE COMMANDMENTS OF STORYTELLING

Inciting Incident: Casual. The faithful party tends to business after the pirate attack, and the leaders form a plan.

Turning Point Progressive Complication: Revelatory. Jim finds the boat is seaworthy and the ship almost unguarded.

Crisis: Best bad choice. If Jim returns to the stockade, he may not have another opportunity to cut the *Hispaniola* free, and the pirates will leave them stranded. If he attempts the mission, he might drown or be killed by pirates.

Climax: Jim decides he'll try to cut the ship adrift and sits to eat and wait for nightfall.

Resolution: Once it's dark, the pirates on shore are occupied, and he can see a light in the cabin on the ship.

NOTES

- Jim's situation changes in several ways during this scene. We could say he is protected to unprotected, supervised to unsupervised, and obedient to disobedient. He's miserable and then feels lighter and happier once outside the confines of the stockade. These micro changes relate to his immediate survival concerns. While some risk is associated with being outside the stockade, overall, his actions here help. When the luminary agent doesn't face the threat of immediate death, we look at survival for Jim's cohort because his long-term survival is tied to theirs.

- The general belief (confirmed by Jim) is that the pirates are otherwise occupied during this scene. Silver has had a tenuous hold on the other pirates since they arrived on the island, and the conditions and events since haven't improved that situation. He won't be able to keep the other pirates away from the rum, so they will be distracted.
- Livesey is seeing to more immediate survival needs dealing with the pirates, but they need the ship as well because they lack provisions to last until the Blandly's consort arrives.
- Had Jim spoken up during the council to decide on next steps, he could have mentioned that someone should go look for the coracle. Jim often possesses more information than the adults. They recognize this on the ship when they first learn of the pirates' treachery.
- Jim leaves, in part because he envies Livesey's trip outside the stockade. But it is wise to confirm the coracle's location and condition. The point is well taken that he left the others shorthanded in the stockade, but Jim takes a calculated risk, gathers valuable intelligence along the way, and contributes to the long-term survival of the group, same as Livesey.
- Events since learning of Silver's treachery have meant a loss of innocence for Jim, but he gains an ability to better navigate within his physical and social environment.

23

THE EBB-TIDE RUNS

The coracle—as I had ample reason to know before I was done with her—was a very safe boat for a person of my height and weight, both buoyant and clever in a seaway; but she was the most cross-grained, lop-sided craft to manage. Do as you pleased, she always made more leeway than anything else, and turning round and round was the manoeuvre she was best at. Even Ben Gunn himself has admitted that she was "queer to handle till you knew her way."

Certainly I did not know her way. She turned in every direction but the one I was bound to go; the most part of the time we were broadside on, and I am very sure I never should have made the ship at all but for the tide. By good fortune, paddle as I pleased, the tide was still sweeping me down; and there lay the *Hispaniola* right in the fairway, hardly to be missed.

First she loomed before me like a blot of something yet blacker than darkness, then her spars and hull began to take shape, and the next moment, as it seemed (for, the farther I went, the brisker grew the current of the ebb), I was alongside of her hawser and had laid hold.

The hawser was as taut as a bowstring, and the current so strong she pulled upon her anchor. All round the hull, in the blackness, the rippling current bubbled and chattered like a little mountain stream.

One cut with my sea-gully and the *Hispaniola* would go humming down the tide.

So far so good, but it next occurred to my recollection that a taut hawser, suddenly cut, is a thing as dangerous as a kicking horse. Ten to one, if I were so foolhardy as to cut the *Hispaniola* from her anchor, I and the coracle would be knocked clean out of the water. [*Jim is remembering knowledge he's picked up along the way and attuning to the environment.*]

This brought me to a full stop, and if fortune had not again particularly favoured me, I should have had to abandon my design. But the light airs which had begun blowing from the south-east and south had hauled round after nightfall into the south-west. Just while I was meditating, a puff came, caught the *Hispaniola*, and forced her up into the current; and to my great joy, I felt the hawser slacken in my grasp, and the hand by which I held it dip for a second under water.

With that I made my mind up, took out my gully, opened it with my teeth, and cut one strand after another, till the vessel swung only by two. Then I lay quiet, waiting to sever these last when the strain should be once more lightened by a breath of wind.

All this time I had heard the sound of loud voices from the cabin, but to say truth, my mind had been so entirely taken up with other thoughts that I had scarcely given ear. Now, however, when I had nothing else to do, I began to pay more heed.

One I recognized for the coxswain's, **Israel Hands**, that had been **Flint's** gunner in former days. The other was, of course, **my friend of the red night-cap**. Both men were plainly the worse of drink, and they were still drinking, for even while I was listening, one of them, with a drunken cry, opened the stern window and threw out something, which I divined to be an empty bottle. But they were not only tipsy; it was plain that they were furiously angry. Oaths flew like hailstones, and every now and then there came forth such an explosion as I thought was sure to end in blows. But each time the quarrel passed off and the voices grumbled lower for a while, until the next crisis came and in its turn passed away without result.

On shore, I could see the glow of the great camp-fire burning warmly through the shore-side trees. **Someone** was singing, a dull, old, droning sailor's song, with a droop and a quaver at the end of every verse, and seemingly no end to it at all but the patience of the singer. I had heard it on the voyage more than once and remembered these words:

"But one man of her crew alive,
What put to sea with seventy-five."

And I thought it was a ditty rather too dolefully appropriate for a company that had met such cruel losses in the morning. But, indeed, from what I saw, all **these buccaneers** were as callous as the sea they sailed on. [*Jim is recognizing the impact the environment has on people and their behavior.*]

At last the breeze came; the schooner sidled and drew nearer in the dark; I felt the hawser slacken once more, and with a good, tough effort, cut the last fibres through.

The breeze had but little action on the coracle, and I was almost instantly swept against the bows of the *Hispaniola*. At the same time, the schooner began to turn upon her heel, spinning slowly, end for end, across the current.

I wrought like a fiend, for I expected every moment to be swamped; and since I found I could not push the coracle directly off, I now shoved straight astern. At length I was clear of my dangerous neighbour, and just as I gave the last impulsion, my hands came across a light cord that was trailing overboard across the stern bulwarks. Instantly I grasped it.

Why I should have done so I can hardly say. It was at first mere instinct, but once I had it in my hands and found it fast, curiosity began to get the upper hand, and I determined I should have one look through the cabin window. [*Worldview-Revelation moment: Jim doesn't dwell on the choice here. He simply acts on instincts that have developed in order to survive.*]

I pulled in hand over hand on the cord, and when I judged myself near enough, rose at infinite risk to about half my height and thus commanded the roof and a slice of the interior of the cabin.

By this time the schooner and her little consort were gliding pretty swiftly through the water; indeed, we had already fetched up level with the camp-fire. The ship was talking, as sailors say, loudly, treading the innumerable ripples with an incessant weltering splash; and until I got my eye above the window-sill I could not comprehend why the watchmen had taken no alarm. One glance, however, was sufficient; and it was only one glance that I durst take from that unsteady skiff. It showed me Hands and his companion locked together in deadly wrestle, each with a hand upon the other's throat.

I dropped upon the thwart again, none too soon, for I was near overboard. I could see nothing for the moment but these two furious, encrimsoned faces swaying together under the smoky lamp, and I shut my eyes to let them grow once more familiar with the darkness.

The endless ballad had come to an end at last, and the whole diminished company about the camp-fire had broken into the chorus I had heard so often:

"Fifteen men on the dead man's chest—
Yo-ho-ho, and a bottle of rum!
Drink and the devil had done for the rest—
Yo-ho-ho, and a bottle of rum!"

I was just thinking how busy drink and the devil were at that very moment in the cabin of the *Hispaniola*, when I was surprised by a sudden lurch of the coracle. At the same moment, she yawed sharply and seemed to change her course. The speed in the meantime had strangely increased.

I opened my eyes at once. All round me were little ripples, combing over with a sharp, bristling sound and slightly phosphorescent. The *Hispaniola* herself, a few yards in whose wake I was still being whirled along, seemed to stagger in her course, and I saw her spars toss a little against the blackness of the night; nay, as I looked longer, I made sure she also was wheeling to the southward.

I glanced over my shoulder, and my heart jumped against my ribs. There, right behind me, was the glow of the camp-fire. The current had turned at right angles, sweeping round along with it the tall schooner and the little dancing coracle; ever quickening, ever bubbling higher, ever muttering louder, it went spinning through the narrows for the open sea.

Suddenly the schooner in front of me gave a violent yaw, turning, perhaps, through twenty degrees; and almost at the same moment one shout followed another from on board; I could hear feet pounding on the companion ladder and I knew that the two drunkards had at last been interrupted in their quarrel and awakened to a sense of their disaster.

I lay down flat in the bottom of that wretched skiff and devoutly recommended my spirit to **its Maker.** At the end of the straits, I made sure we must fall into some bar of raging breakers, where all my troubles would be ended speedily; and though I could, perhaps, bear to die, I could not bear to look upon my fate as it approached.

So I must have lain for hours, continually beaten to and fro upon the billows, now and again wetted with flying sprays, and never ceasing to expect death at the next plunge. Gradually weariness grew upon me; a numbness, an occasional stupor, fell upon my mind even in the midst of my terrors, until sleep at last supervened and in my sea-tossed coracle I lay and dreamed of home and the old Admiral Benbow.

• ANALYZING THE SCENE •

STORY EVENT

A Story Event is an active change of a universal human value for one or more characters as a result of conflict (one character's desires clash with another's, or an environmental shift changes the value positively or negatively).

A Working Scene contains at least one Story Event. To determine a scene's Story Event, answer these four Socratic questions:

1. What are the characters literally doing—that is, what are their micro on-the-surface actions?

Jim rows the coracle out to the *Hispaniola* and cuts the ship loose from its anchor. He spies on the two hands left on the ship, who are drinking and fighting, and then floats and sleeps in the coracle.

2. What is the essential tactic of the characters—that is, what above-the-surface macro behaviors are they employing that are linked to a universal human value?

Jim wants to prevent the pirates from leaving the island with the ship. Hands and O'Brien ("red cap"), like most of the pirates ashore, are violent forces of destruction willing to kill to get what they want. Some disagreement has caused them to fight each other instead of watching for threats.

3. What beyond-the-surface universal human values have changed for one or more characters in the scene? Which one of those value changes is most important and should be included in the Story Grid Spreadsheet?

Jim has accomplished what he set out to do. Even though Hands and O'Brien are aware of what's happened, they lack the ability to remedy the situation. Jim has prevented the pirates from sailing away at least for the near future.

We know Jim survives to tell his tale. So we're curious about how he does it. He knows he must prevent the pirates from sailing the ship away from the island. And he accomplishes that here. Within these actions is the wisdom we need to go on ourselves when we can't know how the story turns out. He expects he will encounter large waves that will swamp or destroy the coracle. As an individual, he was feeling bold and confident, but now he's giving up.

Confident to Giving Up

4. The Scene Event Synthesis: What Story Event sums up the scene's on-the-surface, above-the-surface, and beyond-the-surface change? We will enter that event in the Story Grid Spreadsheet.

Jim cuts the ship lose from its anchor.

HOW THE SCENE ABIDES BY THE FIVE COMMANDMENTS OF STORYTELLING

Inciting Incident: Jim begins his mission in the coracle.

Turning Point Progressive Complication: Active. After cutting the hawser, Jim discovers a rope hanging from the ship that he's able to grab. From that vantage point, he sees the pirates trying to kill one another.

Crisis: Best bad choice. Jim could try to pull himself aboard, but he might be killed by Hands or O'Brien. Or he can drop back into the coracle, though he won't be able to control it and could go out to sea.

Climax: Jim drops into the coracle.

Resolution: The ship and coracle drift seaward toward rough water. Hands and O'Brien eventually notice the ship is afloat. Jim is convinced he's going to die.

NOTES

- Securing the ship is necessary. Although Jim's friends lost fewer people in the most recent attack, they had fewer to lose, and they now lack sufficient numbers to defend the stockade against armed pirates. The adults wouldn't have been able to maneuver the coracle, and they probably wouldn't have allowed Jim to do it if he'd asked for permission. Jim's quick decisions here make survival possible.
- Notice that the two vessels, the coracle with the luminary

agent and the *Hispaniola* with shadow agents, are adrift in this moment.

- Stories are full of lessons large and small. This scene contains wisdom for us all. Sometimes the best thing to do is get some sleep and see how things are in the morning.

24

THE CRUISE OF THE CORACLE

It was broad day when I awoke and found myself tossing at the southwest end of Treasure Island. The sun was up but was still hid from me behind the great bulk of the Spy-glass, which on this side descended almost to the sea in formidable cliffs.

Haulbowline Head and Mizzen-mast Hill were at my elbow, the hill bare and dark, the head bound with cliffs forty or fifty feet high and fringed with great masses of fallen rock. I was scarce a quarter of a mile to seaward, and it was my first thought to paddle in and land.

That notion was soon given over. Among the fallen rocks the breakers spouted and bellowed; loud reverberations, heavy sprays flying and falling, succeeded one another from second to second; and I saw myself, if I ventured nearer, dashed to death upon the rough shore or spending my strength in vain to scale the beetling crags.

Nor was that all, for crawling together on flat tables of rock or letting themselves drop into the sea with loud reports I beheld huge slimy monsters—soft snails, as it were, of incredible bigness—two or three score of them together, making the rocks to echo with their barkings. [*Jim hasn't completely lost his sense of wonder and appreciation for the natural world. Attuning to the environment means knowing how to approach the moment as it arrives.*]

I have understood since that they were sea lions, and entirely harmless. But the look of them, added to the difficulty of the shore and the high running of the surf, was more than enough to disgust me of that landing-place. I felt willing rather to starve at sea than to confront such perils.

In the meantime I had a better chance, as I supposed, before me. North of Haulbowline Head, the land runs in a long way, leaving at low tide a long stretch of yellow sand. To the north of that, again, there comes another cape—Cape of the Woods, as it was marked upon the chart—buried in tall green pines, which descended to the margin of the sea.

I remembered what **Silver** had said about the current that sets northward along the whole west coast of Treasure Island, and seeing from my position that I was already under its influence, I preferred to leave Haulbowline Head behind me and reserve my strength for an attempt to land upon the kindlier-looking Cape of the Woods. [*Studying the map early on and paying attention is serving him well now.*]

There was a great, smooth swell upon the sea. The wind blowing steady and gentle from the south, there was no contrariety between that and the current, and the billows rose and fell unbroken.

Had it been otherwise, I must long ago have perished; but as it was, it is surprising how easily and securely my little and light boat could ride. Often, as I still lay at the bottom and kept no more than an eye above the gunwale, I would see a big blue summit heaving close above me; yet the coracle would but bounce a little, dance as if on springs, and subside on the other side into the trough as lightly as a bird.

I began after a little to grow very bold and sat up to try my skill at paddling. But even a small change in the disposition of the weight will produce violent changes in the behaviour of a coracle. And I had hardly moved before the boat, giving up at once her gentle dancing movement, ran straight down a slope of water so steep that it made me giddy, and struck her nose, with a spout of spray, deep into the side of the next wave.

I was drenched and terrified, and fell instantly back into my old position, whereupon the coracle seemed to find her head again and led me as softly as before among the billows. It was plain she was not to be interfered with, and at that rate, since I could in no way influence her course, what hope had I left of reaching land? I began to be horribly frightened, but I kept my head, for all that. First, moving with all care, I gradually baled out the coracle with my sea-cap; then, getting my eye once more above the gunwale, I set myself to study how it was she managed to slip so quietly through the rollers. [*When Jim can't change his situation, he pauses and pays attention to the environment, looking for causes and effects.*]

I found each wave, instead of the big, smooth glossy mountain it looks from shore or from a vessel's deck, was for all the world like any range of hills on dry land, full of peaks and smooth places and valleys. The coracle, left to herself, turning from side to side, threaded, so to speak, her way through these lower parts and avoided the steep slopes and higher, toppling summits of the wave.

"Well, now," thought I to myself, "it is plain I must lie where I am and not disturb the balance; but it is plain also that I can put the paddle over the side and from time to time, in smooth places, give her a shove or two towards land." No sooner thought upon than done. There I lay on my elbows in the most trying attitude, and every now and again gave a weak stroke or two to turn her head to shore.

It was very tiring and slow work, yet I did visibly gain ground; and as we drew near the Cape of the Woods, though I saw I must infallibly miss that point, I had still made some hundred yards of easting. I was, indeed, close in. I could see the cool green tree-tops swaying together in the breeze, and I felt sure I should make the next promontory without fail.

It was high time, for I now began to be tortured with thirst. The glow of the sun from above, its thousandfold reflection from the waves, the sea-water that fell and dried upon me, caking my very lips with salt, combined to make my throat burn and my brain ache. The sight of the trees so near at hand had almost made me sick with longing, but the current had soon carried me past the point, and as the next reach of sea opened out, I beheld a sight that changed the nature of my thoughts.

Right in front of me, not half a mile away, I beheld the *Hispaniola* under sail. I made sure, of course, that I should be taken; but I was so distressed for want of water that I scarce knew whether to be glad or sorry at the thought, and long before I had come to a conclusion, surprise had taken entire possession of my mind and I could do nothing but stare and wonder.

The *Hispaniola* was under her main-sail and two jibs, and the beautiful white canvas shone in the sun like snow or silver. When I first sighted her, all her sails were drawing; she was lying a course about north-west, and I presumed **the men on board** were going round the island on their way back to the anchorage. Presently she began to fetch more and more to the westward, so that I thought they had sighted me and were going about in chase. At last, however, she fell right into the wind's eye, was taken dead aback, and stood there awhile helpless, with her sails shivering.

"Clumsy fellows," said I; "they must still be drunk as owls." And I thought how Captain Smollett would have set them skipping.

Meanwhile the schooner gradually fell off and filled again upon another tack, sailed swiftly for a minute or so, and brought up once more dead in the wind's eye. Again and again was this repeated. To and fro, up and down, north, south, east, and west, the *Hispaniola* sailed by swoops and dashes, and at each repetition ended as she had begun, with idly flapping canvas. It became plain to me that nobody was steering. And if so, where were the men? Either they were dead drunk or had deserted her, I thought, and perhaps if I could get on board I might return the vessel to her captain.

The current was bearing coracle and schooner southward at an equal rate. As for the latter's sailing, it was so wild and intermittent, and she hung each time so long in irons, that she certainly gained nothing, if she did not even lose. If only I dared to sit up and paddle, I made sure that I could overhaul her. The scheme had an air of adventure that inspired me, and the thought of the water breaker beside the fore companion doubled my growing courage.

Up I got, was welcomed almost instantly by another cloud of spray, but this time stuck to my purpose and set myself, with all my strength and caution, to paddle after the unsteered *Hispaniola*. Once I shipped a sea so heavy that I had to stop and bail, with my heart fluttering like a bird, but gradually I got into the way of the thing and guided my coracle among the waves, with only now and then a blow upon her bows and a dash of foam in my face.

I was now gaining rapidly on the schooner; I could see the brass glisten on the tiller as it banged about, and still no soul appeared upon her decks. I could not choose but suppose she was deserted. If not, the men were lying drunk below, where I might batten them down, perhaps, and do what I chose with the ship.

For some time she had been doing the worse thing possible for me —standing still. She headed nearly due south, yawing, of course, all the time. Each time she fell off, her sails partly filled, and these brought her in a moment right to the wind again. I have said this was the worst thing possible for me, for helpless as she looked in this situation, with the canvas cracking like cannon and the blocks trundling and banging on the deck, she still continued to run away from me, not only with the speed of the current, but by the whole amount of her leeway, which was naturally great.

But now, at last, I had my chance. The breeze fell for some seconds, very low, and the current gradually turning her, the Hispaniola revolved slowly round her centre and at last presented me her stern, with the cabin window still gaping open and the lamp over the table still burning on into the day. The main-sail hung drooped like a banner. She was stock-still but for the current.

For the last little while I had even lost, but now redoubling my efforts, I began once more to overhaul the chase.

I was not a hundred yards from her when the wind came again in a clap; she filled on the port tack and was off again, stooping and skimming like a swallow.

My first impulse was one of despair, but my second was towards joy. Round she came, till she was broadside on to me—round still till she had covered a half and then two thirds and then three quarters of the distance that separated us. I could see the waves boiling white under her forefoot. Immensely tall she looked to me from my low station in the coracle.

And then, of a sudden, I began to comprehend. I had scarce time to think—scarce time to act and save myself. I was on the summit of one swell when the schooner came stooping over the next. The bowsprit was over my head. I sprang to my feet and leaped, stamping the coracle under water. With one hand I caught the jib-boom, while my foot was lodged between the stay and the brace; and as I still clung there panting, a dull blow told me that the schooner had charged down upon and struck the coracle and that I was left without retreat on the Hispaniola.

STORY EVENT

A Story Event is an active change of a universal human value for one or more characters as a result of conflict (one character's desires clash with another's, or an environmental shift changes the value positively or negatively).

A Working Scene contains at least one Story Event. To determine a scene's Story Event, answer these four Socratic questions:

1. What are the characters literally doing—that is, what are their micro on-the-surface actions?

Jim wakes up in the coracle southwest of Treasure Island. He attempts to paddle to shore and observes the movement of the coracle on the waves when he can't maneuver.

2. What is the essential tactic of the characters—that is, what above-the-surface macro behaviors are they employing that are linked to a universal human value?

Jim needs water to survive. No other characters oppose him, but the nature of the movement of water around the island means he can't easily approach the shore again. In this scene the conflict is "person against nature."

3. What beyond-the-surface universal human values have changed for one or more characters in the scene? Which one of those value changes is most important and should be included in the Story Grid Spreadsheet?

Jim begins adrift in the coracle, but he learns to maneuver it and reaches the *Hispaniola*.

Adrift to Aboard Ship

4. The Scene Event Synthesis: What Story Event sums up the scene's on-the-surface, above-the-surface, and beyond-the-surface change? We will enter that event in the Story Grid Spreadsheet.

Jim can't reach the shore easily and needs water. He maneuvers the coracle to the Hispaniola where he catches the jib boom before the coracle is smashed.

. . .

HOW THE SCENE ABIDES BY THE FIVE COMMANDMENTS OF STORYTELLING

Inciting Incident: Jim wakes in the coracle.

Turning Point Progressive Complication: Revelatory. Because of the heat and sun, Jim will die if he doesn't get water soon.

Crisis: If he tries to go for land, he might get smashed on the rocks, but if he goes for the *Hispaniola* there is no guarantee he'll be able to board it.

Climax: Jim maneuvers the coracle toward the *Hispaniola*.

Resolution: An opportunity comes when the ship swings around, and Jim is able to catch the jib-boom. The coracle is smashed by the schooner moments later.

NOTES

- Jim is alone in this scene, and the primary external force of antagonism is the environment. But notice how other characters are "with him" in his mind nonetheless. We carry our past experiences with the environment and people, and they inform the actions we take in the present. Including these elements helps create a richer narrative that feels authentic.
- Notice the power dynamic in this scene. The environment has the upper hand, and Jim must learn to work with it. When he resists, he is less successful than when he goes with the flow. Jim pays attention and responds. This is his gift.
- Livesey mentions overlooking the need for water in the scene when he discovers the spring inside the stockade (scene 16). When Livesey was on the ship, he hadn't remembered they didn't have enough water to last very long. Similarly, Jim remembers to bring food on this adventure, but he doesn't consider his need for water. Imagine being thirsty while surrounded by water you can't drink.

25

I STRIKE THE JOLLY ROGER

I had scarce gained a position on the bowsprit, when the flying jib flapped and filled upon the other tack, with a report like a gun. The schooner trembled to her keel under the reverse, but next moment, the other sails still drawing, the jib flapped back again and hung idle.

This had nearly tossed me off into the sea; and now I lost no time, crawled back along the bowsprit, and tumbled head foremost on the deck.

I was on the lee side of the forecastle, and the mainsail, which was still drawing, concealed from me a certain portion of the after-deck. Not a soul was to be seen. The planks, which had not been swabbed since the mutiny, bore the print of many feet, and an empty bottle, broken by the neck, tumbled to and fro like a live thing in the scuppers.

Suddenly the *Hispaniola* came right into the wind. The jibs behind me cracked aloud, the rudder slammed to, the whole ship gave a sickening heave and shudder, and at the same moment the main-boom swung inboard, the sheet groaning in the blocks, and showed me the lee after-deck.

There were the two watchmen, sure enough: **red-cap** on his back, as stiff as a handspike, with his arms stretched out like those of a crucifix and his teeth showing through his open lips; **Israel Hands** propped against the bulwarks, his chin on his chest, his hands lying open before him on the deck, his face as white, under its tan, as a tallow candle.

For a while the ship kept bucking and sidling like a vicious horse, the sails filling, now on one tack, now on another, and the boom swinging to and fro till the mast groaned aloud under the strain. Now and again too there would come a cloud of light sprays over the bulwark and a heavy blow of the ship's bows against the swell; so much heavier weather was made of it by this great rigged ship than by my home-made, lop-sided coracle, now gone to the bottom of the sea.

At every jump of the schooner, red-cap slipped to and fro, but—what was ghastly to behold—neither his attitude nor his fixed teeth-disclosing grin was anyway disturbed by this rough usage. At every jump too, Hands appeared still more to sink into himself and settle down upon the deck, his feet sliding ever the farther out, and the whole body canting towards the stern, so that his face became, little by little, hid from me; and at last I could see nothing beyond his ear and the frayed ringlet of one whisker.

At the same time, I observed, around both of them, splashes of dark blood upon the planks and began to feel sure that they had killed each other in their drunken wrath.

While I was thus looking and wondering, in a calm moment, when the ship was still, Israel Hands turned partly round and with a low moan writhed himself back to the position in which I had seen him first. The moan, which told of pain and deadly weakness, and the way in which his jaw hung open went right to my heart. But when I remembered the talk I had overheard from the apple barrel, all pity left me.

I walked aft until I reached the main-mast.

"Come aboard, Mr. Hands," I said ironically.

He rolled his eyes round heavily, but he was too far gone to express surprise. All he could do was to utter one word, "Brandy."

It occurred to me there was no time to lose, and dodging the boom as it once more lurched across the deck, I slipped aft and down the companion stairs into the cabin.

It was such a scene of confusion as you can hardly fancy. All the lockfast places had been broken open in quest of the chart. The floor was thick with mud where ruffians had sat down to drink or consult after wading in the marshes round their camp. The bulkheads, all painted in clear white and beaded round with gilt, bore a pattern of dirty hands. Dozens of empty bottles clinked together in corners to the rolling of the ship. One of the doctor's medical books lay open on the table, half of the leaves gutted out, I suppose, for pipelights. In the midst of all this the lamp still cast a smoky glow, obscure and brown as umber.

I went into the cellar; all the barrels were gone, and of the bottles a most surprising number had been drunk out and thrown away. Certainly, since the mutiny began, not a man of them could ever have been sober.

Foraging about, I found a bottle with some brandy left, for Hands; and for myself I routed out some biscuit, some pickled fruits, a great bunch of raisins, and a piece of cheese. With these I came on deck, put down my own stock behind the rudder head and well out of the coxswain's reach, went forward to the water-breaker, and had a good deep drink of water, and then, and not till then, gave Hands the brandy.

He must have drunk a gill before he took the bottle from his mouth.

"Aye," said he, "by thunder, but I wanted some o' that!"

I had sat down already in my own corner and begun to eat.

"Much hurt?" I asked him.

He grunted, or rather, I might say, he barked.

"If **that doctor** was aboard," he said, "I'd be right enough in a couple of turns, but I don't have no manner of luck, you see, and that's what's the matter with me. As for that swab, he's good and dead, he is," he added, indicating the man with the red cap. "He warn't no **seaman** anyhow. And where mought you have come from?"

"Well," said I, "I've come aboard to take possession of this ship, Mr. Hands; and you'll please regard me as your captain until further notice."

He looked at me sourly enough but said nothing. Some of the colour had come back into his cheeks, though he still looked very sick and still continued to slip out and settle down as the ship banged about.

"By the by," I continued, "I can't have these colours, Mr. Hands; and by your leave, I'll strike 'em. Better none than these."

And again dodging the boom, I ran to the colour lines, handed down their cursed black flag, and chucked it overboard.

"God save **the king**!" said I, waving my cap. "And there's an end to **Captain Silver**!"

He watched me keenly and slyly, his chin all the while on his breast.

"I reckon," he said at last, "I reckon, **Cap'n Hawkins**, you'll kind of want to get ashore now. S'pose we talks."

"Why, yes," says I, "with all my heart, Mr. Hands. Say on." And I went back to my meal with a good appetite.

"This man," he began, nodding feebly at the corpse—"**O'Brien** were his name, a rank **Irelander**—this man and me got the canvas on her, meaning for to sail her back. Well, *he's* dead now, he is—as dead as bilge; and who's to sail this ship, I don't see. Without I gives you a hint, you ain't that man, as far's I can tell. Now, look here, you gives me food and drink and a old scarf or ankecher to tie my wound up, you do, and I'll tell you how to sail her, and that's about square all round, I take it."

"I'll tell you one thing," says I: "I'm not going back to **Captain Kidd's** anchorage. I mean to get into North Inlet and beach her quietly there."

"To be sure you did," he cried. "Why, I ain't sich an infernal lubber after all. I can see, can't I? I've tried my fling, I have, and I've lost, and it's you has the wind of me. North Inlet? Why, I haven't no ch'ice, not I! I'd help you sail her up to **Execution Dock**, by thunder! So I would."

Well, as it seemed to me, there was some sense in this. We struck our bargain on the spot. In three minutes I had the *Hispaniola* sailing easily before the wind **along the coast of Treasure Island**, with good hopes of turning the northern point ere noon and beating down again as far as North Inlet before high water, when we might beach her safely and wait till the subsiding tide permitted us to land.

Then I lashed the tiller and went below to my own chest, where I got a soft silk handkerchief of my mother's. With this, and with my aid, Hands bound up the great bleeding stab he had received in the thigh, and after he had eaten a little and had a swallow or two more of the brandy, he began to pick up visibly, sat straighter up, spoke louder and clearer, and looked in every way another man.

The breeze served us admirably. We skimmed before it like a bird, the coast of the island flashing by and the view changing every minute. Soon we were past the high lands and bowling beside low, sandy country, sparsely dotted with dwarf pines, and soon we were beyond that again and had turned the corner of the rocky hill that ends the island on the north.

I was greatly elated with my new command, and pleased with the bright, sunshiny weather and these different prospects of the coast. I had now plenty of water and good things to eat, and my conscience, which had smitten me hard for my desertion, was quieted by the great conquest I had made. I should, I think, have had nothing left me to desire but for the eyes of the coxswain as they followed me derisively about the deck and the odd smile that appeared continually on his face. It was a smile that had in it something both of pain and weakness—a haggard old man's smile; but there was, besides that, a grain of derision, a shadow of treachery, in his expression as he craftily watched, and watched, and watched me at my work.

• ANALYZING THE SCENE •

STORY EVENT

A Story Event is an active change of a universal human value for one or more characters as a result of conflict (one character's desires clash with another's, or an environmental shift changes the value positively or negatively).

A Working Scene contains at least one Story Event. To determine a scene's Story Event, answer these four Socratic questions:

1. What are the characters literally doing—that is, what are their micro on-the-surface actions?

Jim gets aboard the *Hispaniola*, obtains food and water, and negotiates with Hands for help in sailing the ship.

2. What is the essential tactic of the characters—that is, what above-the-surface macro behaviors are they employing that are linked to a universal human value?

Jim wants to take possession of the ship, and Hands wants to avoid death.

3. What beyond-the-surface universal human values have changed for one or more characters in the scene? Which one of those value changes is most important and should be included in the Story Grid Spreadsheet?

The ship was unattended with the Jolly Roger flying, and now Jim is in charge and has taken down the flag. Hands was unconscious and wounded but regained consciousness and tended his wound.

Ship Unattended to Ship under control

4. The Scene Event Synthesis: What Story Event sums up the scene's on-the-surface, above-the-surface, and beyond-the-surface change? We will enter that event in the Story Grid Spreadsheet.

Jim takes charge of the Hispaniola *and, with the help of Hands, sails it toward the north side of the island.*

HOW THE SCENE ABIDES BY THE FIVE COMMANDMENTS OF STORYTELLING

Inciting Incident: Causal. Jim gets aboard the *Hispaniola*.

Turning Point Progressive Complication: Active. Hand offers to help with the sailing if Jim will give him food and drink and bandage his injury.

Crisis: Best bad choice. If Jim doesn't accept help, he'll find it difficult to sail the ship to a safer place. But if he accepts help, Hands could attack him.

Climax: Jim agrees to the deal but dictates the location—the beach at the North Inlet.

Resolution: Together they easily sail the ship, but Jim can tell Hands is looking for an opening to take advantage of him.

NOTES

- Notice that Jim is not the naïve boy who encountered Silver weeks before. He makes a deal with Hands, but that doesn't mean he trusts him.
- It's not unusual for the luminary agent in any story to find allies in unlikely places. When the luminary agent's interests align with the shadow agent, they can preserve energy and resources by working together.
- The ship has been ransacked just as the inn had been after the pirates searched for the map there.
- Remember Trelawney's letter back in scene 7? He wrote, "a child might sail her" when describing the *Hispaniola*.

26

ISRAEL HANDS

The wind, serving us to a desire, now hauled into the west. We could run so much the easier from the north-east corner of the island to the mouth of the North Inlet. Only, as we had no power to anchor and dared not beach her till the tide had flowed a good deal farther, time hung on our hands. The coxswain told me how to lay the ship to; after a good many trials I succeeded, and we both sat in silence over another meal.

"Cap'n," said he at length with that same uncomfortable smile, "here's my old shipmate, O'Brien; s'pose you was to heave him overboard. I ain't partic'lar as a rule, and I don't take no blame for settling his hash, but I don't reckon him ornamental now, do you?"

"I'm not strong enough, and I don't like the job; and there he lies, for me," said I.

"This here's an unlucky ship, this *Hispaniola*, Jim," he went on, blinking. "There's a power of men been killed in this *Hispaniola*—a sight o' poor seamen dead and gone since you and me took ship to Bristol. I never seen sich dirty luck, not I. There was this here O'Brien now—he's dead, ain't he? Well now, I'm no scholar, and you're a lad as can read and figure, and to put it straight, do you take it as a dead man is dead for good, or do he come alive again?"

"You can kill the body, Mr. Hands, but not the spirit; you must know that already," I replied. "O'Brien there is in another world, and may be watching us."

"Ah!" says he. "Well, that's unfort'nate—appears as if killing parties was a waste of time. Howsomever, sperrits don't reckon for much, by what I've seen. I'll chance it with the sperrits, Jim. And now, you've spoke up free, and I'll take it kind if you'd step down into that there cabin and get me a—well, a—shiver my timbers! I can't hit the name on 't; well, you get me a bottle of wine, Jim—this here brandy's too strong for my head."

Now, the coxswain's hesitation seemed to be unnatural, and as for the notion of his preferring wine to brandy, I entirely disbelieved it. The whole story was a pretext. He wanted me to leave the deck—so much was plain; but with what purpose I could in no way imagine. His eyes never met mine; they kept wandering to and fro, up and down, now with a look to the sky, now with a flitting glance upon the dead O'Brien. All the time he kept smiling and putting his tongue out in the most guilty, embarrassed manner, so that **a child** could have told that he was bent on some deception. I was prompt with my answer, however, for I saw where my advantage lay and that with a fellow so densely stupid I could easily conceal my suspicions to the end.

"Some wine?" I said. "Far better. Will you have white or red?"

"Well, I reckon it's about the blessed same to me, shipmate," he replied; "so it's strong, and plenty of it, what's the odds?"

"All right," I answered. "I'll bring you port, Mr. Hands. But I'll have to dig for it."

With that I scuttled down the companion with all the noise I could, slipped off my shoes, ran quietly along the sparred gallery, mounted the forecastle ladder, and popped my head out of the fore companion. I knew he would not expect to see me there, yet I took every precaution possible, and certainly the worst of my suspicions proved too true.

He had risen from his position to his hands and knees, and though his leg obviously hurt him pretty sharply when he moved—for I could hear him stifle a groan—yet it was at a good, rattling rate that he trailed himself across the deck. In half a minute he had reached the port scuppers and picked, out of a coil of rope, a long knife, or rather a short dirk, discoloured to the hilt with blood. He looked upon it for a moment, thrusting forth his under jaw, tried the point upon his hand, and then, hastily concealing it in the bosom of his jacket, trundled back again into his old place against the bulwark.

This was all that I required to know. Israel could move about, he was now armed, and if he had been at so much trouble to get rid of me, it was plain that I was meant to be the victim. What he would do afterwards—whether he would try to crawl right across the island from North Inlet to the camp among the swamps or whether he would fire Long Tom, trusting that **his own comrades** might come first to help him—was, of course, more than I could say.

Yet I felt sure that I could trust him in one point, since in that our interests jumped together, and that was in the disposition of the schooner. **We both desired to have her stranded safe enough, in a sheltered place, and so that, when the time came, she could be got off again with as little labour and danger as might be; and until that was done I considered that my life would certainly be spared.**

While I was thus turning the business over in my mind, I had not been idle with my body. I had stolen back to the cabin, slipped once more into my shoes, and laid my hand at random on a bottle of wine, and now, with this for an excuse, I made my reappearance on the deck.

Hands lay as I had left him, all fallen together in a bundle and with his eyelids lowered as though he were too weak to bear the light. He looked up, however, at my coming, knocked the neck off the bottle like a man who had done the same thing often, and took a good swig, with his favourite toast of "Here's luck!" Then he lay quiet for a little, and then, pulling out a stick of tobacco, begged me to cut him a quid.

"Cut me a junk o' that," says he, "for I haven't no knife and hardly strength enough, so be as I had. Ah, Jim, Jim, I reckon I've missed stays! Cut me a quid, as'll likely be the last, lad, for I'm for my long home, and no mistake."

"Well," said I, "I'll cut you some tobacco, but if I was you and thought myself so badly, I would go to my prayers like **a Christian man**."

"Why?" said he. "Now, you tell me why."

"Why?" I cried. "You were asking me just now about the dead. You've broken your trust; you've lived in sin and lies and blood; there's a man you killed lying at your feet this moment, and you ask me why! For God's mercy, Mr. Hands, that's why."

I spoke with a little heat, thinking of the bloody dirk he had hidden in his pocket and designed, in his ill thoughts, to end me with. He, for his part, took a great draught of the wine and spoke with the most unusual solemnity.

"For thirty years," he said, "I've sailed the seas and seen good and bad, better and worse, fair weather and foul, provisions running out, knives going, and what not. Well, now I tell you, I never seen good come o' goodness yet. Him as strikes first is my fancy; dead men don't bite; them's my views—amen, so be it. And now, you look here," he added, suddenly changing his tone, "we've had about enough of this foolery. The tide's made good enough by now. You just take my orders, Cap'n Hawkins, and we'll sail slap in and be done with it." [*Hands expresses his worldview clearly.*]

All told, we had scarce two miles to run; but the navigation was delicate, the entrance to this northern anchorage was not only narrow and shoal, but lay east and west, so that the schooner must be nicely handled to be got in. I think I was a good, prompt subaltern, and I am very sure that Hands was an excellent pilot, for we went about and about and dodged in, shaving the banks, with a certainty and a neatness that were a pleasure to behold. [*Even though he's in a stressful situation, Jim is able to appreciate craft.*]

Scarcely had we passed the heads before the land closed around us. The shores of North Inlet were as thickly wooded as those of the southern anchorage, but the space was longer and narrower and more like, what in truth it was, the estuary of a river. Right before us, at the southern end, we saw the wreck of a ship in the last stages of dilapidation. It had been a great vessel of three masts but had lain so long exposed to the injuries of the weather that it was hung about with great webs of dripping seaweed, and on the deck of it shore bushes had taken root and now flourished thick with flowers. It was a sad sight, but it showed us that the anchorage was calm.

"Now," said Hands, "look there; there's a pet bit for to beach a ship in. Fine flat sand, never a cat's paw, trees all around of it, and flowers a-blowing like a garding on that old ship."

"And once beached," I inquired, "how shall we get her off again?"

"Why, so," he replied: "you take a line ashore there on the other side at low water, take a turn about one of them big pines; bring it back, take a turn around the capstan, and lie to for the tide. Come high water, all hands take a pull upon the line, and off she comes as sweet as natur'. And now, boy, you stand by. We're near the bit now, and she's too much way on her. Starboard a little—so—steady—starboard—larboard a little--steady—steady!"

So he issued his commands, which I breathlessly obeyed, till, all of a sudden, he cried, "Now, my hearty, luff!" And I put the helm hard up, and the *Hispaniola* swung round rapidly and ran stem on for the low, wooded shore.

The excitement of these last manoeuvres had somewhat interfered with the watch I had kept hitherto, sharply enough, upon the coxswain. Even then I was still so much interested, waiting for the ship to touch, that I had quite forgot the peril that hung over my head and stood craning over the starboard bulwarks and watching the ripples spreading wide before the bows. I might have fallen without a struggle for my life had not a sudden disquietude seized upon me and made me turn my head. Perhaps I had heard a creak or seen his shadow moving with the tail of my eye; perhaps it was an instinct like a cat's; but, sure enough, when I looked round, there was Hands, already half-way towards me, with the dirk in his right hand.

We must both have cried out aloud when our eyes met, but while mine was the shrill cry of terror, his was a roar of fury like a charging bully's. At the same instant, he threw himself forward and I leapt sideways towards the bows. As I did so, I let go of the tiller, which sprang sharp to leeward, and I think this saved my life, for it struck Hands across the chest and stopped him, for the moment, dead.

Before he could recover, I was safe out of the corner where he had me trapped, with all the deck to dodge about. Just forward of the main-mast I stopped, drew a pistol from my pocket, took a cool aim, though he had already turned and was once more coming directly after me, and drew the trigger. The hammer fell, but there followed neither flash nor sound; the priming was useless with sea-water. I cursed myself for my neglect. Why had not I, long before, reprimed and reloaded my only weapons? Then I should not have been as now, a mere fleeing sheep before this butcher.

Wounded as he was, it was wonderful how fast he could move, his grizzled hair tumbling over his face, and his face itself as red as a red ensign with his haste and fury. I had no time to try my other pistol, nor indeed much inclination, for I was sure it would be useless. One thing I saw plainly: I must not simply retreat before him, or he would speedily hold me boxed into the bows, as a moment since he had so nearly boxed me in the stern. Once so caught, and nine or ten inches of the blood-stained dirk would be my last experience on this side of eternity. I placed my palms against the main-mast, which was of a goodish bigness, and waited, every nerve upon the stretch.

Seeing that I meant to dodge, he also paused; and a moment or two passed in feints on his part and corresponding movements upon mine. It was such a game as I had often played at home about the rocks of Black Hill Cove, but never before, you may be sure, with such a wildly beating heart as now. Still, as I say, it was a boy's game, and I thought I could hold my own at it against an elderly seaman with a wounded thigh. Indeed my courage had begun to rise so high that I allowed myself a few darting thoughts on what would be the end of the affair, and while I saw certainly that I could spin it out for long, I saw no hope of any ultimate escape.

Well, while things stood thus, suddenly the *Hispaniola* struck, staggered, ground for an instant in the sand, and then, swift as a blow, canted over to the port side till the deck stood at an angle of forty-five degrees and about a puncheon of water splashed into the scupper holes and lay, in a pool, between the deck and bulwark.

We were both of us capsized in a second, and both of us rolled, almost together, into the scuppers, the dead red-cap, with his arms still spread out, tumbling stiffly after us. So near were we, indeed, that my head came against the coxswain's foot with a crack that made my teeth rattle. Blow and all, I was the first afoot again, for Hands had got involved with the dead body. The sudden canting of the ship had made the deck no place for running on; I had to find some new way of escape, and that upon the instant, for my foe was almost touching me. Quick as thought, **I sprang into the mizzen shrouds, rattled up hand over hand, and did not draw a breath till I was seated on the cross-trees.**

I had been saved by being prompt; the dirk had struck not half a foot below me as I pursued my upward flight; and there stood Israel Hands with his mouth open and his face upturned to mine, a perfect statue of surprise and disappointment.

Now that I had a moment to myself, I lost no time in changing the priming of my pistol, and then, having one ready for service, and to make assurance doubly sure, I proceeded to draw the load of the other and recharge it afresh from the beginning.

My new employment struck Hands all of a heap; he began to see the dice going against him, and after an obvious hesitation, he also hauled himself heavily into the shrouds, and with the dirk in his teeth, began slowly and painfully to mount. It cost him no end of time and groans to haul his wounded leg behind him, and I had quietly finished my arrangements before he was much more than a third of the way up. Then, with a pistol in either hand, I addressed him.

"One more step, Mr. Hands," said I, "and I'll blow your brains out! Dead men don't bite, you know," I added with a chuckle.

He stopped instantly. I could see by the working of his face that he was trying to think, and the process was so slow and laborious that, in my new-found security, I laughed aloud. At last, with a swallow or two, he spoke, his face still wearing the same expression of extreme perplexity. In order to speak he had to take the dagger from his mouth, but in all else he remained unmoved.

"Jim," says he, "I reckon we're fouled, you and me, and we'll have to sign articles. I'd have had you but for that there lurch, but I don't have no luck, not I; and I reckon I'll have to strike, which comes hard, you see, for a master mariner to a ship's younker like you, Jim."

I was drinking in his words and smiling away, as conceited as a cock upon a wall, when, all in a breath, back went his right hand over his shoulder. Something sang like an arrow through the air; I felt a blow and then a sharp pang, and there I was pinned by the shoulder to the mast. In the horrid pain and surprise of the moment—I scarce can say it was by my own volition, and I am sure it was without a conscious aim—both my pistols went off, and both escaped out of my hands. They did not fall alone; with a choked cry, the coxswain loosed his grasp upon the shrouds and plunged head first into the water.

• ANALYZING THE SCENE •

STORY EVENT

A Story Event is an active change of a universal human value for one or more characters as a result of conflict (one character's desires clash with another's, or an environmental shift changes the value positively or negatively).

A Working Scene contains at least one Story Event. To determine a scene's Story Event, answer these four Socratic questions:

1. What are the characters literally doing—that is, what are their micro on-the-surface actions?

Jim and Hands work together to sail the ship to the northern inlet. When they reach it, Hands attacks Jim, who must defend himself.

2. What is the essential tactic of the characters—that is, what above-the-surface macro behaviors are they employing that are linked to a universal human value?

Jim wants to secure the ship and stay alive. Hands wants the same. One will need to kill the other to survive.

3. What beyond-the-surface universal human values have changed for one or more characters in the scene? Which one of those value changes is most important and should be included in the Story Grid Spreadsheet?

The ship is moved around the island to the northern inlet. Jim learns that Hands has a dirk and plans to kill him. Jim experiences a further loss of innocence. He must be willing to kill to survive. Hands attacks and is injured and then killed. While that is on the life-death gradient of value, Jim's life and the survival of his friends are most important. The change with the greatest impact on the survival of Jim's cohort is his shift from threat of imminent death to injured.

Threat of Imminent Death to Injured

4. The Scene Event Synthesis: What Story Event sums up the scene's on-the-surface, above-the-surface, and beyond-the-surface change? We will enter that event in the Story Grid Spreadsheet.

Jim and Hands maneuver the ship to the northern anchorage, and Jim is able to get away long enough to service his gun and kill Hands.

HOW THE SCENE ABIDES BY THE FIVE COMMANDMENTS OF STORYTELLING

Inciting Incident: Causal. Hands directs Jim to steer the ship to the northern inlet.

Turning Point Progressive Complication: Active. Jim observes Hands pick up a dagger and realizes the pirate plans to kill him.

Crisis: Best bad choice. When Hands attacks, Jim will be killed if he doesn't release his shadow agency, but if he does, he'll be a killer.

Climax: Jim climbs into the rigging and primes his pistols.

Resolution: Hands throws his dagger, pinning Jim to the mast and causing him to fire his pistols involuntarily. Hands falls dead into the water.

NOTES

- Similar to when Dorothy kills the Wicked Witch of the West in *The Wonderful Wizard of Oz*, Jim kills Hands accidentally. This is more acceptable in a story about an adolescent that young people will read. Jim had to be willing to kill to survive, though.
- Jim now knows he's capable of taking a life, and this will change his relationship to himself and with his friends. Because of this, he is a full agent and a formidable opponent, even if he prefers not to kill.
- Notice that Jim's decision to deny Hands's request and do nothing with O'Brien's body pays off.

27

"PIECES OF EIGHT"

Owing to the cant of the vessel, the masts hung far out over the water, and from my perch on the cross-trees I had nothing below me but the surface of the bay. **Hands**, who was not so far up, was in consequence nearer to the ship and fell between me and the bulwarks. He rose once to the surface in a lather of foam and blood and then sank again for good. As the water settled, I could see him lying huddled together on the clean, bright sand in the shadow of the vessel's sides. A fish or two whipped past his body. Sometimes, by the quivering of the water, he appeared to move a little, as if he were trying to rise. But he was dead enough, for all that, being both shot and drowned, and was food for fish in the very place where he had designed my slaughter.

I was no sooner certain of this than I began to feel sick, faint, and terrified. The hot blood was running over my back and chest. The dirk, where it had pinned my shoulder to the mast, seemed to burn like a hot iron; yet it was not so much these real sufferings that distressed me, for these, it seemed to me, I could bear without a murmur; **it was the horror I had upon my mind of falling from the cross-trees into that still green water, beside the body of the coxswain.**

I clung with both hands till my nails ached, and I shut my eyes as if to cover up the peril. Gradually my mind came back again, my pulses quieted down to a more natural time, and I was once more in possession of myself.

It was my first thought to pluck forth the dirk, but either it stuck too hard or my nerve failed me, and I desisted with a violent shudder. Oddly enough, that very shudder did the business. The knife, in fact, had come the nearest in the world to missing me altogether; it held me by a mere pinch of skin, and this the shudder tore away. The blood ran down the faster, to be sure, but I was my own master again and only tacked to the mast by my coat and shirt.

These last I broke through with a sudden jerk, and then regained the deck by the starboard shrouds. For nothing in the world would I have again ventured, shaken as I was, upon the overhanging port shrouds from which Israel had so lately fallen.

I went below and did what I could for my wound; it pained me a good deal and still bled freely, but it was neither deep nor dangerous, nor did it greatly gall me when I used my arm. Then I looked around me, and as the ship was now, in a sense, my own, I began to think of clearing it from its last passenger—the dead man, **O'Brien.**

He had pitched, as I have said, against the bulwarks, where he lay like some horrible, ungainly sort of puppet, life-size, indeed, but how different from life's colour or life's comeliness! In that position I could easily have my way with him, and as the habit of tragical adventures had worn off almost all my terror for the dead, I took him by the waist as if he had been a sack of bran and with one good heave, tumbled him overboard. He went in with a sounding plunge; the red cap came off and remained floating on the surface; and as soon as the splash subsided, I could see him and Israel lying side by side, both wavering with the tremulous movement of the water. O'Brien, though still quite a young man, was very bald. There he lay, with that bald head across the knees of the man who had killed him and the quick fishes steering to and fro over both.

I was now alone upon the ship; the tide had just turned. [*Jim doesn't feel alone on the ship until O'Brien's body has been removed.*] The sun was within so few degrees of setting that already the shadow of the pines upon the western shore began to reach right across the anchorage and fall in patterns on the deck. The evening breeze had sprung up, and

240

though it was well warded off by the hill with the two peaks upon the east, the cordage had begun to sing a little softly to itself and the idle sails to rattle to and fro.

I began to see a danger to the ship. The jibs I speedily doused and brought tumbling to the deck, but the main-sail was a harder matter. Of course, when the schooner canted over, the boom had swung outboard, and the cap of it and a foot or two of sail hung even under water. I thought this made it still more dangerous; yet the strain was so heavy that I half feared to meddle. At last I got my knife and cut the halyards. The peak dropped instantly, a great belly of loose canvas floated broad upon the water, and since, pull as I liked, I could not budge the downhall, that was the extent of what I could accomplish. For the rest, the *Hispaniola* must trust to luck, like myself.

By this time the whole anchorage had fallen into shadow—the last rays, I remember, falling through a glade of the wood and shining bright as jewels on the flowery mantle of the wreck. It began to be chill; the tide was rapidly fleeting seaward, the schooner settling more and more on her beam-ends.

I scrambled forward and looked over. It seemed shallow enough, and holding the cut hawser in both hands for a last security, I let myself drop softly overboard. The water scarcely reached my waist; the sand was firm and covered with ripple marks, and I waded ashore in great spirits, leaving the *Hispaniola* on her side, with her main-sail trailing wide upon the surface of the bay. About the same time, the sun went fairly down and the breeze whistled low in the dusk among the tossing pines.

At least, and at last, I was off the sea, nor had I returned thence empty-handed. There lay the schooner, clear at last from **buccaneers** and ready for **our own men** to board and get to sea again. I had nothing nearer my fancy than to get home to the stockade and boast of my achievements. Possibly I might be blamed a bit for my truantry, but the recapture of the *Hispaniola* was a clenching answer, and I hoped that even **Captain Smollett** would confess I had not lost my time.

So thinking, and in famous spirits, I began to set my face homeward for the block house and my companions. I remembered that the most easterly of the rivers which drain into **Captain Kidd**'s anchorage ran from the two-peaked hill upon my left, and I bent my course in that direction that I might pass the stream while it was small. The wood was pretty open, and keeping along the lower spurs, I had soon turned the corner of that hill, and not long after waded to the mid-calf across the watercourse.

This brought me near to where I had encountered **Ben Gunn**, the maroon; and I walked more circumspectly, keeping an eye on every side. The dusk had come nigh hand completely, and as I opened out the cleft between the two peaks, I became aware of a wavering glow against the sky, where, as I judged, the man of the island was cooking his supper before a roaring fire. And yet I wondered, in my heart, that he should show himself so careless. For if I could see this radiance, might it not reach the eyes of **Silver** himself where he camped upon the shore among the marshes? [*Jim is assuming that the situation onshore remained the same in his absence.*]

Gradually the night fell blacker; it was all I could do to guide myself even roughly towards my destination; the double hill behind me and the Spy-glass on my right hand loomed faint and fainter; the stars were few and pale; and in the low ground where I wandered I kept tripping among bushes and rolling into sandy pits.

Suddenly a kind of brightness fell about me. I looked up; a pale glimmer of moonbeams had alighted on the summit of the Spy-glass, and soon after I saw something broad and silvery moving low down behind the trees, and knew the moon had risen.

With this to help me, I passed rapidly over what remained to me of my journey, and sometimes walking, sometimes running, impatiently drew near to the stockade. Yet, as I began to thread the grove that lies before it, I was not so thoughtless but that I slacked my pace and went a trifle warily. It would have been a poor end of my adventures to get shot down by my own party in mistake.

The moon was climbing higher and higher, its light began to fall here and there in masses through the more open districts of the wood, and right in front of me a glow of a different colour appeared among the trees. It was red and hot, and now and again it was a little darkened —as it were, the embers of a bonfire smouldering.

For the life of me I could not think what it might be.

At last I came right down upon the borders of the clearing. The western end was already steeped in moonshine; the rest, and the block house itself, still lay in a black shadow chequered with long silvery streaks of light. On the other side of the house an immense fire had burned itself into clear embers and shed a steady, red reverberation, contrasted strongly with the mellow paleness of the moon. There was not a soul stirring nor a sound beside the noises of the breeze.

I stopped, with much wonder in my heart, and perhaps a little terror also. It had not been our way to build great fires; we were, indeed, by the captain's orders, somewhat niggardly of firewood, and I began to fear that something had gone wrong while I was absent.

I stole round by the eastern end, keeping close in shadow, and at a convenient place, where the darkness was thickest, crossed the palisade.

To make assurance surer, I got upon my hands and knees and crawled, without a sound, towards the corner of the house. As I drew nearer, my heart was suddenly and greatly lightened. It is not a pleasant noise in itself, and I have often complained of it at other times, but just then it was like music to hear **my friends** snoring together so loud and peaceful in their sleep. The sea-cry of the watch, that beautiful "All's well," never fell more reassuringly on my ear.

In the meantime, there was no doubt of one thing; they kept an infamous bad watch. If it had been **Silver and his lads** that were now creeping in on them, not a soul would have seen daybreak. That was what it was, thought I, to have the captain wounded; and again I blamed myself sharply for leaving them in that danger with so few to mount guard.

By this time I had got to the door and stood up. All was dark within, so that I could distinguish nothing by the eye. As for sounds, there was the steady drone of the snorers and a small occasional noise, a flickering or pecking that I could in no way account for.

With my arms before me I walked steadily in. I should lie down in my own place (I thought with a silent chuckle) and enjoy their faces when they found me in the morning.

My foot struck something yielding—it was **a sleeper**'s leg; and he turned and groaned, but without awaking.

And then, all of a sudden, a shrill voice broke forth out of the darkness:

"Pieces of eight! Pieces of eight! Pieces of eight! Pieces of eight! Pieces of eight!" and so forth, without pause or change, like the clacking of a tiny mill.

Silver's green parrot, **Captain Flint**! It was she whom I had heard pecking at a piece of bark; it was she, keeping better watch than any human being, who thus announced my arrival with her wearisome refrain.

I had no time left me to recover. At the sharp, clipping tone of the parrot, the sleepers awoke and sprang up; and with a mighty oath, the voice of **Silver** cried, "Who goes?"

I turned to run, struck violently against one person, recoiled, and ran full into the arms of a second, who for his part closed upon and held me tight.

"Bring a torch, **Dick**," said Silver when my capture was thus assured.

And one of the men left the log-house and presently returned with a lighted brand.

STORY EVENT

A Story Event is an active change of a universal human value for one or more characters as a result of conflict (one character's desires clash with another's, or an environmental shift changes the value positively or negatively).

A Working Scene contains at least one Story Event. To determine a scene's Story Event, answer these four Socratic questions:

1. What are the characters literally doing—that is, what are their micro on-the-surface actions?

Jim deals with his injury and puts the ship to rights before making his way back to the stockade.

2. What is the essential tactic of the characters—that is, what above-the-surface macro behaviors are they employing that are linked to a universal human value?

Jim wants to ensure the ship is safe and return to the stockade and the community of his friends. He's distracted by his desire to let his friends know about his conquest.

3. What beyond-the-surface universal human values have changed for one or more characters in the scene? Which one of those value changes is most important and should be included in the Story Grid Spreadsheet?

In this scene, Jim begins in shock and soon recovers, but he is captured by the pirates who now have possession of the stockade.

In Shock to Recovered to Captured

4. The Scene Event Synthesis: What Story Event sums up the scene's on-the-surface, above-the-surface, and beyond-the-surface change? We will enter that event in the Story Grid Spreadsheet.

Jim deals with his injury and puts the ship to right, then he makes his way ashore and falls into the hands of the enemy inside the stockade.

HOW THE SCENE ABIDES BY THE FIVE COMMANDMENTS OF STORYTELLING

Inciting Incident: Causal. Hands is dead, but Jim has a wound he must tend to.

Turning Point Progressive Complication: Revelatory. Jim spots a big fire near where he met Gunn and assumes Gunn is being careless.

Crisis: Best bad choice. Should Jim delay returning to his friends to investigate the fire or go directly to the cabin without finding out what's going on?

Climax: Jim is tired and eager to return to his friends, so he immediately returns to the cabin and enters despite other anomalies including the lack of a guard.

Resolution: The pirates hold the cabin and grab Jim before he can escape.

NOTES

- Jim has applied new wisdom when dealing with the pirates, but he still has a blind spot when it comes to his cohort. He is so eager to return to his friends—which makes sense because he's been through a traumatic event and has news that changes their situation drastically—but he's not paying attention to the clues that would alert him to the danger. He's still misreading the situation to a certain extent.
- What's the nature of Jim's confusion here? He assumed things stayed the same while he was away because there has been no evidence of fighting (sound or destruction). His failure to pick up on the clues and interpret them correctly lead him to danger.

PART SIX: CAPTAIN SILVER

28

IN THE ENEMY'S CAMP

The red glare of the torch, lighting up the interior of the block house, showed me the worst of my apprehensions realized. The pirates were in possession of the house and stores: there was the cask of cognac, there were the pork and bread, as before, and what tenfold increased my horror, not a sign of any prisoner. I could only judge that all had perished, and my heart smote me sorely that I had not been there to perish with them.

There were **six of the buccaneers**, all told; not another man was left alive. Five of them were on their feet, flushed and swollen, suddenly called out of the first sleep of drunkenness. The sixth had only risen upon his elbow; he was deadly pale, and the blood-stained bandage round his head told that he had recently been wounded, and still more recently dressed. I remembered the man who had been shot and had run back among the woods in the great attack, and doubted not that this was he.

The **parrot** sat, preening her plumage, on **Long John's** shoulder. He himself, I thought, looked somewhat paler and more stern than I was used to. He still wore the fine broadcloth suit in which he had fulfilled his mission, but it was bitterly the worse for wear, daubed with clay and torn with the sharp briers of the wood.

"So," said he, "here's **Jim Hawkins**, shiver my timbers! Dropped in, like, eh? Well, come, I take that friendly."

And thereupon he sat down across the brandy cask and began to fill a pipe.

"Give me a loan of the link, **Dick**," said he; and then, when he had a good light, "That'll do, lad," he added; "stick the glim [*candle or lantern*] in the wood heap; and you, gentlemen, bring yourselves to! You needn't stand up for Mr. Hawkins; *he'll* excuse you, you may lay to that. And so, Jim"—stopping the tobacco—"here you were, and quite a pleasant surprise for **poor old John**. I see you were smart when first I set my eyes on you, but this here gets away from me clean, it do."

To all this, as may be well supposed, I made no answer. They had set me with my back against the wall, and I stood there, looking Silver in the face, pluckily enough, I hope, to all outward appearance, but with black despair in my heart.

Silver took a whiff or two of his pipe with great composure and then ran on again.

"Now, you see, Jim, so be as you *are* here," says he, "I'll give you a piece of my mind. I've always liked you, I have, for a lad of spirit, and the picter of my own self when I was young and handsome. I always wanted you to jine and take your share, and die a gentleman, and now, my cock, you've got to. **Cap'n Smollett**'s a fine seaman, as I'll own up to any day, but stiff on discipline. 'Dooty is dooty,' says he, and right he is. Just you keep clear of the cap'n. The doctor himself is gone dead against you—'ungrateful scamp' was what he said; and the short and the long of the whole story is about here: you can't go back to your own lot, for they won't have you; and without you start a third ship's company all by yourself, which might be lonely, you'll have to jine with Cap'n Silver."

So far so good. **My friends**, then, were still alive, and though I partly believed the truth of Silver's statement, that the cabin party were incensed at me for my desertion, I was more relieved than distressed by what I heard.

"I don't say nothing as to your being in our hands," continued Silver, "though there you are, and you may lay to it. I'm all for argyment; I never seen good come out o' threatening. If you like the service, well, you'll jine; and if you don't, Jim, why, you're free to answer no—free and welcome, **shipmate**; and if fairer can be said by **mortal seaman**, shiver my sides!"

"Am I to answer, then?" I asked with a very tremulous voice. Through all this sneering talk, I was made to feel the threat of death that overhung me, and my cheeks burned and my heart beat painfully in my breast.

"Lad," said Silver, "no one's a-pressing of you. Take your bearings. None of us won't hurry you, mate; time goes so pleasant in your company, you see."

"Well," says I, growing a bit bolder, "if I'm to choose, I declare I have a right to know what's what, and why you're here, and where my friends are."

"Wot's wot?" repeated one of the buccaneers in a deep growl. "Ah, he'd be a lucky one as knowed that!"

"You'll perhaps batten down your hatches till you're spoke to, my friend," cried Silver truculently to this speaker. And then, in his first gracious tones, he replied to me, "Yesterday morning, Mr. Hawkins," said he, "in the dog-watch, down came **Doctor Livesey** with a flag of truce. Says he, 'Cap'n Silver, you're sold out. Ship's gone.' Well, maybe we'd been taking a glass, and a song to help it round. I won't say no. Leastways, none of us had looked out. We looked out, and by thunder, the old ship was gone! I never seen a pack o' fools look fishier; and you may lay to that, if I tells you that looked the fishiest. 'Well,' says the doctor, 'let's bargain.' We bargained, him and I, and here we are: stores, brandy, block house, the firewood you was thoughtful enough to cut, and in a manner of speaking, the whole blessed boat, from cross-trees to kelson. As for them, they've tramped; I don't know where's they are."

He drew again quietly at his pipe.

"And lest you should take it into that head of yours," he went on, "that you was included in the treaty, here's the last word that was said: 'How many are you,' says I, 'to leave?' **'Four,'** says he; 'four, **and one of us wounded.** As for **that boy**, I don't know where he is, confound him,' says he, 'nor I don't much care. We're about sick of him.' These was his words.

"Is that all?" I asked.

"Well, it's all that you're to hear, my son," returned Silver.

"And now I am to choose?"

"And now you are to choose, and you may lay to that," said Silver.

"Well," said I, "I am not such a fool but I know pretty well what I have to look for. Let the worst come to the worst, it's little I care. I've seen too many die since I fell in with you. But there's a thing or two I have to tell you," I said, and by this time I was quite excited; "and the first is this: here you are, in a bad way—ship lost, treasure lost, men lost, your whole business gone to wreck; and if you want to know who did it —it was I! I was in the apple barrel the night we sighted land, and I heard you, **John**, and you, Dick Johnson, and **Hands**, who is now at the bottom of the sea, and told every word you said before the hour was out. And as for the schooner, it was I who cut her cable, and it was I that killed **the men you had aboard of her**, and it was I who brought her where you'll never see her more, not one of you. The laugh's on my side; I've had the top of this business from the first; I no more fear you than I fear a fly. Kill me, if you please, or spare me. But one thing I'll say, and no more; if you spare me, bygones are bygones, and when you fellows are in court for piracy, I'll save you all I can. It is for you to choose. Kill another and do yourselves no good, or spare me and keep a witness to save you from the gallows."

I stopped, for, I tell you, I was out of breath, and to my wonder, not a man of them moved, but all sat staring at me like as many sheep. And while they were still staring, I broke out again, "And now, Mr. Silver," I said, "I believe you're the best man here, and if things go to the worst, I'll take it kind of you to let the doctor know the way I took it."

"I'll bear it in mind," said Silver with an accent so curious that I could not, for the life of me, decide whether he were laughing at my request or had been favourably affected by my courage.

"I'll put one to that," cried the old mahogany-faced seaman —**Morgan** by name—whom I had seen in Long John's public-house upon the quays of Bristol. "It was him that knowed **Black Dog**."

"Well, and see here," added the sea-cook. "I'll put another again to that, by thunder! For it was this same boy that faked the chart from **Billy Bones**. First and last, we've split upon Jim Hawkins!"

"Then here goes!" said Morgan with an oath.

And he sprang up, drawing his knife as if he had been twenty.

"Avast, there!" cried Silver. "Who are you, Tom Morgan? Maybe you thought you was cap'n here, perhaps. By the powers, but I'll teach you better! Cross me, and you'll go where many a good man's gone before you, first and last, these thirty year back—some to the yard-arm, shiver my timbers, and some by the board, and all to feed the fishes. There's never a man looked me between the eyes and seen a good day a'terwards, Tom Morgan, you may lay to that."

Morgan paused, but a hoarse murmur rose from the others.

"Tom's right," said one.

"I stood hazing long enough from one," added another. "I'll be hanged if I'll be hazed by you, John Silver."

"Did any of you gentlemen want to have it out with *me*?" roared Silver, bending far forward from his position on the keg, with his pipe still glowing in his right hand. "Put a name on what you're at; you ain't dumb, I reckon. Him that wants shall get it. Have I lived this many years, and a son of a rum puncheon cock his hat athwart my hawse at the latter end of it? You know the way; you're all **gentlemen o' fortune**, by your account. Well, I'm ready. Take a cutlass, him that dares, and I'll see the colour of his inside, crutch and all, before that pipe's empty."

Not a man stirred; not a man answered.

"That's your sort, is it?" he added, returning his pipe to his mouth. "Well, you're a gay lot to look at, anyway. Not much worth to fight, you ain't. P'r'aps you can understand **King George**'s English. I'm cap'n here by 'lection. I'm cap'n here because I'm the best man by a long sea-mile. You won't fight, as gentlemen o' fortune should; then, by thunder, you'll obey, and you may lay to it! I like that boy, now; I never seen a better boy than that. He's more a man than any pair of rats of you in this here house, and what I say is this: let me see him that'll lay a hand on him— that's what I say, and you may lay to it." [*This feels more authentic than Silver's earlier praise of Jim.*]

There was a long pause after this. I stood straight up against the wall, my heart still going like a sledge-hammer, but with a ray of hope now shining in my bosom. Silver leant back against the wall, his arms crossed, his pipe in the corner of his mouth, as calm as though he had been in church; yet his eye kept wandering furtively, and he kept the tail of it on his unruly followers. They, on their part, drew gradually together towards the far end of the block house, and the low hiss of their whispering sounded in my ear continuously, like a stream. One after another, they would look up, and the red light of the torch would fall for a second on their nervous faces; but it was not towards me, it was towards Silver that they turned their eyes.

"You seem to have a lot to say," remarked Silver, spitting far into the air. "Pipe up and let me hear it, or lay to."

"Ax your pardon, sir," returned one of the men; "you're pretty free with some of the rules; maybe you'll kindly keep an eye upon the rest. This crew's dissatisfied; this crew don't vally bullying a marlin-spike; this crew has its rights like other crews, I'll make so free as that; and by your own rules, I take it we can talk together. I ax your pardon, sir, acknowledging you for to be captaing at this present; but I claim my right, and steps outside for a council."

And with an elaborate sea-salute, this fellow, a long, ill-looking, yellow-eyed man of five and thirty, stepped coolly towards the door and disappeared out of the house. One after another the rest followed his example, each making a salute as he passed, each adding some apology. "According to rules," said one. "Forecastle council," said Morgan. And so with one remark or another all marched out and left Silver and me alone with the torch.

The sea-cook instantly removed his pipe.

"Now, look you here, Jim Hawkins," he said in a steady whisper that was no more than audible, "you're within half a plank of death, and what's a long sight worse, of torture. They're going to throw me off. But, you mark, I stand by you through thick and thin. I didn't mean to; no, not till you spoke up. I was about desperate to lose that much blunt, and be hanged into the bargain. But I see you was the right sort. I says to myself, you stand by Hawkins, John, and Hawkins'll stand by you. You're his last card, and by the living thunder, John, he's yours! Back to back, says I. You save your witness, and he'll save your neck!"

I began dimly to understand.

"You mean all's lost?" I asked.

"Aye, by gum, I do!" he answered. "Ship gone, neck gone—that's the size of it. Once I looked into that bay, Jim Hawkins, and seen no schooner—well, I'm tough, but I gave out. As for that lot and their council, mark me, they're outright fools and cowards. I'll save your life —if so be as I can—from them. But, see here, Jim—tit for tat—you save Long John from swinging."

I was bewildered; it seemed a thing so hopeless he was asking—he, the old buccaneer, the ringleader throughout.

"What I can do, that I'll do," I said.

"It's a bargain!" cried Long John. "You speak up plucky, and by thunder, I've a chance!"

He hobbled to the torch, where it stood propped among the firewood, and took a fresh light to his pipe.

"Understand me, Jim," he said, returning. "I've a head on my shoulders, I have. I'm on **squire's** side now. I know you've got that ship safe somewheres. How you done it, I don't know, but safe it is. I guess Hands and **O'Brien** turned soft. I never much believed in neither of *them*. Now you mark me. I ask no questions, nor I won't let others. I know when a game's up, I do; and I know a lad that's staunch. Ah, you that's young—you and me might have done a power of good together!"

He drew some cognac from the cask into a tin cannikin.

"Will you taste, messmate?" he asked; and when I had refused: "Well, I'll take a drain myself, Jim," said he. "I need a caulker, for there's trouble on hand. And talking o' trouble, why did that doctor give me the chart, Jim?"

My face expressed a wonder so unaffected that he saw the needlessness of further questions.

"Ah, well, he did, though," said he. "And there's something under that, no doubt—something, surely, under that, Jim—bad or good."

And he took another swallow of the brandy, shaking his great fair head like a man who looks forward to the worst.

• ANALYZING THE SCENE •

STORY EVENT

A Story Event is an active change of a universal human value for one or more characters as a result of conflict (one character's desires clash with another's, or an environmental shift changes the value positively or negatively).

A Working Scene contains at least one Story Event. To determine a scene's Story Event, answer these four Socratic questions:

1. What are the characters literally doing—that is, what are their micro on-the-surface actions?

Jim and the pirates are discussing what should happen to Jim. Silver gives Jim the option to join them or die. The other pirates challenge Silver and refuse to include him in their discussions. Jim and Silver strike a deal for mutual benefit.

2. What is the essential tactic of the characters—that is, what above-the-surface macro behaviors are they employing that are linked to a universal human value?

Silver is hedging his bets and making a deal because he doesn't understand why Livesey gave him the map, and he sees Jim as a formidable opponent or ally. Jim wants to know of the condition of his friends and stay alive, and he is taking stock of the situation. The other pirates are upset with the way the mission is going and are ready for a change in leadership.

3. What beyond-the-surface universal human values have changed for one or more characters in the scene? Which one of those value changes is most important and should be included in the Story Grid Spreadsheet?

Jim and Silver improve their prospects by agreeing to help one another. This is dangerous for Jim because Silver is not trustworthy, but this is the only viable option to stay alive. The other pirates move from satisfaction to suspicion, but Silver secures a temporary reprieve for Jim.

Imminent Death to Reprieve

4. The Scene Event Synthesis: What Story Event sums up the

scene's on-the-surface, above-the-surface, and beyond-the-surface change? We will enter that event in the Story Grid Spreadsheet.

Jim and Silver size one another up and make a deal that upsets the other pirates, who discuss their options out of hearing.

HOW THE SCENE ABIDES BY THE FIVE COMMANDMENTS OF STORYTELLING

Inciting Incident: Causal. Silver questions Jim hoping to gain some information and leverage.

Turning Point Progressive Complication: Active. Silver offers a better deal to Jim while the other pirates are speaking outside. If Jim agrees to help Silver, Silver will keep him alive.

Crisis: Best bad choice. Jim risks death either way. The other pirates want to kill him and possibly torture him already. Silver is not trustworthy, but they share a common enemy right now.

Climax: Silver stands up for Jim and threatens the other pirates.

Resolution: The other pirates leave to discuss the situation while Silver tells Jim they don't have much of a chance but promises to help if he promises to speak up for him if they make it back to England. Neither knows why Livesey gave up the map.

NOTES

- This is similar to the situation when Jim was dealing with Hands (scenes 25 and 26). He can't trust Silver beyond where their interests are aligned, but when they want the same thing, he can count on Silver.
- Jim is recognized as a fully agentic being by Silver. He possesses luminary and shadow *agency*, which means he can use his skills to create or destroy according to the situation. But as a luminary *agent*, he acts to increase the agency of others because this is for the common good. As a shadow agent, Silver acts only for himself.

29

THE BLACK SPOT AGAIN

The council of **buccaneers** had lasted some time, when one of them re-entered the house, and with a repetition of the same salute, which had in my eyes an ironical air, begged for a moment's loan of the torch. **Silver** briefly agreed, and this emissary retired again, leaving us together in the dark.

"There's a breeze coming, **Jim**," said Silver, who had by this time adopted quite a friendly and familiar tone.

I turned to the loophole nearest me and looked out. The embers of the great fire had so far burned themselves out and now glowed so low and duskily that I understood why these conspirators desired a torch. About half-way down the slope to the stockade, they were collected in a group; one held the light, another was on his knees in their midst, and I saw the blade of an open knife shine in his hand with varying colours in the moon and torchlight. The rest were all somewhat stooping, as though watching the manoeuvres of this last. I could just make out that he had a book as well as a knife in his hand, and was still wondering how anything so incongruous had come in their possession when the kneeling figure rose once more to his feet and the whole party began to move together towards the house.

"Here they come," said I; and I returned to my former position, for it seemed beneath my dignity that they should find me watching them.

"Well, let 'em come, lad—let 'em come," said Silver cheerily. "I've still a shot in my locker."

The door opened, and the five men, standing huddled together just inside, pushed one of their number forward. In any other circumstances it would have been comical to see his slow advance, hesitating as he set down each foot, but holding his closed right hand in front of him.

"Step up, lad," cried Silver. "I won't eat you. Hand it over, lubber. I know the rules, I do; I won't hurt a depytation."

Thus encouraged, the buccaneer stepped forth more briskly, and having passed something to Silver, from hand to hand, slipped yet more smartly back again to his companions.

The sea-cook looked at what had been given him.

"The black spot! I thought so," he observed. "Where might you have got the paper? Why, hillo! Look here, now; this ain't lucky! You've gone and cut this out of a Bible. What fool's cut a Bible?"

"Ah, there!" said **Morgan**. "There! Wot did I say? No good'll come o' that, I said."

"Well, you've about fixed it now, among you," continued Silver. "You'll all swing now, I reckon. What soft-headed lubber had a Bible?"

"It was **Dick**," said one.

"Dick, was it? Then Dick can get to prayers," said Silver. "He's seen his slice of luck, has Dick, and you may lay to that."

But here the long man with the yellow eyes struck in.

"Belay that talk, John Silver," he said. "This crew has tipped you the black spot in full council, as in dooty bound; just you turn it over, as in dooty bound, and see what's wrote there. Then you can talk."

"Thanky, **George**," replied the sea-cook. "You always was brisk for business, and has the rules by heart, George, as I'm pleased to see. Well, what is it, anyway? Ah! 'Deposed'—that's it, is it? Very pretty wrote, to be sure; like print, I swear. Your hand o' write, George? Why, you was gettin' quite a leadin' man in this here crew. You'll be cap'n next, I shouldn't wonder. Just oblige me with that torch again, will you? This pipe don't draw."

"Come, now," said George, "you don't fool this crew no more. You're a funny man, by your account; but you're over now, and you'll maybe step down off that barrel and help vote."

"I thought you said you knowed the rules," returned Silver contemptuously. "Leastways, if you don't, I do; and I wait here—and I'm still your cap'n, mind—till you outs with your grievances and I reply; in the meantime, your black spot ain't worth a biscuit. After that, we'll see."

"Oh," replied George, "you don't be under no kind of apprehension; *we're* all square, we are. First, you've made a hash of this cruise—you'll be a bold man to say no to that. Second, you let **the enemy** out o' this here trap for nothing. Why did they want out? I dunno, but it's pretty plain they wanted it. Third, you wouldn't let us go at them upon the march. Oh, we see through you, John Silver; you want to play booty, that's what's wrong with you. And then, fourth, there's this here boy."

"Is that all?" asked Silver quietly.

"Enough, too," retorted George. "We'll all swing and sun-dry for your bungling."

"Well now, look here, I'll answer these four p'ints; one after another I'll answer 'em. I made a hash o' this cruise, did I? Well now, you all know what I wanted, and you all know if that had been done that we'd 'a been aboard the *Hispaniola* this night as ever was, every man of us alive, and fit, and full of good plum-duff, and the treasure in the hold of her, by thunder! Well, who crossed me? Who forced my hand, as was the lawful cap'n? Who tipped me the black spot the day we landed and began this dance? Ah, it's a fine dance—I'm with you there—and looks mighty like a hornpipe in a rope's end at Execution Dock by London town, it does. But who done it? Why, it was **Anderson**, and **Hands**, and you, George Merry! And you're the last above board of that same meddling crew; and you have the **Davy Jones's** insolence to up and stand for cap'n over me—you, that sank the lot of us! By the powers! But this tops the stiffest yarn to nothing."

Silver paused, and I could see by the faces of George and his late comrades that these words had not been said in vain.

"That's for number one," cried the accused, wiping the sweat from his brow, for he had been talking with a vehemence that shook the house. "Why, I give you my word, I'm sick to speak to you. You've neither sense nor memory, and I leave it to fancy where **your mothers** was that let you come to sea. Sea! **Gentlemen o' fortune!** I reckon tailors is your trade."

"Go on, John," said Morgan. "Speak up to the others."

"Ah, the others!" returned John. "They're a nice lot, ain't they? You say this cruise is bungled. Ah! By gum, if you could understand how bad it's bungled, you would see! We're that near the gibbet that my neck's stiff with thinking on it. You've seen 'em, maybe, hanged in chains, birds about 'em, seamen p'inting 'em out as they go down with the tide. 'Who's that?' says one. 'That! Why, that's John Silver. I knowed him well,' says another. And you can hear the chains a-jangle as you go about and reach for the other buoy. Now, that's about where we are, every mother's son of us, thanks to him, and Hands, and Anderson, and other ruination fools of you. And if you want to know about number four, and that boy, why, shiver my timbers, isn't he **a hostage**? Are we a-going to waste a hostage? No, not us; he might be our last chance, and I shouldn't wonder. Kill that boy? Not me, mates! And number three? Ah, well, there's a deal to say to number three. Maybe you don't count it nothing to have a real college doctor to see you every day—you, John, with your head broke—or you, George Merry, that had the ague shakes upon you not six hours agone, and has your eyes the colour of lemon peel to this same moment on the clock? And maybe, perhaps, you didn't know there was **a consort** coming either? But there is, and not so long till then; and we'll see who'll be glad to have a hostage when it comes to that. And as for number two, and why I made a bargain—well, you came crawling on your knees to me to make it—on your knees you came, you was that downhearted—and you'd have starved too if I hadn't—but that's a trifle! You look there—that's why!"

And he cast down upon the floor a paper that I instantly recognized —none other than the chart on yellow paper, with the three red crosses, that I had found in the oilcloth at the bottom of **the captain's** chest. Why the doctor had given it to him was more than I could fancy.

But if it were inexplicable to me, the appearance of the chart was incredible to the surviving mutineers. They leaped upon it like cats upon a mouse. It went from hand to hand, one tearing it from another; and by the oaths and the cries and the childish laughter with which they accompanied their examination, you would have thought, not only they were fingering the very gold, but were at sea with it, besides, in safety.

"Yes," said one, "that's **Flint**, sure enough. J. F., and a score below, with a clove hitch to it; so he done ever."

"Mighty pretty," said George. "But how are we to get away with it, and us no ship."

Silver suddenly sprang up, and supporting himself with a hand against the wall: "Now I give you warning, George," he cried. "One more word of your sauce, and I'll call you down and fight you. How? Why, how do I know? You had ought to tell me that—**you and the rest**, that lost me my schooner, with your interference, burn you! But not you, you can't; you hain't got the invention of a cockroach. But civil you can speak, and shall, George Merry, you may lay to that."

"That's fair enow," said the old man Morgan.

"Fair! I reckon so," said the sea-cook. "You lost the ship; I found the treasure. Who's the better man at that? And now I resign, by thunder! Elect whom you please to be your cap'n now; I'm done with it."

"Silver!" they cried. "Barbecue forever! Barbecue for cap'n!"

"So that's the toon, is it?" cried the cook. "George, I reckon you'll have to wait another turn, friend; and lucky for you as I'm not a revengeful man. But that was never my way. And now, shipmates, this black spot? 'Tain't much good now, is it? Dick's crossed his luck and spoiled his Bible, and that's about all."

"It'll do to kiss the book on still, won't it?" growled Dick, who was evidently uneasy at the curse he had brought upon himself.

"A Bible with a bit cut out!" returned Silver derisively. "Not it. It don't bind no more'n a ballad-book."

"Don't it, though?" cried Dick with a sort of joy. "Well, I reckon that's worth having too."

"Here, Jim—here's a cur'osity for you," said Silver, and he tossed me the paper.

It was around about the size of a crown piece. One side was blank, for it had been the last leaf; the other contained a verse or two of Revelation—these words among the rest, which struck sharply home upon my mind: "Without are dogs and murderers." The printed side had been blackened with wood ash, which already began to come off and soil my fingers; on the blank side had been written with the same material the one word "Depposed." I have that curiosity beside me at this moment, but not a trace of writing now remains beyond a single scratch, such as a man might make with his thumb-nail.

That was the end of the night's business. Soon after, with a drink all round, we lay down to sleep, and the outside of Silver's vengeance was to put George Merry up for sentinel and threaten him with death if he should prove unfaithful.

It was long ere I could close an eye, and heaven knows I had matter enough for thought in the man whom I had slain that afternoon, in my own most perilous position, and above all, in the remarkable game that I saw Silver now engaged upon—keeping the mutineers together with one hand and grasping with the other after every means, possible and impossible, to make his peace and save his miserable life. He himself slept peacefully and snored aloud, yet my heart was sore for him, wicked as he was, to think on the dark perils that environed and the shameful gibbet that awaited him.

• ANALYZING THE SCENE •

STORY EVENT

A Story Event is an active change of a universal human value for one or more characters as a result of conflict (one character's desires clash with another's, or an environmental shift changes the value positively or negatively).

A Working Scene contains at least one Story Event. To determine a scene's Story Event, answer these four Socratic questions:

1. What are the characters literally doing—that is, what are their micro on-the-surface actions?

Jim and Silver wait while the other pirates have a private discussion outside. They return with a list of grievances against Silver. Silver defends himself and produces the map. When he tries to resign as captain, the others want him to stay.

2. What is the essential tactic of the characters—that is, what above-the-surface macro behaviors are they employing that are linked to a universal human value?

Silver wants to persuade the others to follow him. Merry is trying to wrest power from Silver. Jim is observing. His fate is in the hands of others.

3. What beyond-the-surface universal human values have changed for one or more characters in the scene? Which one of those value changes is most important and should be included in the Story Grid Spreadsheet?

Jim is a bit wary of Silver but ends with respect and sympathy for him. Silver's position is threatened, but he convinces the other pirates that he should remain their captain. Jim faces torture and death if the other pirates succeed in deposing Silver, but when Silver maintains his position, Jim is safe for the time being.

Certain Death to Temporary Safety

4. The Scene Event Synthesis: What Story Event sums up the scene's on-the-surface, above-the-surface, and beyond-the-surface change? We will enter that event in the Story Grid Spreadsheet.

The other pirates challenge Silver's authority and deliver the black spot, but he shows them the map, and they back down.

HOW THE SCENE ABIDES BY THE FIVE COMMANDMENTS OF STORYTELLING

Inciting Incident: Causal. The pirates discuss Silver's fate in a council outside the cabin.

Turning Point Progressive Complication: Active. Silver produces Flint's map.

Crisis: Best bad choice. If the pirates depose Silver, they will gain power but make an enemy of Silver. If they don't depose Silver, they must follow Silver's orders, including allowing Jim to live.

Climax: The pirates choose Silver. "Barbecue forever!"

Resolution: Silver gives Jim the piece of paper with the black spot, which Jim keeps, noting the Bible verse on the back. Merry is punished by having to stand watch. Jim remarks on how he has trouble sleeping but Silver sleeps soundly.

NOTES

- Jim is a passive observer in this scene. His fate is tied to Silver, and that is decided by the other pirates in this scene. Silver is pretty sure they will present him with the black spot, so it's not an unexpected event. Silver is waiting to hear their complaints to decide whether he needs to reveal his last advantage—the treasure map.
- This event is an echo of the scene in the beginning hook when Pew delivers the black spot to Bones. Repeating similar circumstances in later scenes is a great tool for showing how a character has changed. Jim is watching as he did in scene 3, but he's actively calculating too.
- Why did Jim keep the piece of paper? The word deposed and the black spot itself are gone by the time he writes his account, but the Bible verse probably reminds him when

you leave home and go adventuring, you are outside the law and in someone else's territory. "Without are dogs and murderers."

30

ON PAROLE

I was wakened—indeed, we were all wakened, for I could see even **the sentinel** shake himself together from where he had fallen against the door-post—by a clear, hearty voice hailing us from the margin of the wood:

"Block house, ahoy!" it cried. "Here's the doctor."

And the doctor it was. Although I was glad to hear the sound, yet my gladness was not without admixture. I remembered with confusion my insubordinate and stealthy conduct, and when I saw where it had brought me—among what companions and surrounded by what dangers—I felt ashamed to look him in the face.

He must have risen in the dark, for the day had hardly come; and when I ran to a loophole and looked out, I saw him standing, like Silver once before, up to the mid-leg in creeping vapour.

"You, doctor! Top o' the morning to you, sir!" cried **Silver**, broad awake and beaming with good nature in a moment. "Bright and early, to be sure; and it's the early bird, as the saying goes, that gets the rations. **George**, shake up your timbers, son, and help **Dr. Livesey** over the ship's side. All a-doin' well, your patients was—all well and merry."

So he pattered on, standing on the hilltop with his crutch under his elbow and one hand upon the side of the log-house—quite the old John in voice, manner, and expression.

"We've quite a surprise for you too, sir," he continued. "We've a little stranger here—he! he! A noo boarder and lodger, sir, and looking fit and taut as a fiddle; slep' like a supercargo, he did, right alongside of John—stem to stem we was, all night."

Dr. Livesey was by this time across the stockade and pretty near the cook, and I could hear the alteration in his voice as he said, "Not Jim?"

"The very same Jim as ever was," says Silver.

The doctor stopped outright, although he did not speak, and it was some seconds before he seemed able to move on.

"Well, well," he said at last, "duty first and pleasure afterwards, as you might have said yourself, Silver. Let us overhaul these patients of yours."

A moment afterwards he had entered the block house and with one grim nod to me proceeded with his work among the sick. He seemed under no apprehension, though he must have known that his life, among these treacherous demons, depended on a hair; and he rattled on to his patients as if he were paying an ordinary professional visit in a **quiet English family.** His manner, I suppose, reacted on the men, for they behaved to him as if nothing had occurred, as if he were still **ship's doctor** and they still **faithful hands before the mast.**

"You're doing well, my friend," he said to **the fellow with the bandaged head**, "and if ever any person had a close shave, it was you; your head must be as hard as iron. Well, George, how goes it? You're a pretty colour, certainly; why, your liver, man, is upside down. Did you take that medicine? Did he take that medicine, men?"

"Aye, aye, sir, he took it, sure enough," returned **Morgan.**

"Because, you see, since I am **mutineers' doctor**, or **prison doctor** as I prefer to call it," says Doctor Livesey in his pleasantest way, "I make it a point of honour not to lose **a man for King George** (**God** bless him!) and the gallows."

The rogues looked at each other but swallowed the home-thrust in silence.

"**Dick** don't feel well, sir," said **one.**

"Don't he?" replied the doctor. "Well, step up here, Dick, and let me see your tongue. No, I should be surprised if he did! The man's tongue is fit to frighten **the French**. Another fever."

"Ah, there," said Morgan, "that comed of sp'iling Bibles."

"That comes—as you call it—of being arrant asses," retorted the doctor, "and not having sense enough to know honest air from poison, and the dry land from a vile, pestiferous slough. I think it most probable—though of course it's only an opinion—that you'll all have the deuce to pay before you get that malaria out of your systems. Camp in a bog, would you? Silver, I'm surprised at you. You're less of a fool than many, take you all round; but you don't appear to me to have the rudiments of a notion of the rules of health.

"Well," he added after he had dosed them round and they had taken his prescriptions, with really laughable humility, more like **charity schoolchildren** than **blood-guilty mutineers and pirates**—" well, that's done for today. And now I should wish to have a talk with that boy, please."

And he nodded his head in my direction carelessly.

George Merry was at the door, spitting and spluttering over some bad-tasted medicine; but at the first word of the doctor's proposal he swung round with a deep flush and cried "No!" and swore.

Silver struck the barrel with his open hand.

"Si-lence!" he roared and looked about him positively like a lion. "Doctor," he went on in his usual tones, "I was a-thinking of that, knowing as how you had a fancy for the boy. We're all humbly grateful for your kindness, and as you see, puts faith in you and takes the drugs down like that much grog. And I take it I've found a way as'll suit all. Hawkins, will you give me your word of honour as a young gentleman —for a young gentleman you are, although poor born—your word of honour not to slip your cable?"

I readily gave the pledge required.

"Then, doctor," said Silver, "you just step outside o' that stockade, and once you're there I'll bring the boy down on the inside, and I reckon you can yarn through the spars. Good day to you, sir, and all our dooties to **the squire** and **Cap'n Smollett**."

The explosion of disapproval, which nothing but Silver's black looks had restrained, broke out immediately the doctor had left the house. Silver was roundly accused of playing double—of trying to make a separate peace for himself, of sacrificing the interests of his accomplices and victims, and, in one word, of the identical, exact thing that he was doing. It seemed to me so obvious, in this case, that I could not imagine how he was to turn their anger. But he was twice the man the rest were, and his last night's victory had given him a huge preponderance on their minds. He called them all the fools and dolts you can imagine, said it was necessary I should talk to the doctor, fluttered the chart in their faces, asked them if they could afford to break the treaty the very day they were bound a-treasure-hunting.

"No, by thunder!" he cried. "It's us must break the treaty when the time comes; and till then I'll gammon that doctor, if I have to ile his boots with brandy."

And then he bade them get the fire lit, and stalked out upon his crutch, with his hand on my shoulder, leaving them in a disarray, and silenced by his volubility rather than convinced.

"Slow, lad, slow," he said. "They might round upon us in a twinkle of an eye if we was seen to hurry."

Very deliberately, then, did we advance across the sand to where the doctor awaited us on the other side of the stockade, and as soon as we were within easy speaking distance Silver stopped.

"You'll make a note of this here also, doctor," says he, "and the boy'll tell you how I saved his life, and were deposed for it too, and you may lay to that. Doctor, when a man's steering as near the wind as me—playing chuck-farthing with the last breath in his body, like—you wouldn't think it too much, mayhap, to give him one good word? You'll please bear in mind it's not my life only now—it's that boy's into the bargain; and you'll speak me fair, doctor, and give me a bit o' hope to go on, for the sake of mercy."

Silver was a changed man once he was out there and had his back to his friends and the block house; his cheeks seemed to have fallen in, his voice trembled; never was a soul more dead in earnest.

"Why, John, you're not afraid?" asked Dr. Livesey.

"Doctor, I'm no coward; no, not I—not *so* much!" and he snapped his fingers. "If I was I wouldn't say it. But I'll own up fairly, I've the shakes upon me for the gallows. You're a good man and a true; I never seen a better man! And you'll not forget what I done good, not any more than you'll forget the bad, I know. And I step aside—see here—

and leave you and Jim alone. And you'll put that down for me too, for it's a long stretch, is that!"

So saying, he stepped back a little way, till he was out of earshot, and there sat down upon a tree-stump and began to whistle, spinning round now and again upon his seat so as to command a sight, sometimes of me and the doctor and sometimes of his unruly ruffians as they went to and fro in the sand between the fire—which they were busy rekindling—and the house, from which they brought forth pork and bread to make the breakfast.

"So, Jim," said the doctor sadly, "here you are. As you have brewed, so shall you drink, my boy. Heaven knows, I cannot find it in my heart to blame you, but this much I will say, be it kind or unkind: when Captain Smollett was well, you dared not have gone off; and when he was ill and couldn't help it, by George, it was downright cowardly!"

I will own that I here began to weep. "Doctor," I said, "you might spare me. I have blamed myself enough; my life's forfeit anyway, and I should have been dead by now if Silver hadn't stood for me; and doctor, believe this, I can die—and I dare say I deserve it—but what I fear is torture. If they come to torture me—"

"Jim," the doctor interrupted, and his voice was quite changed, "Jim, I can't have this. Whip over, and we'll run for it."

"Doctor," said I, "I passed my word."

"I know, I know," he cried. "We can't help that, Jim, now. I'll take it on my shoulders, holus bolus, blame and shame, my boy; but stay here, I cannot let you. Jump! One jump, and you're out, and we'll run for it like antelopes."

"No," I replied; "you know right well you wouldn't do the thing yourself—neither you nor squire nor captain; and no more will I. Silver trusted me; I passed my word, and back I go. But, doctor, you did not let me finish. If they come to torture me, I might let slip a word of where the ship is, for I got the ship, part by luck and part by risking, and she lies in North Inlet, on the southern beach, and just below high water. At half tide she must be high and dry."

"The ship!" exclaimed the doctor.

Rapidly I described to him my adventures, and he heard me out in silence.

"There is a kind of fate in this," he observed when I had done. "Every step, it's you that saves our lives; and do you suppose by any chance that we are going to let you lose yours? That would be a poor return, my boy. You found out the plot; you found Ben Gunn—the best deed that ever you did, or will do, though you live to ninety. Oh, by Jupiter, and talking of Ben Gunn! Why, this is the mischief in person. Silver!" he cried. "Silver! I'll give you a piece of advice," he continued as the cook drew near again; "don't you be in any great hurry after that treasure."

"Why, sir, I do my possible, which that ain't," said Silver. "I can only, asking your pardon, save my life and the boy's by seeking for that treasure; and you may lay to that."

"Well, Silver," replied the doctor, "if that is so, I'll go one step further: look out for squalls when you find it." [*Squalls are short, violent storms, but here, Livesey is warning of a short-lived commotion or harsh cry.*]

"Sir," said Silver, "as between man and man, that's too much and too little. What you're after, why you left the block house, why you given me that there chart, I don't know, now, do I? And yet I done your bidding with my eyes shut and never a word of hope! But no, this here's too much. If you won't tell me what you mean plain out, just say so and I'll leave the helm."

"No," said the doctor musingly; "I've no right to say more; it's not my secret, you see, Silver, or, I give you my word, I'd tell it you. But I'll go as far with you as I dare go, and a step beyond, for I'll have my wig sorted by the captain or I'm mistaken! And first, I'll give you a bit of hope; Silver, if we both get alive out of this wolf-trap, I'll do my best to save you, short of perjury."

Silver's face was radiant. "You couldn't say more, I'm sure, sir, not if you was **my mother**," he cried.

"Well, that's my first concession," added the doctor. "My second is a piece of advice: keep the boy close beside you, and when you need help, halloo. I'm off to seek it for you, and that itself will show you if I speak at random. Good-bye, Jim."

And Dr. Livesey shook hands with me through the stockade, nodded to Silver, and set off at a brisk pace into the wood.

• ANALYZING THE SCENE •

STORY EVENT

A Story Event is an active change of a universal human value for one or more characters as a result of conflict (one character's desires clash with another's, or an environmental shift changes the value positively or negatively).

A Working Scene contains at least one Story Event. To determine a scene's Story Event, answer these four Socratic questions:

1. What are the characters literally doing—that is, what are their micro on-the-surface actions?

Livesey comes to the stockade to check on the sick and injured pirates and is permitted to speak with Jim over the objections of the pirates (other than Silver).

2. What is the essential tactic of the characters—that is, what above-the-surface macro behaviors are they employing that are linked to a universal human value?

Jim wants to tell Livesey about where he stowed the ship because he's worried he'll reveal the location if tortured. Silver is hoping to hedge his bets and gain information to stay alive and in charge. Livesey wants to save Jim's life and is willing to encourage him to break his word to do so.

3. What beyond-the-surface universal human values have changed for one or more characters in the scene? Which one of those value changes is most important and should be included in the Story Grid Spreadsheet?

Identifying the most important value change in a scene is sometimes difficult. This scene begins with Jim in the stockade, a prisoner of the pirates, and it ends in much the same way. But Silver has managed to keep control of the pirates, and Jim is able to exchange vital information with Livesey. When in doubt, the Story Grid rule of thumb is to highlight the shift that best aligns with the global value.

Jim cannot get home on his own, so the party's survival is important. Silver makes it possible for Jim to tell Livesey where the ship is. This makes it more likely they will regain the ship so everyone in the party can survive.

Stranded to Access to Transport

4. The Scene Event Synthesis: What Story Event sums up the scene's on-the-surface, above-the-surface, and beyond-the-surface change? We will enter that event in the Story Grid Spreadsheet.

Livesey visits the stockade to check on his patients among the pirates. Jim refuses to run away but tells Livesey where the ship is so he can take possession.

HOW THE SCENE ABIDES BY THE FIVE COMMANDMENTS OF STORYTELLING

Inciting Incident: Causal. Livesey arrives to tend to the sick pirates.

Turning Point Progressive Complication: Active. Silver speaks up for Jim and allows him a private word with Livesey.

Crisis: Irreconcilable goods choice. Livesey tells Jim to jump the stockade and run, which is good for Jim if he can escape, but it's bad for Silver to whom Jim gave his word.

Climax: Jim refuses, explaining that his honor won't allow him and that Livesey would not have done it either.

Resolution: Livesey vows to save Jim, who lets him know about the ship's location. Livesey offers a clue to Silver and promises to speak for Silver in court if they all survive.

NOTES

- In this scene, Jim shows what a fate worse than death would be for him. He's resigned to his own death, but he now fears torture most because if he were to reveal the location, his death would not save his friends.
- Livesey is critical of Jim for not running at first but then admits that without Jim's contributions, they would all be dead. Livesey's presence offers Jim a chance to escape, but Jim chooses to stay with the pirates.
- Given Livesey's action in encouraging Jim to run, which

would mean breaking his word, Jim was right to suspect the adults would have stopped him from going to look for the coracle and cutting the ship loose.

- Jim's choice to stay is set up in scene 4 when does not run with the money after his mother suggests it. He defies the adults to do what he believes is right.

31

THE TREASURE-HUNT: FLINT'S POINTER

"**Jim**," said Silver, when we were alone, "if I saved your life, you saved mine; and I'll not forget it. I seen **the doctor** waving you to run for it—with the tail of my eye, I did; and I seen you say no, as plain as hearing. Jim, that's one to you. This is the first glint of hope I had since the attack failed, and I owe it you. And now, Jim, we're to go in for this here treasure-hunting, with sealed orders too, and I don't like it; and you and me must stick close, back to back like, and we'll save our necks in spite o' fate and fortune."

Just then **a man hailed us from the fire** that breakfast was ready, and we were soon seated here and there about the sand over biscuit and fried junk. They had lit a fire fit to roast an ox, and it was now grown so hot that they could only approach it from the windward, and even there not without precaution. In the same wasteful spirit, they had cooked, I suppose, three times more than we could eat; and **one of them**, with an empty laugh, threw what was left into the fire, which blazed and roared again over this unusual fuel. I never in my life saw men so careless of the morrow; hand to mouth is the only word that can describe their way of doing; and what with wasted food and sleeping sentries, though they were bold enough for a brush and be done with it, I could see their entire unfitness for anything like a prolonged campaign.

Even Silver, eating away, with **Captain Flint** upon his shoulder, had not a word of blame for their recklessness. And this the more surprised me, for I thought he had never shown himself so cunning as he did then.

"Aye, mates," said he, "it's lucky you have Barbecue to think for you with this here head. I got what I wanted, I did. Sure enough, they have the ship. Where they have it, I don't know yet; but once we hit the treasure, we'll have to jump about and find out. And then, mates, us that has the boats, I reckon, has the upper hand."

Thus he kept running on, with his mouth full of the hot bacon; thus he restored their hope and confidence, and, I more than suspect, repaired his own at the same time. [*Jim not only notices what Silver is doing, but he's making note of Silver's essential tactics driving his actions. Jim no longer takes anything at face value or makes assumptions.*]

"As for hostage," he continued, "that's his last talk, I guess, **with them he loves so dear.** I've got my piece o' news, and thanky to him for that; but it's over and done. I'll take him in a line when we go treasure-hunting, for we'll keep him like so much gold, in case of accidents, you mark, and in the meantime. Once we got the ship and treasure both and off to sea like jolly companions, why then we'll talk Mr. Hawkins over, we will, and we'll give him his share, to be sure, for all his kindness." [*Silver is keeping Jim close and offering the other pirates a reason to let Jim live.*]

It was no wonder the men were in a good humour now. For my part, I was horribly cast down. Should the scheme he had now sketched prove feasible, Silver, already doubly a traitor, would not hesitate to adopt it. He had still a foot in either camp, and there was no doubt he would prefer wealth and freedom with the pirates to a bare escape from hanging, which was the best he had to hope on our side.

Nay, and even if things so fell out that he was forced to keep his faith with **Dr. Livesey**, even then what danger lay before us! What a moment that would be when the suspicions of his followers turned to certainty and he and I should have to fight for dear life—**he a cripple and I a boy**—against **five strong and active seamen!** [*This is another passage that lets us know Silver is a dangerous shadow agent.*]

Add to this double apprehension the mystery that still hung over

280

the behaviour of **my friends**, their unexplained desertion of the stockade, their inexplicable cession of the chart, or harder still to understand, the doctor's last warning to Silver, "Look out for squalls when you find it," and you will readily believe how little taste I found in my breakfast and with how uneasy a heart I set forth behind my captors on the quest for treasure.

We made a curious figure, had anyone been there to see us—all in soiled sailor clothes and all but me armed to the teeth. Silver had two guns slung about him—one before and one behind—besides the great cutlass at his waist and a pistol in each pocket of his square-tailed coat. To complete his strange appearance, Captain Flint sat perched upon his shoulder and gabbling odds and ends of purposeless sea-talk. I had a line about my waist and followed obediently after the sea-cook, who held the loose end of the rope, now in his free hand, now between his powerful teeth. For all the world, I was led like a dancing bear.

The other men were variously burthened [*variant of burdened*], some carrying picks and shovels—for that had been the very first necessary they brought ashore from the *Hispaniola*—others laden with pork, bread, and brandy for the midday meal. All the stores, I observed, came from our stock, and I could see the truth of Silver's words the night before. Had he not struck a bargain with the doctor, he and his mutineers, deserted by the ship, must have been driven to subsist on clear water and the proceeds of their hunting. Water would have been little to their taste; a sailor is not usually a good shot; and besides all that, when they were so short of eatables, it was not likely they would be very flush of powder.

Well, thus equipped, we all set out—**even the fellow with the broken head**, who should certainly have kept in shadow—and straggled, one after another, to the beach, where the two gigs awaited us. Even these bore trace of the drunken folly of the pirates, one in a broken thwart, and both in their muddy and unbailed condition. Both were to be carried along with us for the sake of safety; and so, with our numbers divided between them, we set forth upon the bosom of the anchorage.

As we pulled over, there was some discussion on the chart. The red cross was, of course, far too large to be a guide; and the terms of the note on the back, as you will hear, admitted of some ambiguity. They ran, the reader may remember, thus:

Tall tree, Spy-glass shoulder, bearing a point to the N. of N.N.E. Skeleton Island E.S.E. and by E. Ten feet.

A tall tree was thus the principal mark. Now, right before us the anchorage was bounded by a plateau from two to three hundred feet high, adjoining on the north the sloping southern shoulder of the Spy-glass and rising again towards the south into the rough, cliffy eminence called the Mizzen-mast Hill. The top of the plateau was dotted thickly with pine-trees of varying height. Every here and there, one of a different species rose forty or fifty feet clear above its neighbours, and which of these was the particular "tall tree" of Captain Flint could only be decided on the spot, and by the readings of the compass.

Yet, although that was the case, every man on board the boats had picked a favourite of his own ere we were half-way over, Long John alone shrugging his shoulders and bidding them wait till they were there.

We pulled easily, by Silver's directions, not to weary the hands prematurely, and after quite a long passage, landed at the mouth of the second river—that which runs down a woody cleft of the Spy-glass. Thence, bending to our left, we began to ascend the slope towards the plateau.

At the first outset, heavy, miry ground and a matted, marish vegetation greatly delayed our progress; but by little and little the hill began to steepen and become stony under foot, and the wood to change its character and to grow in a more open order. It was, indeed, a most pleasant portion of the island that we were now approaching. A heavy-scented broom and many flowering shrubs had almost taken the place of grass. Thickets of green nutmeg-trees were dotted here and there with the red columns and the broad shadow of the pines; and the first mingled their spice with the aroma of the others. The air, besides, was fresh and stirring, and this, under the sheer sunbeams, was a wonderful refreshment to our senses.

The party spread itself abroad, in a fan shape, shouting and leaping to and fro. About the centre, and a good way behind the rest, Silver and I followed—I tethered by my rope, he ploughing, with deep pants, among the sliding gravel. From time to time, indeed, I had to lend him a hand, or he must have missed his footing and fallen backward down the hill.

We had thus proceeded for about half a mile and were approaching the brow of the plateau when **the man upon the farthest left** began to cry aloud, as if in terror. Shout after shout came from him, and the others began to run in his direction.

"He can't 'a found the treasure," said **old Morgan**, hurrying past us from the right, "for that's clean a-top."

Indeed, as we found when we also reached the spot, it was something very different. At the foot of a pretty big pine and involved in a green creeper, which had even partly lifted some of the smaller bones, a human skeleton lay, with a few shreds of clothing, on the ground. I believe a chill struck for a moment to every heart.

"He was a seaman," said George Merry, who, bolder than the rest, had gone up close and was examining the rags of clothing. "Leastways, this is good sea-cloth."

"Aye, aye," said Silver; "like enough; you wouldn't look to find **a bishop** here, I reckon. But what sort of a way is that for bones to lie? 'Tain't in natur'."

Indeed, on a second glance, it seemed impossible to fancy that the body was in a natural position. But for some disarray (the work, perhaps, of the birds that had fed upon him or of the slow-growing creeper that had gradually enveloped his remains) the man lay perfectly straight—his feet pointing in one direction, his hands, raised above his head like a diver's, pointing directly in the opposite.

"I've taken a notion into my old numbskull," observed Silver. "Here's the compass; there's the tip-top p'int o' Skeleton Island, stickin' out like a tooth. Just take a bearing, will you, along the line of them bones."

It was done. The body pointed straight in the direction of the island, and the compass read duly E.S.E. and by E.

"I thought so," cried the cook; "this here is a p'inter. Right up there is our line for the Pole Star and the jolly dollars. But, by thunder! If it don't make me cold inside to think of **Flint**. This is one of *his* jokes, and no mistake. Him and these six was alone here; he killed 'em, every man;

and this one he hauled here and laid down by compass, shiver my timbers! They're long bones, and the hair's been yellow. Aye, that would be **Allardyce**. You mind Allardyce, **Tom Morgan**?"

"Aye, aye," returned Morgan; "I mind him; he owed me money, he did, and took my knife ashore with him."

"Speaking of knives," said another, "why don't we find his'n lying round? Flint warn't the man to pick a seaman's pocket; and the birds, I guess, would leave it be."

"By the powers, and that's true!" cried Silver.

"There ain't a thing left here," said Merry, still feeling round among the bones; "not a copper doit nor a baccy box. It don't look nat'ral to me."

"No, by gum, it don't," agreed Silver; "not nat'ral, nor not nice, says you. Great guns! Messmates, but if Flint was living, this would be a hot spot for you and me. Six they were, and six are we; and bones is what they are now."

"I saw him dead with these here deadlights," said Morgan. "Billy took me in. There he laid, with penny-pieces on his eyes."

"Dead—aye, sure enough he's dead and gone below," said the fellow with the bandage; "but if ever sperrit walked, it would be Flint's. Dear heart, but he died bad, did Flint!"

"Aye, that he did," observed another; "now he raged, and now he hollered for the rum, and now he sang. 'Fifteen Men' were his only song, mates; and I tell you true, I never rightly liked to hear it since. It was main hot, and the windy was open, and I hear that old song comin' out as clear as clear—and the death-haul on the man already."

"Come, come," said Silver; "stow this talk. He's dead, and he don't walk, that I know; leastways, he won't walk by day, and you may lay to that. Care killed a cat. Fetch ahead for the doubloons."

We started, certainly; but in spite of the hot sun and the staring daylight, the pirates no longer ran separate and shouting through the wood, but kept side by side and spoke with bated breath. The terror of the dead buccaneer had fallen on their spirits.

• ANALYZING THE SCENE •

STORY EVENT

A Story Event is an active change of a universal human value for one or more characters as a result of conflict (one character's desires clash with another's, or an environmental shift changes the value positively or negatively).

A Working Scene contains at least one Story Event. To determine a scene's Story Event, answer these four Socratic questions:

1. What are the characters literally doing—that is, what are their micro on-the-surface actions?

Silver keeps Jim close as the pirates follow the map and instructions to find the treasure and encounter a skeleton arranged as a pointer.

2. What is the essential tactic of the characters—that is, what above-the-surface macro behaviors are they employing that are linked to a universal human value?

Jim needs to pay attention so he can stay alive. His fate is tied to Silver, who can't be trusted. Silver is still hedging. He wants to control the situation to have a chance of obtaining the treasure and staying alive. Keeping Jim alive gives Silver a way to negotiate with Livesey if he must later on.

3. What beyond-the-surface universal human values have changed for one or more characters in the scene? Which one of those value changes is most important and should be included in the Story Grid Spreadsheet?

The pirates begin confidently but are shaken and scared by the skeleton. Their fear gives Silver more leverage but could also make the men less predictable. Jim is unsure of whether to trust Silver and then realizes he cannot let down his guard.

Overconfidence to Doubts

4. The Scene Event Synthesis: What Story Event sums up the scene's on-the-surface, above-the-surface, and beyond-the-surface change? We will enter that event in the Story Grid Spreadsheet.

The pirates seek the treasure and are unnerved when they discover an unnaturally arranged skeleton. Jim realizes he still can't trust Silver even though Jim depends on him for his safety.

HOW THE SCENE ABIDES BY THE FIVE COMMANDMENTS OF STORYTELLING

Inciting Incident: Causal. The pirates eat breakfast before leaving the cabin to seek the treasure. Silver tells Jim they need to stick together to stay alive.

Turning Point Progressive Complication: Active. The party encounters a skeleton that points in the direction of the treasure (according to the instructions). The other pirates are spooked.

Crisis: Best bad choice. If Silver acts on Livesey's earlier advice and uses the pointer as a delay tactic, the other pirates could catch on and revolt. If Silver continues, he may be walking into a trap.

Climax: Silver tells the men that Flint is dead, and his spirit isn't coming for them during the day at least. He orders them to keep going.

Resolution: The other pirates are spooked, but they follow Silver's orders.

NOTES

- Two major threads are operating in this scene. On the surface, the pirates and Jim are following the map. Above the surface, Jim is looking for opportunities to help him stay alive. That means trying to read Silver and the other pirates. As Jim mentions, the odds are against him and Silver in a fight with the other pirates, and Jim knows Silver is keeping one foot in each camp. Jim's fate is tied to Silver, but Jim can't turn over his agency to him like he has done in the past with other adults in his life.
- When Jim faces off with Hands on the ship (scenes 25 and 26), they are faking each other out. Notice that in this scene Jim and Silver are both doing their best to predict what the other will do and not give away much themselves.

- Jim's new skills have earned him Silver's respect. It is likely he sees Jim as a useful pirate crew member. If not for Jim's morals and the examples of good men in his life, he could have ended up like Silver or Bones.

32

THE TREASURE-HUNT: THE VOICE AMONG THE TREES

Partly from the damping influence of this alarm, partly to rest **Silver** and **the sick folk**, the whole party sat down as soon as they had gained the brow of the ascent.

The plateau being somewhat tilted towards the west, this spot on which we had paused commanded a wide prospect on either hand. Before us, over the tree-tops, we beheld the **Cape of the Woods** fringed with surf; behind, we not only looked down upon **the anchorage and Skeleton Island**, but saw—clear across the spit and the eastern lowlands—a great field of open sea upon the east. Sheer above us rose the **Spyglass**, here dotted with single pines, there black with precipices. There was no sound but that of the distant breakers, mounting from all round, and the chirp of countless insects in the brush. Not a man, not a sail, upon the sea; the very largeness of the view increased the sense of solitude.

Silver, as he sat, took certain bearings with his compass.

"There are three 'tall trees'" said he, "about in the right line from Skeleton Island. 'Spy-glass shoulder,' I take it, means that lower p'int there. It's child's play to find the stuff now. I've half a mind to dine first."

"I don't feel sharp," growled **Morgan**. "Thinkin' o' **Flint**—I think it were—as done me."

"Ah, well, my son, you praise your stars he's dead," said Silver.

"He were an ugly devil," cried **a third pirate** with a shudder; "that blue in the face too!"

"That was how the rum took him," added **Merry**. "Blue! Well, I reckon he was blue. That's a true word."

Ever since they had found the skeleton and got upon this train of thought, they had spoken lower and lower, and they had almost got to whispering by now, so that the sound of their talk hardly interrupted the silence of the wood. All of a sudden, out of the middle of the trees in front of us, a thin, high, trembling voice struck up the well-known air and words:

"Fifteen men on the dead man's chest—
Yo-ho-ho, and a bottle of rum!"

I never have seen men more dreadfully affected than the pirates. The colour went from their six faces like enchantment; some leaped to their feet, some clawed hold of others; Morgan grovelled on the ground.

"It's Flint, by—!" cried Merry.

The song had stopped as suddenly as it began—broken off, you would have said, in the middle of a note, as though someone had laid his hand upon the singer's mouth. Coming through the clear, sunny atmosphere among the green tree-tops, I thought it had sounded airily and sweetly; and the effect on my companions was the stranger.

"Come," said Silver, struggling with his ashen lips to get the word out; "this won't do. Stand by to go about. This is a rum start, and I can't name the voice, but it's someone skylarking—someone that's flesh and blood, and you may lay to that."

His courage had come back as he spoke, and some of the colour to his face along with it. Already the others had begun to lend an ear to this encouragement and were coming a little to themselves, when the same voice broke out again—not this time singing, but in a faint distant hail that echoed yet fainter among the clefts of the Spy-glass.

"**Darby M'Graw**," it wailed—for that is the word that best describes the sound—"Darby M'Graw! Darby M'Graw!" again and again and again; and then rising a little higher, and with an oath that I leave out: "Fetch aft the rum, Darby!"

The buccaneers remained rooted to the ground, their eyes starting from their heads. Long after the voice had died away they still stared in silence, dreadfully, before them.

"That fixes it!" gasped one. "Let's go."

"They was his last words," moaned Morgan, "his last words above board."

Dick had his Bible out and was praying volubly. He had been well brought up, had Dick, before he came to sea and fell among bad companions.

Still Silver was unconquered. I could hear his teeth rattle in his head, but he had not yet surrendered.

"Nobody in this here island ever heard of Darby," he muttered; "not one but us that's here." And then, making a great effort: "Shipmates," he cried, "I'm here to get that stuff, and I'll not be beat by man or devil. I never was feared of Flint in his life, and, by the powers, I'll face him dead. There's seven hundred thousand pound not a quarter of a mile from here. When did ever **a gentleman o' fortune** show his stern to that much dollars for **a boozy old seaman with a blue mug**—and him dead too?"

But there was no sign of reawakening courage in his followers, rather, indeed, of growing terror at the irreverence of his words.

"Belay there, John!" said Merry. "Don't you cross a sperrit."

And the rest were all too terrified to reply. They would have run away severally had they dared; but fear kept them together, and kept them close by John, as if his daring helped them. He, on his part, had pretty well fought his weakness down.

"Sperrit? Well, maybe," he said. "But there's one thing not clear to me. There was an echo. Now, no man ever seen a sperrit with a shadow; well then, what's he doing with an echo to him, I should like to know? That ain't in natur', surely?"

This argument seemed weak enough to me. But you can never tell what will affect the superstitious, and to my wonder, George Merry was greatly relieved.

"Well, that's so," he said. "You've a head upon your shoulders, John, and no mistake. 'Bout ship, mates! This here crew is on a wrong tack, I do believe. And come to think on it, it was like Flint's voice, I grant you, but not just so clear-away like it, after all. It was liker somebody else's voice now—it was liker—"

"By the powers, **Ben Gunn!**" roared Silver.

"Aye, and so it were," cried Morgan, springing on his knees. "Ben Gunn it were!"

"It don't make much odds, do it, now?" asked Dick. "Ben Gunn's not here in the body any more'n Flint."

But the older hands greeted this remark with scorn.

"Why, nobody minds Ben Gunn," cried Merry; "dead or alive, nobody minds him."

It was extraordinary how their spirits had returned and how the natural colour had revived in their faces. Soon they were chatting together, with intervals of listening; and not long after, hearing no further sound, they shouldered the tools and set forth again, Merry walking first with Silver's compass to keep them on the right line with Skeleton Island. He had said the truth: dead or alive, nobody minded Ben Gunn.

Dick alone still held his Bible, and looked around him as he went, with fearful glances; but he found no sympathy, and Silver even joked him on his precautions.

"I told you," said he—"I told you you had sp'iled your Bible. If it ain't no good to swear by, what do you suppose a sperrit would give for it? Not that!" and he snapped his big fingers, halting a moment on his crutch.

But Dick was not to be comforted; indeed, it was soon plain to me that the lad was falling sick; hastened by heat, exhaustion, and the shock of his alarm, the fever, predicted by **Dr. Livesey**, was evidently growing swiftly higher.

It was fine open walking here, upon the summit; our way lay a little downhill, for, as I have said, the plateau tilted towards the west. The pines, great and small, grew wide apart; and even between the clumps of nutmeg and azalea, wide open spaces baked in the hot sunshine. Striking, as we did, pretty near north-west across the island, we drew, on the one hand, ever nearer under the shoulders of the Spy-glass, and on the other, looked ever wider over that western bay where I had once tossed and trembled in the coracle.

The first of the tall trees was reached, and by the bearings proved the wrong one. So with the second. The third rose nearly two hundred feet into the air above a clump of underwood—a giant of a vegetable, with a red column as big as a cottage, and a wide shadow around in which a company could have manoeuvred. It was conspicuous far to sea both on the east and west and might have been entered as a sailing mark upon the chart.

But it was not its size that now impressed my companions; it was the knowledge that seven hundred thousand pounds in gold lay somewhere buried below its spreading shadow. The thought of the money, as they drew nearer, swallowed up their previous terrors. Their eyes burned in their heads; their feet grew speedier and lighter; their whole soul was bound up in that fortune, that whole lifetime of extravagance and pleasure, that lay waiting there for each of them. [*This is their ultimate concern.*]

Silver hobbled, grunting, on his crutch; his nostrils stood out and quivered; he cursed like a madman when the flies settled on his hot and shiny countenance; he plucked furiously at the line that held me to him and from time to time turned his eyes upon me with a deadly look. Certainly he took no pains to hide his thoughts, and certainly I read them like print. **In the immediate nearness of the gold, all else had been forgotten: his promise and the doctor's warning were both things of the past, and I could not doubt that he hoped to seize upon the treasure, find and board the *Hispaniola* under cover of night, cut every honest throat about that island, and sail away as he had at first intended, laden with crimes and riches.**

Shaken as I was with these alarms, it was hard for me to keep up with the rapid pace of the treasure-hunters. Now and again I stumbled, and it was then that Silver plucked so roughly at the rope and launched at me his murderous glances. Dick, who had dropped behind us and now brought up the rear, was babbling to himself both prayers and curses as his fever kept rising. This also added to my wretchedness, and to crown all, I was haunted by the thought of the tragedy that had once been acted on that plateau, when that ungodly buccaneer with the blue face—he who died at Savannah [*Flint*], singing and shouting for drink —had there, with his own hand, cut down his six accomplices. This grove that was now so peaceful must then have rung with cries, I thought; and even with the thought I could believe I heard it ringing still.

We were now at the margin of the thicket.

"Huzza, mates, all together!" shouted Merry; and the foremost broke into a run.

And suddenly, not ten yards further, we beheld them stop. A low cry arose. Silver doubled his pace, digging away with the foot of his crutch like one possessed; and next moment he and I had come also to a dead halt.

Before us was a great excavation, not very recent, for the sides had fallen in and grass had sprouted on the bottom. In this were the shaft of a pick broken in two and the boards of several packing-cases strewn around. On one of these boards I saw, branded with a hot iron, the name *Walrus*—the name of Flint's ship.

All was clear to probation. The *cache* had been found and rifled; the seven hundred thousand pounds were gone!

• ANALYZING THE SCENE •

STORY EVENT

A Story Event is an active change of a universal human value for one or more characters as a result of conflict (one character's desires clash with another's, or an environmental shift changes the value positively or negatively).

A Working Scene contains at least one Story Event. To determine a scene's Story Event, answer these four Socratic questions:

I. What are the characters literally doing—that is, what are their micro on-the-surface actions?

The pirates, with Jim in tow, continue slowly toward the place where they believe the treasure will be. They hear strange voices, but Silver convinces them to keep moving. When they get close, most of the pirates break into a run.

2. What is the essential tactic of the characters—that is, what above-the-surface macro behaviors are they employing that are linked to a universal human value?

Jim wants to stay alive. Physically, he's constrained, but he can employ his mind to identify and solve problems. He must rely on his powers of observation so he can act when he's able. Silver wants to get to the treasure, and the closer they get, the more Jim sees he can't rely on Silver's promises to influence his behavior. The other pirates want the treasure also, but at first, they're afraid of the spirit of Flint. Gunn wants to disrupt them.

3. What beyond-the-surface universal human values have changed for one or more characters in the scene? Which one of those value changes is most important and should be included in the Story Grid Spreadsheet?

Jim is unsure of Silver at first but soon confirms that Silver is as powerless over his desire for the treasure as the others are. The pirates are anxious as the scene opens, but they become crazed as they near the treasure site. This scene turns when Silver speaks with authority and identifies Gunn's voice. Nothing of consequence stands between them and the treasure. Which value shift is the most relevant to the survival of Jim and his friends? Jim needs Silver to keep his head and influence the behavior of the other pirates. The closer they get to the treasure, the less control Silver has over his own emotions and actions let alone that of the others, even though they are following his orders at this point. I would identify the shift on a gradient of fear.

Terrified to No Fear

4. The Scene Event Synthesis: What Story Event sums up the scene's on-the-surface, above-the-surface, and beyond-the-surface change? We will enter that event in the Story Grid Spreadsheet.

The pirates hear a strange voice that preys on their resolve, but Silver's reassurance and their own greed allow them to overcome their fear and superstition to reach the site only to find the treasure is missing.

HOW THE SCENE ABIDES BY THE FIVE COMMANDMENTS OF STORYTELLING

Inciting Incident: Causal. The pirates continue toward the treasure after finding the pointer.

Turning Point Progressive Complication: Revelation. Silver realizes they are hearing Gunn's voice.

Crisis: Best Bad Choice. Silver risks losing the treasure if he heeds Livesey's warning about squalls, but he risks everything if he abandons his caution and gives in to lust for wealth.

Climax: Silver ignores the warning and is as eager to reach the treasure as the others.

Resolution: They reach the cave, and the treasure has been removed.

NOTES

- In this sequence of scenes (beginning with scene 28), Jim's moment-by-moment survival depends on Silver's good will toward him, which depends on how much Silver thinks he might need Jim. Without the treasure to placate and distract the crew, Jim's position and Silver's is significantly worse.
- Notice that Silver disregards Livesey's warning to delay the

pirates. That's not to say this isn't a difficult line to walk, but Silver doesn't take advantage of the opportunities he has to slow the pirates down. In other words, he's still playing both sides in pursuit of his ultimate concern—the treasure.

- This scene is reminiscent of two earlier scenes that show proximity to a highly desirable goal sometimes causes people to lose sight of everything else. In scene 4, Jim's mother suffers from this goal-directed blindness as she tries to get what she is due from the captain's bag of money. In scene 5, Pew is caught in the same trap and meets a tragic end. Jim is blinded by his goals when he first meets Silver, but he's operating at a much higher and safer level now.

33

THE FALL OF A CHIEFTAIN

There never was such an overturn in this world. Each of these six men was as though he had been struck. But with **Silver** the blow passed almost instantly. Every thought of his soul had been set full-stretch, like a racer, on that money; well, he was brought up, in a single second, dead; and he kept his head, found his temper, and changed his plan before the others had had time to realize the disappointment.

"**Jim**," he whispered, "take that, and stand by for trouble."

And he passed me a double-barrelled pistol.

At the same time, he began quietly moving northward, and in a few steps had put the hollow between us two and the other five. Then he looked at me and nodded, as much as to say, "Here is a narrow corner," as, indeed, I thought it was. His looks were not quite friendly, and I was so revolted at these constant changes that I could not forbear whispering, "So you've changed sides again."

There was no time left for him to answer in. The buccaneers, with oaths and cries, began to leap, one after another, into the pit and to dig with their fingers, throwing the boards aside as they did so. **Morgan** found a piece of gold. He held it up with a perfect spout of oaths. It was a two-guinea piece, and it went from hand to hand among them for a quarter of a minute.

"Two guineas!" roared **Merry**, shaking it at Silver. "That's your seven hundred thousand pounds, is it? You're the man for bargains, ain't you? You're him that never bungled nothing, you wooden-headed lubber!"

"Dig away, boys," said Silver with the coolest insolence; "you'll find some pig-nuts and I shouldn't wonder."

"Pig-nuts!" repeated Merry, in a scream. "Mates, do you hear that? I tell you now, that man there knew it all along. Look in the face of him and you'll see it wrote there."

"Ah, Merry," remarked Silver, "standing for cap'n again? You're a pushing lad, to be sure."

But this time everyone was entirely in Merry's favour. They began to scramble out of the excavation, darting furious glances behind them. One thing I observed, which looked well for us: they all got out upon the opposite side from Silver.

Well, there we stood, two on one side, five on the other, the pit between us, and nobody screwed up high enough to offer the first blow. Silver never moved; he watched them, very upright on his crutch, and looked as cool as ever I saw him. He was brave, and no mistake.

At last Merry seemed to think a speech might help matters.

"Mates," says he, "there's two of them alone there; one's the old cripple that brought us all here and blundered us down to this; the other's that cub that I mean to have the heart of. Now, mates—"

He was raising his arm and his voice, and plainly meant to lead a charge. But just then—*crack! crack! crack!*—three musket-shots flashed out of the thicket. Merry tumbled head foremost into the excavation; **the man with the bandage** spun round like a teetotum and fell all his length upon his side, where he lay dead, but still twitching; and the other three turned and ran for it with all their might.

Before you could wink, Long John had fired two barrels of a pistol into the struggling Merry, and as the man rolled up his eyes at him in the last agony, "George," said he, "I reckon I settled you."

At the same moment, **the doctor**, **Gray**, and **Ben Gunn** joined us, with smoking muskets, from among the nutmeg-trees.

"Forward!" cried the doctor. "Double quick, my lads. We must head 'em off the boats."

And we set off at a great pace, sometimes plunging through the bushes to the chest.

I tell you, but Silver was anxious to keep up with us. **The work that man went through, leaping on his crutch till the muscles of his chest were fit to burst, was work no sound man ever equalled; and so thinks the doctor.** As it was, he was already thirty yards behind us and on the verge of strangling when we reached the brow of the slope.

"Doctor," he hailed, "see there! No hurry!"

Sure enough there was no hurry. In a more open part of the plateau, we could see the three survivors still running in the same direction as they had started, right for **Mizzenmast Hill.** We were already between them and the boats; and so we four sat down to breathe, while Long John, mopping his face, came slowly up with us.

"Thank ye kindly, doctor," says he. "You came in in about the nick, I guess, for me and Hawkins. And so it's you, Ben Gunn!" he added. "Well, you're a nice one, to be sure."

"I'm Ben Gunn, I am," replied the maroon, wriggling like an eel in his embarrassment. "And," he added, after a long pause, "how do, Mr. Silver? Pretty well, I thank ye, says you."

"Ben, Ben," murmured Silver, "to think as you've done me!"

The doctor sent back Gray for one of the pick-axes deserted, in their flight, by the mutineers, and then as we proceeded leisurely downhill to where the boats were lying, related in a few words what had taken place. It was a story that profoundly interested Silver; and Ben Gunn, the half-idiot maroon, was the hero from beginning to end.

Ben, in his long, lonely wanderings about the island, had found the skeleton—it was he that had rifled it; he had found the treasure; he had dug it up (it was the haft of his pick-axe that lay broken in the excavation); he had carried it on his back, in many weary journeys, from the foot of the tall pine to a cave he had on the two-pointed hill at the north-east angle of the island, and there it had lain stored in safety **since two months before the arrival of the** *Hispaniola.*

When the doctor had wormed this secret from him on the afternoon of the attack, and when next morning he saw the anchorage deserted, he had gone to Silver, given him the chart, which was now useless—given him the stores, for Ben Gunn's cave was well supplied with goats' meat salted by himself—given anything and everything to get a chance of moving in safety from the stockade to the two-pointed hill, there to be clear of malaria and keep a guard upon the money.

"As for you, Jim," he said, "it went against my heart, but I did what I thought best for those who had stood by their duty; and if you were not one of these, whose fault was it?"

That morning, finding that I was to be involved in the horrid disappointment he had prepared for the mutineers, he had run all the way to the cave, and leaving **the squire** to guard **the captain**, had taken Gray and the maroon and started, making the diagonal across the island to be at hand beside the pine. Soon, however, he saw that our party had the start of him; and Ben Gunn, being fleet of foot, had been dispatched in front to do his best alone. Then it had occurred to him to work upon the superstitions of **his former shipmates**, and he was so far successful that Gray and the doctor had come up and were already ambushed before the arrival of the treasure-hunters.

"Ah," said Silver, "it were fortunate for me that I had Hawkins here. You would have let old John be cut to bits, and never given it a thought, doctor."

"Not a thought," replied Dr. Livesey cheerily.

And by this time we had reached the gigs. The doctor, with the pick-axe, demolished one of them, and then we all got aboard the other and set out to go round by sea for North Inlet.

This was a run of eight or nine miles. Silver, though he was almost killed already with fatigue, was set to an oar, like the rest of us, and we were soon skimming swiftly over a smooth sea. Soon we passed out of the straits and doubled the south-east corner of the island, round which, four days ago, we had towed the Hispaniola.

As we passed the two-pointed hill, we could see the black mouth of Ben Gunn's cave and a figure standing by it, leaning on a musket. It was the squire, and we waved a handkerchief and gave him three cheers, in which the voice of Silver joined as heartily as any.

Three miles farther, just inside the mouth of North Inlet, what should we meet but the *Hispaniola*, cruising by herself? The last flood had lifted her, and had there been much wind or a strong tide current, as in the southern anchorage, we should never have found her more, or found her stranded beyond help. As it was, there was little amiss beyond the wreck of the main-sail. Another anchor was got ready and dropped in a fathom and a half of water. We all pulled round again to **Rum Cove**, the nearest point for Ben Gunn's treasure-house; and then Gray, single-handed, returned with the gig to the *Hispaniola*, where he was to pass the night on guard.

A gentle slope ran up from the beach to the entrance of the cave. At the top, **the squire** met us. To me he was cordial and kind, saying nothing of my escapade either in the way of blame or praise. At Silver's polite salute he somewhat flushed.

"John Silver," he said, "you're a prodigious villain and imposter—a monstrous imposter, sir. I am told I am not to prosecute you. Well, then, I will not. But **the dead men**, sir, hang about your neck like mill-stones."

"Thank you kindly, sir," replied Long John, again saluting.

"I dare you to thank me!" cried the squire. "It is a gross dereliction of my duty. Stand back."

And thereupon we all entered the cave. It was a large, airy place, with a little spring and a pool of clear water, overhung with ferns. The floor was sand. Before a big fire lay **Captain Smollett**; and in a far corner, only duskily flickered over by the blaze, I beheld great heaps of coin and quadrilaterals built of bars of gold. That was **Flint's** treasure that we had come so far to seek and that had cost already the lives of **seventeen men from the *Hispaniola***. How many it had cost in the amassing, what blood and sorrow, what good ships scuttled on the deep, what brave men walking the plank blindfold, what shot of cannon, what shame and lies and cruelty, perhaps no man alive could tell. Yet there were still three upon that island—Silver, and old Morgan, and Ben Gunn—who had each taken his share in these crimes, as each had hoped in vain to share in the reward.

"Come in, Jim," said the captain. "You're a good boy in your line, Jim, but I don't think you and me'll go to sea again. You're too much of the born favourite for me. Is that you, John Silver? What brings you here, man?"

"Come back to my dooty, sir," returned Silver.

"Ah!" said the captain, and that was all he said.

What a supper I had of it that night, with all my friends around me; and what a meal it was, with Ben Gunn's salted goat and some delicacies and a bottle of old wine from the *Hispaniola*. Never, I am sure, were people gayer or happier. And there was Silver, sitting back almost out of the firelight, but eating heartily, prompt to spring forward when anything was wanted, even joining quietly in our laughter—**the same bland, polite, obsequious seaman of the voyage out.**

• ANALYZING THE SCENE •

STORY EVENT

A Story Event is an active change of a universal human value for one or more characters as a result of conflict (one character's desires clash with another's, or an environmental shift changes the value positively or negatively).

A Working Scene contains at least one Story Event. To determine a scene's Story Event, answer these four Socratic questions:

1. What are the characters literally doing—that is, what are their micro on-the-surface actions?

After they learn the treasure is missing, Silver arms Jim, and they move away from the other pirates. Pirate trash talking commences, and Merry and the others are about to charge when shots are fired (by Livesey, Gray, and Gunn). Merry and one other pirate are killed. The three remaining pirates escape. Jim, Silver and the others talk while they walk to the boats and row to secure the *Hispaniola* (where Gray is left as a guard). They travel to Gunn's cave where they eat and rest.

2. What is the essential tactic of the characters—that is, what above-the-surface macro behaviors are they employing that are linked to a universal human value?

Livesey wants to secure survival for as many people as he can, and this drives all his actions in this scene. Jim is attempting to survive and applying all of his powers to that end. Silver also wants to survive, and we see him adapting to each new situation as it comes. Merry and the other pirates want revenge at first, not realizing they need to focus on survival.

3. What beyond-the-surface universal human values have changed for one or more characters in the scene? Which one of those value changes is most important and should be included in the Story Grid Spreadsheet?

The pirates who attempt to attack have moved from life to death. Although three survive, we've seen they don't have the skills and mindset to think about long-term survival or the sense to surrender so they might not be stranded on the island. Livesey, Gray, and Gunn are at risk of death, but they have the advantage of surprise and cover. Jim and Silver move from imminent death to safety.

Imminent Death to Safety

4. **The Scene Event Synthesis: What Story Event sums up the scene's on-the-surface, above-the-surface, and beyond-the-surface change? We will enter that event in the Story Grid Spreadsheet.**

Jim is saved by the timely action of Livesey, Gray, and Gunn. They keep their word and allow Silver to join them as they retrieve the boats, secure the ship, and return to Gunn's cave.

HOW THE SCENE ABIDES BY THE FIVE COMMANDMENTS OF STORYTELLING

Inciting Incident: Causal. The treasure is gone, and Silver maneuvers as the other pirates prepare to attack.

Turning Point Progressive Complication: Active. Livesey, Gray, and Gunn attack, killing two pirates and chasing the three others.

Crisis: Best bad choice. If they kill or abandon Silver, they will break their word and cause another death in pursuit of the treasure, but if they allow him to live, he could turn on them again.

Climax: No one is glad to have Silver with them, but they choose to honor their word.

Resolution: They retrieve a boat, secure the ship, and return to Gunn's cave.

NOTES

- This scene is the core event, a scene we call the *luminary agent at the mercy of the shadow agent*. If we zoom out, we see that Jim is held by the pirates for most of the ending payoff. Pull back further and we see that Jim has been at their mercy since the beginning when Bones arrived at the inn. Jim gets out of jeopardy by attuning to his environment and exercising his agency as dictated by the circumstances. He uses his existing powers of observation, but he applies them more effectively.

- Jim has a crisis here—to accept the gun and join Silver or not. He accepts the gun but doesn't turn over his agency. He lets Silver know he's not fooled by his act.
- Livesey's global need is to preserve life. He wants the treasure, but he already lives a good life pursuing what matters most to him. Our human need to mature doesn't end, and even adults can misread the call to adventure.

34

AND LAST

The next morning we fell early to work, for the transportation of this great mass of gold near a mile by land to the beach, and thence three miles by boat to the *Hispaniola*, was a considerable task for so small a number of workmen. **The three fellows** still abroad upon the island did not greatly trouble us; a single sentry on the shoulder of the hill was sufficient to ensure us against any sudden onslaught, and we thought, besides, they had had more than enough of fighting.

Therefore the work was pushed on briskly. **Gray** and **Ben Gunn** came and went with the boat, while the rest during their absences piled treasure on the beach. Two of the bars, slung in a rope's end, made a good load for **a grown man**—one that he was glad to walk slowly with. For my part, as I was not much use at carrying, I was kept busy all day in the cave packing the minted money into bread-bags.

It was a strange collection, like **Billy Bones**'s hoard for the diversity of coinage, but so much larger and so much more varied that I think I never had more pleasure than in sorting them. English, French, Spanish, Portuguese, Georges, and Louises, doubloons and double guineas and moidores and sequins, the pictures of **all the kings of Europe for the last hundred years**, strange Oriental pieces stamped with what looked like wisps of string or bits of spider's web, round pieces and square pieces, and pieces bored through the middle, as if to wear them round your neck—nearly every variety of money in the world must, I think, have found a place in that collection; and for number, I am sure they were like autumn leaves, so that my back ached with stooping and my fingers with sorting them out.

Day after day this work went on; by every evening a fortune had been stowed aboard, but there was another fortune waiting for the morrow; and all this time we heard nothing of **the three surviving mutineers.**

At last—I think it was on the third night—**the doctor** and I were strolling on the shoulder of the hill where it overlooks the lowlands of the isle, when, from out the thick darkness below, the wind brought us a noise between shrieking and singing. It was only a snatch that reached our ears, followed by the former silence.

"Heaven forgive them," said the doctor; "'tis the mutineers!"

"All drunk, sir," struck in the voice of **Silver** from behind us.

Silver, I should say, was allowed his entire liberty, and in spite of daily rebuffs, seemed to regard himself once more as quite a privileged and friendly dependent. Indeed, it was remarkable how well he bore these slights and with what unwearying politeness he kept on trying to ingratiate himself with all. Yet, I think, none treated him better than a dog, unless it was Ben Gunn, who was still terribly afraid of his old quartermaster, or myself, who had really something to thank him for; although for that matter, I suppose, I had reason to think even worse of him than anybody else, for I had seen him meditating a fresh treachery upon the plateau. Accordingly, it was pretty gruffly that the doctor answered him.

"Drunk or raving," said he.

"Right you were, sir," replied Silver; "and precious little odds which, to you and me."

"I suppose you would hardly ask me to call you a humane man," returned the doctor with a sneer, "and so my feelings may surprise you, Master Silver. But if I were sure they were raving—as I am morally certain one, at least, of them is down with fever—I should leave this camp, and at whatever risk to my own carcass, take them the assistance of my skill."

"Ask your pardon, sir, you would be very wrong," quoth Silver. "You would lose your precious life, and you may lay to that. I'm on your side now, hand and glove; and I shouldn't wish for to see the party weakened, let alone yourself, seeing as I know what I owes you. But these men down there, they couldn't keep their word—no, not supposing they wished to; and what's more, they couldn't believe as you could."

"No," said the doctor. "You're the man to keep your word, we know that."

Well, that was about the last news we had of the three pirates. Only once we heard a gunshot a great way off and supposed them to be hunting. A council was held, and it was decided that we must desert them on the island—to the huge glee, I must say, of Ben Gunn, and with the strong approval of Gray. We left a good stock of powder and shot, the bulk of the salt goat, a few medicines, and some other necessaries, tools, clothing, a spare sail, a fathom or two of rope, and by the particular desire of the doctor, a handsome present of tobacco.

That was about our last doing on the island. Before that, we had got the treasure stowed and had shipped enough water and the remainder of the goat meat in case of any distress; and at last, one fine morning, we weighed anchor, which was about all that we could manage, and stood out of North Inlet, the same colours flying that the captain had flown and fought under at the palisade.

The three fellows must have been watching us closer than we thought for, as we soon had proved. For coming through the narrows, we had to lie very near the southern point, and there we saw all three of them kneeling together on a spit of sand, with their arms raised in supplication. It went to all our hearts, I think, to leave them in that wretched state; but we could not risk another mutiny; and to take them home for the gibbet would have been a cruel sort of kindness. The doctor hailed them and told them of the stores we had left, and where they were to find them. But they continued to call us by name and appeal to us, for God's sake, to be merciful and not leave them to die in such a place.

At last, seeing the ship still bore on her course and was now swiftly drawing out of earshot, one of them—I know not which it was—leapt to his feet with a hoarse cry, whipped his musket to his shoulder, and sent a shot whistling over Silver's head and through the main-sail.

After that, we kept under cover of the bulwarks, and when next I looked out they had disappeared from the spit, and the spit itself had almost melted out of sight in the growing distance. That was, at least, the end of that; and before noon, to my inexpressible joy, the highest rock of Treasure Island had sunk into the blue round of sea.

We were so short of men that **everyone on board** had to bear a hand—only the captain lying on a mattress in the stern and giving his orders, for though greatly recovered he was still in want of quiet. We laid her head for **the nearest port in Spanish America**, for we could not risk the voyage home without **fresh hands**; and as it was, what with baffling winds and a couple of fresh gales, we were all worn out before we reached it.

It was just at sundown when we cast anchor in a most beautiful land-locked gulf, and were immediately surrounded by shore boats full of **Negroes and Mexican Indians and half-bloods** selling fruits and vegetables and offering to dive for bits of money. The sight of so many good-humoured faces (especially the blacks), the taste of the tropical fruits, and above all the lights that began to shine in the town made a most charming contrast to our dark and bloody sojourn on the island; and **the doctor and the squire**, taking me along with them, went ashore to pass the early part of the night. Here they met **the captain of an English man-of-war**, fell in talk with him, went on board his ship, and, in short, had so agreeable a time that day was breaking when we came alongside the *Hispaniola*.

Ben Gunn was on deck alone, and as soon as we came on board he began, with wonderful contortions, to make us a confession. Silver was gone. The maroon had connived at his escape in a shore boat some hours ago, and he now assured us he had only done so to preserve our lives, which would certainly have been forfeit if "that man with the one leg had stayed aboard." But this was not all. The sea-cook had not gone empty-handed. He had cut through a bulkhead unobserved and had removed one of the sacks of coin, worth perhaps three or four hundred guineas, to help him on his further wanderings.

I think we were all pleased to be so cheaply quit of him.

Well, to make a long story short, we got a few hands on board, made a good cruise home, and the *Hispaniola* reached Bristol just as Mr. Blandly was beginning to think of fitting out her consort. Five men only of those who had sailed returned with her. "Drink and the devil had done for the rest," with a vengeance, although, to be sure, we were not quite in so bad a case as that other ship they sang about:

With one man of her crew alive,

What put to sea with seventy-five.

All of us had an ample share of the treasure and used it wisely or foolishly, according to our natures. Captain Smollett is now retired from the sea. Gray not only saved his money, but being suddenly smit with the desire to rise, also studied his profession, and he is now mate and part owner of a fine full-rigged ship, married besides, and the father of a family. As for Ben Gunn, he got a thousand pounds, which he spent or lost in three weeks, or to be more exact, in nineteen days, for he was back begging on the twentieth. Then he was given a lodge to keep, exactly as he had feared upon the island; and he still lives, a great favourite, though something of a butt, with the country boys, and a notable singer in church on Sundays and saints' days.

Of Silver we have heard no more. That formidable seafaring man with one leg has at last gone clean out of my life; but I dare say he met **his old Negress**, and perhaps still lives in comfort with her and **Captain Flint**. It is to be hoped so, I suppose, for his chances of comfort in another world are very small.

The bar silver and the arms still lie, for all that I know, where Flint buried them; and certainly they shall lie there for me. Oxen and wain-ropes would not bring me back again to that accursed island; and the worst dreams that ever I have are when I hear the surf booming about its coasts or start upright in bed with the sharp voice of Captain Flint still ringing in my ears: "Pieces of eight! Pieces of eight!"

• ANALYZING THE SCENE •

STORY EVENT

A Story Event is an active change of a universal human value for one or more characters as a result of conflict (one character's desires clash with another's, or an environmental shift changes the value positively or negatively).

A Working Scene contains at least one Story Event. To determine a scene's Story Event, answer these four Socratic questions:

1. What are the characters literally doing—that is, what are their micro on-the-surface actions?

Jim and his companions pack the treasure and transport it to the ship. As they sail away with Silver, the three now-stranded pirates fire on the *Hispaniola* without causing harm. When the ship reaches a nearby Spanish port, Silver escapes with a small share of the treasure.

2. What is the essential tactic of the characters—that is, what above-the-surface macro behaviors are they employing that are linked to a universal human value?

Livesey and the others want to preserve life, but they realize the three remaining pirates are a danger to them and would only be executed once they arrive in England. Silver wants to escape. Though Livesey and the others have promised to speak for him, he cannot count on English justice going his way. He slips away at the first opportunity.

3. What beyond-the-surface universal human values have changed for one or more characters in the scene? Which one of those value changes is most important and should be included in the Story Grid Spreadsheet?

The risk of death to the crew that remains is minimized because they leave the three pirates behind, but there is some risk that Silver will turn on them. This is eliminated when Silver escapes.

Abroad to Home Safe

4. The Scene Event Synthesis: What Story Event sums up the scene's on-the-surface, above-the-surface, and beyond-the-surface change? We will enter that event in the Story Grid Spreadsheet.

Jim and his companions secure the treasure and leave three pirates on the island. Silver escapes, and Jim is done with adventures.

HOW THE SCENE ABIDES BY THE FIVE COMMANDMENTS OF STORYTELLING

Inciting Incident: Causal. The remaining faithful crew and Silver begin to pack the treasure.

Turning Point Progressive Complication: Active. The ship is loaded, and it's time to return to England.

Crisis: Best bad choice. If the faithful crew abandon the three remaining pirates (other than Silver), they are condemning them to die on the island. But if they take the pirates with them, the crew will remain in danger and the pirates will only be transported to their deaths.

Climax: The leaders choose to abandon the pirates on the island but leave them with food and ammunition they can use to obtain more.

Resolution: Silver slips away while they are stopped in a Spanish port. When they return to England and divvy up the treasure, each individual disposes of it according to their nature.

NOTE

- Jim as the luminary agent changes, but the other characters in the story stay the same with the exception of how they see Jim.

ABOUT THE AUTHOR

LESLIE WATTS is the Editor-in-Chief of Story Grid Publishing, overseeing the acquisition and editing of its fiction and nonfiction titles. A member of the first class of Story Grid certified editors, Leslie is also a *Story Grid Writer's Room* and *Roundtable* podcaster, an instructor, mentor, and proud story nerd. She has written craft-focused articles for the Fundamental Fridays blog and popular books, including *Point of View, Conventions and Obligatory Moments* (with Kimberly Kessler), *What's the Big Idea?* (with Shelley Sperry), and a masterwork analysis guide to Malcolm Gladwell's *The Tipping Point* (with Shelley Sperry).

ABOUT THE EDITOR

ALLISON FAIRHURST is a fiction writer, a book coach, and a story nerd through and through. She studied Literature and Creative Writing at university. After graduating in 2012, she continued on her path to learn the craft of writing and editing through workshops, masterclasses, many books, and of course, Story Grid. Though building her print record, she was last published on Lemonhound.com, in Bone Bouquet 5.1, and in Dirt Magazine. Connect with her at allisonfairhurst.com.

NOTES

INTRODUCTION

1. "Pirates of the Caribbean," Rides and Attractions Disneyland Park, accessed February 27, 2021, https://disneyland.disney.go.com/attractions/disneyland/pirates-of-the-caribbean/.
2. Ker Than, "Talk Like a Pirate Day? Not Even Pirates Spoke Pirate," National Geographic, September 19, 2017, https://www.nationalgeographic.com/culture/article/120919-talk-like-a-pirate-day-news-history.

MAPPING THE ACTION TERRAIN

1. In the Story Grid Universe, we use terms you may not be familiar with yet. For example, when we talk about certain characters in a story, we may refer to *luminary agents* or *shadow agents*. These are terms we use to describe the protagonist and the external antagonist. These unfamiliar terms can take some getting used to, but they aren't technical jargon meant to exclude people. In the Story Grid Universe, our goal is to describe story concepts as precisely as possible to reflect their function and relationships with other elements.

   If this is all new to you, be sure and grab a copy of *Story Grid 101: The Five First Principles of the Story Grid Methodology* by Story Grid founder Shawn Coyne (available free on the site), and a recent title from Story Grid publisher, Tim Grahl, *The Writers' Common Language: A Shared Vocabulary to Tell Better Stories*. Finally, if you want to learn more about Story Grid's tools and how to use them consistently and effectively, read *The Writer's Daily Practice: A Guide to Becoming a Lifelong Storyteller* by Story Grid certified editor Danielle Kiowski.
2. For more information about the Four Core Framework and the core elements for all twelve of Story Grid's content genres, see Shawn Coyne, *The Four Core Framework: Needs, Life Values, Emotions, and Events in Storytelling* (Egremont, MA, Story Grid Publishing 2020).
3. For a deeper exploration of the Action genre, including the conventions and obligatory moments, see Shawn Coyne, *Action Story: The Primal Genre* (Egremont, MA, Story Grid Publishing 2020).

CONVENTIONS

1. For more information about genre conventions and obligatory moments, see Kimberly Kessler and Leslie Watts, *Conventions and Obligatory Moments: The Must-Haves to Meet Audience Requirements* (Egremont, MA, Story Grid Publishing 2020)

SELECTIVE CONSTRAINTS

1. For more on the subgenres and plots of the Action genre, see Shawn Coyne, *Action Story: The Primal Genre* (Egremont, MA, Story Grid Publishing 2020).

ENABLING CONSTRAINTS

1. For more information about these three perennial problems that humans face and how they relate to story, see *The Hobbit by J.R.R. Tolkien: A Story Grid Masterwork Guide* or *The Wonderful Wizard of Oz by L. Frank Baum: A Story Grid Masterwork Guide*, both by Shawn Coyne.